BURIED TR
CHINESE T

Buried Treasures of Chinese Turkestan

Albert von Le Coq

With an Introduction by Peter Hopkirk

HONG KONG
OXFORD UNIVERSITY PRESS
OXFORD NEW YORK

Oxford University Press

*Oxford New York Toronto
Delhi Bombay Calcutta Madras Karachi
Petaling Jaya Singapore Hong Kong Tokyo
Nairobi Dar es Salaam Cape Town
Melbourne Auckland*

*and associated companies in
Berlin Ibadan*

*First published by George Allen & Unwin Ltd. 1928
© George Allen & Unwin Ltd. 1928
Introduction © Oxford University Press 1985*

*All rights reserved. No part of this publication may be reproduced,
stored in a retrieval system, or transmitted, in any form or by any means,
electronic, mechanical, photocopying, recording or otherwise,
without the prior permission of Oxford University Press.*

'Oxford' is a trade mark of Oxford University Press

*First issued, with permission
and with the addition of an Introduction,
as an Oxford in Asia Paperback 1985
Second impression 1987
Reissued in Oxford Paperbacks 1988
Second impression 1989*

0 19 583878 5

*Printed in Hong Kong
Published by Oxford University Press, Warwick House, Hong Kong*

INTRODUCTION

IN the winter of 1895, after a nightmarish crossing of the High Pamir, there arrived in the remote Chinese frontier town of Kashgar a young Swedish explorer named Sven Hedin. From the local oasis-dwellers he heard strange tales of treasure-filled towns lying buried beneath the sands far out in the treacherous Taklamakan desert. According to the natives, Allah had buried these towns with sandstorms many centuries earlier because of the evil ways of their inhabitants. For anyone brave enough to face the terrors, both natural and supernatural, of the desert, there were, he was assured, fabulous treasures for the taking.

Hedin soon became convinced that behind these tales there lay more than a grain of truth. After very nearly dying of thirst on his first foray into the Taklamakan (which means, in the local Uighur tongue, 'Go in — and you won't come out'), he finally stumbled on the ruins of what, long before, had been a small but flourishing township. Of more importance, however, were the artefacts he brought back with him from this first sortie. For these proved that some nine centuries earlier, before the Islamic conquest of Central Asia, this lost city had been a Buddhist community.

It was the first of many such sand-buried ruins which archaeologists from seven countries were to discover along the route of the ancient Silk Road, the great trans-Asian highway once linking the two superpowers of the day, imperial China and distant Rome. For Hedin's startling find was to signal the beginning of an international race or free-for-all for the art treasures of this long-lost Buddhist civilization. Today, to the chagrin of Chinese scholars, these are scattered throughout the museums of at least thirteen countries.

The first excavator to arrive, across the Karakoram from India, was the formidable oriental scholar Aurel Stein, a Hungarian-turned-Englishman, who had long suspected that a lost civilization of some kind lay buried beneath China's western deserts. He was closely followed by archaeologists from Germany, Japan, Russia, France and — finally — America.

Between them they managed to remove, literally by the ton, huge wall-paintings, thousands of sculptures, delicate figured silks, priceless manuscripts and other antiquities from the ruined tombs and temples of this ancient highway. For over the centuries, following the arrival of Buddhism on the Silk Road, its scattered oases had given birth to their own unique style of art. A subtle fusion of Indian, Chinese, Persian and the Greek of Alexander the Great, it became known as Serindian art.

But then had begun the Silk Road's slow decline. Gradually, as the Chinese lost control of the region to the marauding Huns, and other war-like tribes, the traffic slowed. The life-sustaining irrigation systems of the oasis towns around the desert became neglected, and their inhabitants packed their bags and left. Finally, around the tenth century, the region fell to the sword of Islam.

The once-rich settlements now became ghost-towns, inhabited only by howling winds and drifting sand. Before long, as the Taklamakan gradually swallowed them up, both they and the civilization they had once nurtured were forgotten. All that remained were the legends that Hedin came upon so many centuries later.

Among the most successful of the several nationalities to take part in the race which followed were the Germans. Altogether they sent four expeditions to Chinese Turkestan between 1902 and 1914. The first was led by Professor Albert Grünwedel, an eminent Buddhist art historian from the National Ethnological Museum in Berlin, and head of that museum's Indian department.

Largely financed by Friedrich Krupp, the German arms magnate, the three-man expedition was away for a year, excavating in the Turpan (Turfan) region and returning with some forty-six cases of antiquities. A second expedition was planned for 1904, but Grünwedel was unfit to travel, so a substitute leader had to be found. If he recovered in time, it was agreed that Grünwedel would join them later.

The man chosen was Albert von Le Coq, the author of this book. The son of a wealthy Huguenot wine-merchant, he had lived in England and America before returning to Darmstadt to take over the family business. But his heart lay elsewhere, and after thirteen years he threw it up in order to pursue his real love, Central Asian history and languages. Moving to Berlin, he spent several years studying Arabic, Turkish, Persian and Sanskrit. In 1902, at the age of 42, he joined (initially as an unpaid volunteer) the Indian department of the Berlin Ethnological Museum, just as Grünwedel was mounting his first expedition to Chinese Turkestan.

INTRODUCTION

It says much for von Le Coq's ability, not to say his determination, that two years later this inexperienced, middle-aged scholar was leading an important archaeological expedition that enjoyed the personal patronage of the Kaiser himself. Accompanying him to Turfan, where they were to carry out further excavations, was the resourceful Theodor Bartus, the museum's handyman, who had been with Grünwedel on the first expedition.

Eventually, months later, they were joined by Grünwedel, but in the meantime they dug and sawed away at the sites, filling more than a hundred large crates with sections of wall-paintings (carefully cut up by Bartus for easy transportation), sculptures, manuscripts and other treasures. In terms of sheer weight, this was eight times as much as Grünwedel had brought back from the first expedition.

Among their most dazzling finds were the huge, ninth-century murals from the great cliff-face monastery at Bezeklik (Bazaklik), today visited by many travellers to China, but then still unknown, being in the very back-of-beyond. The paintings were cut into three sections to be transported by camel to the nearest railhead in Russian Turkestan, more than a thousand miles to the west.

From just one of Bezeklik's many shrines and temples, von Le Coq and Bartus cut away fifteen large paintings of the Buddha, all of different periods. To save them from unnecessary damage during their rough, twenty-month journey to Berlin, each section was wrapped first in cotton wool, next in felt, and finally in dry reeds. Then, back-to-back in pairs, they were sandwiched between wooden boards, bound securely with ropes, and nailed up in crates stuffed with straw.

Meanwhile, as von Le Coq and Bartus worked feverishly in the heat and dust to remove as many of these treasures as they could, moving on each time they denuded a site, elsewhere on the Silk Road their rivals were doing much the same. In 1906, Stein returned across the Karakoram on the second of his four expeditions, while close on his heels came a new contestant in the race, the brilliant young French scholar, Paul Pelliot, fluent in some thirteen languages, including Chinese. Also at work were the Japanese and the Russians.

I have told the story of the race for the Silk Road treasures in my book, *Foreign Devils on the Silk Road*, and it is too long a saga to repeat here. Also, the adventures and misadventures of the Germans during their excavations are the subject of this book, and are

INTRODUCTION

best told in von Le Coq's own words. However, it is worth recalling how it was that von Le Coq came to miss the greatest of all the Silk Road prizes (not to say the most controversial).

Following their triumph at Bezeklik, von Le Coq and Bartus received a message from Grünwedel, saying that he was now fully recovered and was on his way to Kashgar, a thousand miles to the west, where he asked them to rendezvous with him (why he could not have joined them in the east is not clear).

Just as the two men were loading their camels and preparing to head back to Kashgar, they heard rumours of a huge and mysterious library of ancient manuscripts which a Chinese priest had found hidden behind a wall at the great temple complex of Dunhuang (Tunghwang). Now this lay some seventeen days to the south across the Gobi desert. To get there would have involved at least a month's detour, and they were already running late for their rendezvous with Grünwedel. Moreover, they had investigated such tales before, and had wasted much time on fruitless searches.

Von Le Coq decided to spin a coin, a Chinese gold dollar. It came down tails. And so it was that he handed to his rival, Stein, the triumph of discovering and removing to Britain the great Dunhuang library which included the earliest known printed work. Such a turn of events was hardly calculated to improve von Le Coq's relations with Grünwedel, which were never over-harmonious. This was partly due to temperamental differences, but also to a divergence of view over the removal of wall-paintings from sites.

Grünwedel believed in studying and recording these *in situ*, and not in carrying them away, while von Le Coq was convinced that they must be rescued and transported to safety in the West. This difference in view was to lead to repeated quarrels between the two men, although von Le Coq, being the more forceful personality, tended to win these battles. His case for the wholesale removal of the treasures rested on the damage, described in this book, which was being inflicted on them by both man and nature. There was a bitter irony in this argument, as will be seen, although von Le Coq did not live to witness it.

The outbreak of the First World War put an end to the German expeditions, although Stein was able to continue excavating. In the meantime the Frenchman, Pelliot, had removed from Dunhuang what still remained of the long-lost library. It was this, as much as

INTRODUCTION

anything else, which drew the attention of the authorities in Peking to what was going on in this remote corner of their empire. Eventually, they were to slam the door on all foreign expeditions, but only after most of the great treasures had been removed.

The contestants could hardly complain. They had had an astonishing run for their money, or rather that of their sponsors, having carried away enough treasures to fill the Central Asian galleries of several museums. The Germans, thanks to von Le Coq and the hardworking Bartus, had done particularly well.

But that is not the end of the story. Von Le Coq was to die in 1930, a poor and saddened man. Not only was he financially ruined by the First World War, but he never got over the death of his only son, killed fighting his lifelong friends, albeit archaeological rivals, the British.

His one solace was to wander among his treasures in the Berlin Museum, reliving those heady days on the Silk Road. But mercifully his death spared him one terrible further blow. Between November 1943 and January 1945, during the Second World War, the museum was hit no fewer than seven times in Allied bombing raids. The great building, backing on to where the Berlin Wall now runs, ended as a heap of charred rubble.

The more easily moved treasures had been taken away on the outbreak of war and placed in bunkers or coal-mines for safety. Thus some sixty per cent of the Silk Road collection survived the bombing. But because they were cemented firmly into place, the largest of the wall-paintings could not be moved and had to be left in the museum. All that the staff could do was to cover them with iron shields and sandbags, and hope for the best.

As a result, twenty-eight of the finest of the paintings which von Le Coq and Bartus had so painstakingly cut up and carried out of China, including the ninth-century masterpieces from Bezeklik, were totally destroyed. Had he not died — in an asylum, in 1935 — Albert Grünwedel might have felt vindicated by the ironic fate which befell these works of art. For it was he who had advocated that such treasures were best left where they were found.

Nor were these the only Silk Road treasures removed by the German excavators that were to be lost by the museum (although one day they might still turn up). For in 1945, when the Russians occupied Berlin, they looted at least ten crates of Silk Road sculptures from a bunker they discovered beneath the zoo. These — like Schliemann's gold from Troy, which also vanished from Berlin at this time — have never been seen since, despite repeated requests to the Russians for their return.

The horrifying loss of the huge Bezeklik paintings has led to a widespread belief, especially in China, that *all* the Berlin Silk Road treasures were destroyed during the war. The Chinese cite the loss bitterly when refuting any suggestion that men like Stein, von Le Coq and Pelliot were really *rescuing* these works of art from destruction by peasant farmers, Islamic iconoclasts and earthquakes. A strong case can be made for both arguments, but it ultimately devolves on what would have happened at each particular site had the paintings, sculptures and manuscripts been left *in situ* for present-day Chinese archaeologists to rescue. In many cases they would certainly not have survived, while in others they probably would.

One reason perhaps for the enduring belief (among Chinese scholars anyway) that all the German treasures were destroyed during the war is Berlin's present isolation. For few people are in the fortunate position of being able to jump on a plane and make their way out to the leafy West Berlin suburb of Dahlem where the surviving pieces can be seen in their magnificent new home. At the time of writing, the treasures have only left Berlin once, in 1982, when some of the finest of them were flown to New York for a special Silk Road exhibition at the Metropolitan Museum of Art.

With the bulk of the works of art and manuscripts from this long-lost civilization now spread through more than thirty museums and institutions outside China the question will one day arise as to whether they should be returned to the country of their origin. Indeed, the sympathy Peking has expressed for Greece's demand for the return of the Elgin Marbles suggests that the Chinese might intend to make similar claims for their own cultural heritage in London, Berlin, Delhi, Paris, Tokyo, Leningrad and elsewhere.

But that, in turn, would raise awkward questions. Why, it would be asked, did the Chinese do nothing at the time to prevent the wholesale removal of these works of art from the Silk Road? It could even be argued that senior officials on the spot actually gave assistance to the archaeologists, especially to Stein (who was later knighted by the British government for his work). Many of these treasures, moreover, are not Chinese in origin, but belong, if to anyone, to the Uighur inhabitants of the region, whose ancestors produced them.

INTRODUCTION

Peking's most likely claim would be for the Chinese-language manuscripts removed from Dunhuang by Stein and Pelliot, now in the British Library and the Bibliothèque Nationale in Paris. For these are the very bones of a period of China's history which is poorly documented, and which Peking considers to be its rightful property.

But whatever the rights and wrongs of all this, it is almost certain that we have not heard the last of those caravan-loads of ancient treasures that von Le Coq and Stein, Pelliot and others, removed from China's remote western regions during the early years of this century.

Peter Hopkirk is the author of three books on the Central Asian travellers: *Foreign Devils on the Silk Road*, *Trespassers on the Roof of the World*, and *Setting the East Ablaze*.

BURIED TREASURES OF
CHINESE TURKESTAN

AN ACCOUNT OF THE ACTIVITIES AND ADVENTURES
OF THE SECOND AND THIRD GERMAN
TURFAN EXPEDITIONS

BY

ALBERT von LE COQ

*Departmental Director and Professor of the
National Ethnological Museum, Berlin*

TRANSLATED BY

ANNA BARWELL

LONDON
GEORGE ALLEN & UNWIN LTD
MUSEUM STREET

PREFACE

AFTER the self-sacrificing enterprise of the Berlin publishers, Messrs. Dietrich Reimer (E. Vohsen), made it possible to offer the public the large and valuable plates of our finds in the Turfan oasis, the interest shown by all circles in our discoveries has greatly increased.

Meantime, with the support of those in authority, acting in cordial and friendly co-operation with the architect of the State Museum, the objects thus photographed have, after strenuous effort of an exceedingly varied nature, been most admirably set up for exhibition—a brilliant fulfilment of the wishes I have harboured for many years, often, indeed, mingled with an oppressive feeling of the impossibility of their realization.

By the favour of the Minister, Dr. Becker, we have been enabled to bring the other one hundred and fifteen cases of frescoes and other antiquities out of the Museum cellar where they were stored during the war, and the work of erecting new halls for these paintings, etc., has been begun.

My old friends and helpers at the head of the firm of Dietrich Reimer have held out to me a prospect of the publication of these new and exceedingly valuable paintings in a sixth volume of the series of plates that they have already produced under the title of *The Late Greco-Buddhist Art of Central Asia*. I cannot refrain from expressing my thanks to them for this renewed support, entailing, as it does, in the difficult state of business still prevailing, considerable risk to themselves.

But my warmest thanks are due to the authorities who have provided the means and made the exhibition possible.

It is my pleasant duty to express my deep gratitude to Dr. Becker, the Minister of Public Education in Science and Art, and to his assistant colleague, Dr. Gall, Ministerial Privy Councillor, for so complete a fulfilment of my wishes.

I am also deeply grateful to Herr Wille, architect of the State Museum, for the unfailing readiness with which he has allowed us to benefit by his expert knowledge and unerring taste in achieving such a great success.

8 BURIED TREASURES OF CHINESE TURKESTAN

A certain number of onlookers—members of the Press—have failed in due appreciation of our efforts, but we have found ample compensation for this lack of understanding in the approval of very many visitors, possessing expert knowledge of the subject.

Herr S. C. Bosch-Reitz, the director of the East Asiatic Department of the Metropolitan Museum in New York; Herr Eumorphopoulos of London, the most important collector of East Asiatic art; the Imperial Chancellor, Dr. Luther; Dr. O. Spengler; Sven Hedin, our intrepid pioneer; Sir Aurel Stein, the indefatigable doyen of the archæologists of Central Asia; the members of the Prussian Academy of Sciences in Berlin, especially Herren H. Lüders, Ed. Meyer, F. W. K. Müller, and O. Franke; the Professors of the Universities of Halle (particularly Herren Karo and W. Weber), Göttingen, Hamburg, Heidelberg, Tübingen, Frankfort, Greifswald, Königsberg, Harvard, Yale, Columbia, of the Swedish universities; the members of the Budapest Scientific Institute; and many others well-known in research work, as well as the expert owners of some of the most important antiquity houses, viz. Mrs. Spier of London, Messrs. Yamanaka of New York and London, Herr Worch of Berlin: all these have been unanimous in their unqualified approval both of the objects shown and of an exhibition upon which such care and thought has been expended as to make it worthy of the valuable exhibits.

But if the approval of experts, of the brotherhood, so to speak, was a source of satisfaction, how much more so the spontaneous approval which private individuals, unversed in this branch of knowledge, have accorded to the exhibition and its aims! We have had opportunity to conduct many parties of visitors from foreign and German cities—above all, from Berlin—and to give them the most essential information concerning these discoveries and the new world which they reveal. As time went on, a more and more urgent wish was expressed on every hand for detailed knowledge of the journeys that led to these results—in fact, a popular account in book form of the work, hardships, joys, and sufferings experienced during these expeditions. In accordance with previous arrangements the firm of J. C. Hinrichs in Leipzig kindly undertook to publish such a book and I herewith present it to my readers. It is a personal narrative—free from scientific ballast—of our experiences in those distant sunny lands, which, remote and dusty as they undoubtedly

PREFACE

are, will ever be endeared to us by the memory of many efforts crowned with success and of the many valuable friends that we made during our stay there. This narrative is interspersed with all kinds of remarks referring to the life and character of our native friends—Eastern Turkestan and Chinese alike—and to interesting developments of the history of art, etc. But the main object of the book is to give to the public at large a general idea of our expeditions and their results.

I would refer any reader desiring more detailed information to the great number of publications of quite a popular character and mostly published by Dietrich Reimer, which are given in the bibliography which appears as an appendix to my narrative.

Should the success of this book be such as to justify my doing so, I hope to follow it up by the history of the fourth expedition, which was afterwards undertaken under very different political circumstances.

A. von LE COQ

Dahlem-Berlin, *Autumn* 1926

CONTENTS

	PAGE
PREFACE	7
LIST OF PLATES	13
INTRODUCTORY	17

    (*a*) Historical survey.
    (*b*) Remarks on the expeditions.
    (*c*) The different styles of the paintings.
    (*d*) Manes and his teaching.
    (*e*) The country and people in our time.

THE JOURNEY OF THE SECOND EXPEDITION TO TURFAN-KARAKHOJA	43
OUR LIFE AND WORK IN KARAKHOJA. I	56
OUR LIFE AND WORK IN KARAKHOJA. II	71
THE TEMPLE-SETTLEMENTS OF SANGIM AGHYZ, BAZAKLIK, CHIKKAN KOL, AND TUYOQ	83

    (*a*) The Sangim Ravine.
    (*b*) Tuyoq.

JOURNEY TO KOMUL; STAY THERE; DEPARTURE FOR KASHGAR	102
JOURNEY TO KASHGAR; MEETING WITH GRÜNWEDEL; BEGINNING OF THE THIRD JOURNEY	111
WORK AND EXPERIENCES IN KYZYL	122
WORK IN THE OASIS OF KORLA-KARASHAHR; JOURNEY TO KASHGAR	142
RETURN HOME OVER THE HIMALAYAS	151
ITINERARIES	170
BIBLIOGRAPHY	174
INDEX	179

LIST OF PLATES

PLATE		FOLLOWING PAGE
1.	Rest-house to the north of Urumchi	40
	A dangerous pass near Aighyr Bulak	40
2.	Mosque of Amin Khoja	40
	A street in Urumchi, with execution apparatus	40
3.	A street in the ruined city of Yar-khoto	40
	Cave temples near Yar-khoto	40
4.	Mohammedan tomb with Buddhist wheel symbol, near Turfan	40
	Buddhist terraced pyramid in the ruined town of Khocho	40
	View of Khocho ruins	40
5.	A ruin with Iranian arches, Khocho	49
	The old city walls at Khocho, with our baggage camels	49
6.	The visit of the *Wang* of Lukchun	49
	Our quarters in Karakhoja, 1905	49
7.	Hellenistic heads, Khocho	57
	From Le Coq, "Bilderatlas zur Kunst und Kulturgeschichte Mittelasians."—Dietrich Reimer, Berlin.	
8.	The corpse hall, Ruin K, Khocho	57
	Manichæan vaulted building, Khocho	57
9.	Christian fresco (Palm Sunday?), Khocho	57
	Painting of Manes, Ruin K, Khocho	57
10.	A page of a Turkish-Manichæan book, illuminated, Khocho	57
	Hellenistic Buddha torso, Khocho	57
11.	*Stūpa*, temple *Gamma*, Khocho	64
	Surroundings of ruin *Gamma*, Khocho	64
12.	Splendid floor in fresco style, Khocho	64
13.	Mamasit Mirab, a frequent male type, Karakhoja	70
	Zuwida Khan, a finer female type, Karakhoja	70
	From Le Coq, "Bilderatlas zur Kunst und Kulturgeschichte Mittelasians."—Dietrich Reimer, Berlin.	

PLATE	FOLLOWING PAGE
14. An oven (*tanur, tonur*), with women making bread, Karakhoja	70
A plank-weaver, Karakhoja	70

From G. Rassul Galvan, "Als Karawanenführer bei den Sahib's."—Kurt Vowinckel, Berlin.

15. Burial monuments, Persian vaulted buildings, east of Khocho	70
Large *stūpa*, Syrkyp	70
16. Fortified temple, Sangim Ravine	70
Rock temple in the curve of the Sangim Ravine	70
17. Southern buildings of temples at Bazaklik	78
Northern end of the main terrace, Bazaklik	78
18. Main terrace from the east, Bazaklik	78
Southern end of main terrace, Bazaklik	78
19. Types of early inhabitants on the frescoes, Bazaklik	86
(*a*) Syrians. (*b*) Tochari and Eastern Asiatics.	
20. Types of the early inhabitants on the frescoes, Bazaklik	86
(*a*) Persians. (*b*) Turkish Prince.	
21. Types of early inhabitants (frescoes), Bazaklik	86
(*a*) East Asiatic monks. (*b*) Indian monks.	
22. Exhibition of Bazaklik frescoes in the Ethnological Museum, Berlin	86
23. Mosque of the Seven Sleepers (*ashabu 'l kahf*), Tuyoq	93
24. (*a*) Monastery on the right bank, Tuyoq. (Destroyed by earthquake, 1916)	93
(*b*) Cave-temple in the bend of the left bank, Tuyoq (Find of manuscripts here.)	93
25. Ruins in the bend of the left bank, Tuyoq	101
Summer castle of Ara-Tam belonging to the *Wang* of Komul	101
26. Indian *stūpa* and Persian domed building, Kichik Hasar Shahri	101
Buddhist temple ruins, Ara-Tam, near Komul	101
27. Funeral mosque and tombs of the *Wangs* of Komul	101
Hall with pillars in the funeral mosque, Komul	101
28. Rock temples on the River Muzart, Kum Tura	101
Passage in the temple buildings, Kum Tura	101

LIST OF PLATES

PLATE		FOLLOWING PAGE
29.	Mir Safdar Ali, Prince (*tham*) of Hunza [Descendant of Alexander the Great]	109
	Khalmat Khan, a fine male type from Ferghana	109
30.	Roofed *bazar* street, Bugur	109
	Islam house of prayer, Shahyar	109

From G. Rassul Galvan, "Als Karawanenführer bei den Sahib's."—Kurt Vowinckel, Berlin.

31.	Western part of the temple buildings (*ming-öi*), Kyzyl	115
	Continuation of the same buildings, eastward	115
32.	Bartus and labourers on the temples of the little brook-ravine, Kyzyl	115
	The "step" cave-temple, big brook-ravine, Kyzyl	115
33.	Lunette on the wall of the "step" temple *cella*. Above: Mara's attack;	115
	Below: Scenes from the life of Buddha, Kyzyl	115
34.	The right bank. Entrance to the little brook-ravine, Kyzyl	115
	North end of big brook-ravine. Junction of both valleys. Kyzyl. Temples destroyed by an earthquake, 1916	115
35.	Building with red cupola roof. Pictures of benefactors in presumably European dress on the walls	123
	The "dance of death" (Great find of manuscripts here.)	123

From Waldschmidt, "Gandhara/Kutscha."—Klinkhardt & Bierman, Leipzig.

36.	Frescoes	123

    1. Tocharian lady, Kum Tura.

From Grünwedel, "Altbuddhistische Kultstätten in Chinesisch-Turkistan."—Walter de Gruyter & Co., Berlin.

    2. A white divinity with a dark-skinned musician (with Babylonian harp).

From Waldschmidt, "Gandhara/Kutscha."—Klinkhardt & Bierman, Leipzig.

    3. Tocharian painter in the E. Sassanian dress. Second temple building, Kyzyl.

37.	View from a monk's cell. Second building, Kyzyl	130
	The "crash" temple. Here the author nearly met with disaster, Kyzyl	130

From Waldschmidt, "Gandhara/Kutscha."—Klinkhardt & Bierman, Leipzig.

38.	Further wall of a *cella* with the pedestal of the sacred image and corridors. Second buildings, Kyzyl	130
	Entrance into one of the corridors, *ibid*.	130
39.	Small wooden reliquary, Tuyoq	130
	Painted "lantern" roof, Chikkan Kol	130
	Remains of Hellenistic statues. "Figure cave," Kyzyl	130

From Grünwedel, "Altbuddhistische Kultstätten in Chinesisch-Turkistan."—Walter de Gruyter & Co., Berlin.

16 BURIED TREASURES OF CHINESE TURKESTAN

PLATE	FOLLOWING PAGE
40. Head of a Buddhist saint, after the style of a late antique Hercules' head	130
Indo-Hellenistic fresco, scene from a legend. "Seaman's cave," Kyzyl	130
From Waldschmidt, "Gandhara/Kutscha."—Klinkhardt & Bierman, Leipzig.	
41. Temptation of Buddha by Mara's daughters. "Peacock cave," Kyzyl	140
From Waldschmidt, "Gandhara/Kutscha."—Klinkhardt & Bierman, Leipzig.	
42. Buddha preaching—many signs of late antique influence. "Painter's temple," Kyzyl	140
43. Conventional landscapes with rebirth legends. Chief colours, ultra-marine and bright red. Painting from the dome of a roof, Kyzyl	147
44. Distribution of relics. Fresco, Kyzyl	147
From Waldschmidt, "Gandhara/Kutscha."—Klinkhardt & Bierman, Leipzig.	
45. Cremation of Buddha's body. Fresco, Kyzyl	147
(Mummy bandages. Dragon on coffin lid)	
From Waldschmidt, "Gandhara/Kutscha."—Klinkhardt & Bierman, Leipzig.	
46. Splendid apartment with lantern roof in a house in Hindu-Kush (copied from Sir Aurel Stein)	147
From Le Coq, "Bilderatlas zur Kunst und Kulturgeschichte Mittelasians."—Dietrich Reimer, Berlin.	
47. Statue of a divinity, Shorchuk	153
Caryatid? from a pedestal, elephant pillar, Kyzyl	153
From Le Coq, "Bilderatlas zur Kunst und Kulturgeschichte Mittelasians."—Dietrich Reimer, Berlin.	
48. A view of the ruined town at Shorchuk, near Karashahr	153
49. The house of the English Political Agent, Mr.—now Sir —George Macartney, Kashgar	162
Crossing the River Tiznab with the caravan	162
From G. Rassul Galvan, "Als Karawanenführer bei den Sahib's."—Kurt Vowinckel, Berlin.	
50. Rest-station. *Kulan oldi* (the wild horse died), Karakorum Mountains	162
Tibetan *stūpas*, near Panamik	162
From G. Rassul Galvan, "Als Karawanenführer bei den Sahib's."—Kurt Vowinckel, Berlin.	
51. Inscribed stones ("Mani stones") near Panamik	162
Tibetan monastery, Lamayuru	162
From G. Rassul Galvan, "Als Karawanenführer bei den Sahib's."—Kurt Vowinckel, Berlin.	
52. Group of *stūpas* by the road-side, Lamayuru	162
The fortress of Dras	162
From G. Rassul Galvan, "Als Karawanenführer bei den Sahib's."—Kurt Vowinckel, Berlin.	

BURIED TREASURES OF CHINESE TURKESTAN

INTRODUCTORY

Historical Survey

ALEXANDER's conquest doubtless brought in its train the introduction of Greek culture and art into Bactria and North-West India. Many towns were rearranged and peopled by ex-service Greek and Macedonian mercenaries, who married the native women and thus changed the population to one of mixed nationalities but of Greek civilization. In Bactria the Indians were ultimately subdued by the Greeks, after having achieved a short period of successful opposition to the newcomers' rule, but Grecian supremacy was finally destroyed by the attacks of the Parthians and Sacæ about 130 B.C. After the Sacæ came the Kushans, who established a great empire embracing the district of the Indus as well as part of Bactria and of East and Western Turkestan.

Even before the invasion of these nomadic tribes Buddhism had made its way from India into the Hindu Kush valleys of the river Kabul. This region in ancient times was called Gandhara, and was inhabited by Indian tribes who appear under the names of *Gandarioi* and *Aparytai* in the enumeration of Xerxes's troops, given by Herodotus.

When Buddhism first penetrated these districts the type of Buddha was not yet fixed, since the Indian artists lacked either ability or courage to venture upon a graphical representation of the *All Perfect*. But the artists of Gandhara, by virtue of their mixed parentage, created the image of Buddha after the type of Apollo or Dionysus.

Thus, by the use of all the types of classical mythology, this district became the Pantheon of Buddhistic art, which through the whole of India as far as Java, and through Central Asia up to China, Korea, and Japan, is the foundation of the whole range of Buddhistic art in all these countries.

Wherever decaying Greek art comes into contact with a barbaric (non-Greek) religion, a new form of art arises. Thus, in the West contact with Christianity produced the early Christian art (Greco-Christian), and in the East contact with Buddhism resulted in the earliest Buddhistic art (Greco-Buddhist). The similarity between these two expressions of art is in many cases amazing. Numbers of the relief groups so frequently found in Gandhara, if characteristic Buddhist additions such as figures of Buddha and other Indian gods and saints had been removed, would have represented equally well the carvings on an early Christian sarcophagus.

This art, carried into Turkestan with the Buddhist propaganda, which was especially active in the first century of the Christian era, reached that country by one of two roads, viz. the longer but easier way through Bactria over the Pamir plateau to Kashgar, Yarkand, and Khotan, or by a second route, probably not used until a later date, through Kashmir and over the Karakorum Pass to the same destination. On the first of these routes this art would come under modifying Iranian influence, on the second under Indian.

The Buddhist missionary settlements in Turkestan were many in number, and consisted either of fortified monasteries, built of adobe bricks both on steep cliffs and in level plains, or of temples and monasteries, of varying size, hewn out in the perpendicular sides of high mountain ranges.

These last buildings are modelled more in the Iranian than the Indian style, for even though such cave-like temples are found in India at an earlier date than in Bactria (N.E. Afghanistan), yet the architecture of the excavated temples of Chinese Turkestan bears a much greater resemblance to similar buildings in Afghanistan —e.g. the enormous settlement at Bamian—than they do to those in India.

The name, too, of such rock settlements is in signification the same as in Afghanistan, where they are called *hazār saum* (Persian Arabic) = "a thousand rooms." *Ming-öi*, their customary appellation throughout Chinese Turkestan, has exactly the same meaning. The different settlements are respectively distinguished by the name of the nearest inhabited place—thus the *ming-öi* of Kyzyl, Kumtura, Shorchuk, etc.

From these monasteries the light of Buddhism radiated as far as China, which was enlightened by the new religion exactly as,

INTRODUCTORY

at a considerably later period, the Germanic North received the light of Christianity from the monasteries of Ireland.

Thus Buddhism with its art reached the nations of Chinese Turkestan, and continued its course ever eastwards along the celebrated "silk routes" that in the north follow the course of Tien-shan and in the south of the Kuen Lun. These silk roads cross each other in the oasis of Turfan, where the old town of Khocho is the most important junction. On the way the Hellenistic types suffered continual modifications under the influence of the Indo-European inhabitants of the districts through which they passed. This march of Hellenism from west to east is one of the four great movements of civilization which our expedition was able to establish.

But it is not the first, for in prehistoric times another such movement took place from the West to the Far East, when European peoples of South Russia—the Chinese Yue-chi, to be mentioned later on—passed to the north of the Celestial Mountains along roads that can be traversed even at the present day, and brought their Scythian art from Pontus to Mongolia.

Later on, at the time of the Aryan migration, a pronounced movement of civilization took place from Central Asia to Europe. The Huns and their friends and allies, the Iranian Alani, pressed the Goths on, to the West, and Alanian troops accompanied Germanic tribes on their victorious expeditions through Europe. In these expeditions they must have brought to Europe many objects of Central Asiatic and East Sassanian origin which were incorporated in the new growth of civilization among the Germanic States of Europe; these things were doubtless principally weapons, articles of clothing, and objects connected with funeral customs.

The last movement from east to west is that of the Mongols, who immediately after the consolidation of their empire established their post, thus being the first to bring Peking into greater proximity to the European capitals than was ever achieved, either before or since, until the opening of the Siberian Railway. It can scarcely be doubted that the Mongolians, in spite of their widespread devastations, brought us many varying kinds of Eastern possessions, and that through them Chinese influences reached Europe for the first time. Thus it seems no longer a debatable point that the Chinese were the first inventors of printing, even if only in a rudimentary form, and that these rudiments, brought into Europe by the

Mongols, laid the foundation of the art of printing in Holland and Germany.

At all periods when a strong dynasty occupied the throne, China was compelled to keep garrisons to protect the silk-roads in the countries through which they passed, and China, moreover, held sway over all the numerous small Indo-European principalities. In spite of this power of theirs, however, it is impossible to find anywhere the slightest suggestion of Chinese influence in either the architecture, painting, or sculpture of these subordinate peoples. All their forms are Indian or Iranian on a late classical basis.

It must, therefore, be assumed that until about the fifth century A.D. no form of art had existed in China which could in the least have influenced the nations of Eastern Turkestan, who looked to the works of antique art for their inspiration. Eastern Turkestan is not a fitting name for the country at that time, for it was colonized throughout by people of Indo-European extraction, whilst in the west and southwards, from the neighbourhood of Kashgar, Iranian Sacæ were also in occupation. The southern frontier up to Lop-nor was occupied by Indians who had pressed forward from north-west India over the mountains, and, by intermarriage with the Tibetans there, had perhaps acquired that facial similarity with Eastern Asiatics with which they are credited by Chinese historians. All the northern frontier as far as Kucha and probably much farther to the east—possibly to Komul—was occupied by Iranian Sogdians, whose chief towns, Samarkand and Bokhara, were of ancient renown in the old province of Sogdiana.

From Kucha to Turfan, however, the ruling class were a remarkable race, viz. the Tochari, a people of Indo-European speech, and, curiously enough, their tongue belonged to the European group of the Aryan languages. A hundred is called *kand*, like the Latin *centum*.

How this people got to Central Asia we do not know. Yet to the north of the Celestial Mountains, where pasture and water have enabled nomadic tribes to stay in any spot, there are many burial mounds, crowned by rough stone figures; when opened these mounds are found to contain objects of a bronze age of civilization which correspond to the Scythian antiquities of South Russia and of the Crimea. The stone figures, too, are marked by the same characteristics as are found in similar South Russian figures.

INTRODUCTORY

These burial mounds obviously mark out the path along which, in pre-Christian times, a European tribe (in my opinion the Yue-chi, to be mentioned very shortly) pushed on their way to China.

According to Chinese records, Western China, about the third century B.C., was conquered by a people bearing the name of Yue-chi (horsemen armed with bows and arrows), who pressed on to the bend of the waters of the Hwang Ho. But about 170 B.C. they were defeated by the Huns in a bloody battle and driven back to the West. They marched to the Ili valley, where they defeated the Sacæ, who at that time led a nomadic life there, and drove them off westwards. Soon, however, they had to follow in the same direction themselves, since their old enemies kept on harassing them from the East. Thus the Sacæ marched on to Bactria, which they conquered about 135 B.C., and so brought Greek rule to an end.

They were followed by the Yue-chi, who, after the conquest of India and Sistan by the Sacæ, founded a great empire in Bactria and north-west India, which flourished until the fifth century. The Sacæ and Yue-chi alike accepted the Buddhist religion, and amongst the Kushans, successors of the Yue-chi, Buddhism and its art was most zealously cultivated.

The Tochari, of whom we have already spoken, are in our opinion the survivors of the Yue-chi in Turkestan.

We connect with these people the European heads with blue eyes and red hair on the frescoes, as well as the European language which we found in great quantities of manuscripts in and near the respective temples and for which the name of the "Tocharish" language is in itself a testimony.

In the eighth century, about A.D. 760, the conquest of the country by the Turks began. The Uighurs, a strong Turkish people, eminently gifted in arts of war and peace alike, conquered the north-east of the country and took a firm footing in the town of Khocho near Turfan, the junction of the two trade roads, where they accepted the existing civilization and Buddhism as well.

Their kings, however, embraced the religion of Manes, whilst of their people a small minority, which afterwards increased to great numbers, were converted to Christianity. These people must, like their ancestors, be looked upon as a nation of entirely Western civilization.

22 BURIED TREASURES OF CHINESE TURKESTAN

Their three religions—Buddhist, Manichæan, and Christian—are all of Western origin. Their Sogdian writing is also derived from a Western Semitic source. They wrote with the reed pen of the Western peoples and their medical knowledge, as far as we know it, also came from the West. The Chinese influence upon their civilization was apparent mainly in externals, e.g. they used chopsticks and the Chinese ink-slab [1] and paint-brush for ordinary everyday writing. A certain admixture of Persian elements is apparent in their dress, although their clothing as a whole maintained its distinctive Turkish characteristics.

In a short period—roughly speaking during the next two hundred years—they subdued the whole land, and intermixed to such an extent with the former inhabitants that in the tenth century the country had become a veritable Turkestan, that is a land of the Turks. They further developed the existing civilization, and that, too, with great success.

But since they were evidently an Eastern Asiatic race—and have hence been compared with the Chinese in outward appearance—they changed the forms of art which they adopted in much the same way as did the Chinese. Under their hands the classic faces of the Gods forthwith degenerated into those typical of Eastern Asia.

The splendour of their empire must have come to an end in the ninth century, for at this time the eastern portion of their realm was subjugated by the Kirghiz—at that time a people of great power. But the Uighur Empire in East Turkestan had a recrudescence of prosperity which lasted until the time of Jenghiz Khan.

The Uighurs submitted to the universal conqueror, and continued to exist for some time longer as a dependent State under Mongolian rule.

The Manichæans had familiarized the Uighurs with Manes' art of religious painting for which Manichæism was so renowned. This art goes back to a Sassanian style of painting, resting in the main on an antique foundation. As is customary in sacred representation, the Uighurs also endeavoured to remain as faithful as possible to the style of their Persian models in religious painting.

After the overthrow of the Uighurs, the Mongols adopted their

---

[1] Ink slab is a slab of rough stone with a hollowed surface in which the Chinese rubbed down their ink and mixed it with water.

INTRODUCTORY

more advanced Western civilization, and with it the Manichæan style of painting, bringing it with them when they conquered China, where this school of painting came under Eastern Asiatic influences. Then when the Mongols conquered Persia, and, so it is said, destroyed the former inhabitants in an almost incredible manner, they brought back to this country the art which had originated there, but which had been modified by the Uighurs and still further by the Mongols themselves, and here it then became the chief inspiration of the later Persian and Indian "Islam" miniature painting.

Islam did not get as far as Kashgar until the tenth century, and met with but scant approval amongst the inhabitants of the country. The Buddhists of Khotan and Kucha put up a despairing fight against the Arabian and Persian intruders, achieving, too, such a measure of success that, in post-Mongolian times, Buddhist temples were still standing side by side with Mohammedan mosques in the eastern towns—as, for example, in Turfan. The introduction of Islam had a fatal effect on the civilization, and especially on the art, of the country.

Moreover, trade in general suffered from the discovery of a sea-route from China to Persia. The silk-roads fell into decay, and the country, depopulated by the Mongol wars, gradually declined from its high level of civilization, for when Jenghiz Khan called to his standards all capable of bearing arms amongst the Turks to fill up the gaps in his great forces, those left behind found it no longer possible to maintain in working order the arrangements for irrigation, upon which all agriculture depends in this rainless country. They withdrew to districts that could be cultivated with the least work, and enormous tracts of land formerly under cultivation became deserts once more. In addition to this, the advance of the shifting dunes in many places covered the fruitful fields with sand, and this was apparently accompanied by a gradual drying-up of the rivers. These last-named phenomena seem to have occurred especially along the southern edge of the land.

After the intrusion of Islam in the tenth century there was a gradual decline in the civilization of the country, for it fell under the subjugation of Jagatai, a son of Jenghiz Khan; and remained under the increasing degeneracy of this dynasty until about the middle of the sixteenth century, when a family of saints—descendants of Mohammed—immigrated from Samarkand and attained both wealth and position in Chinese Turkestan.

Under the name of "Khojas" they gradually became the real rulers of the country, but soon divided into two branches, which waged a deadly feud against each other, until at last the chief of one of the branches, with the help of Kalmuck princes of the Dzungaria, conquered Kashgar and assumed the reins of government as a vassal of the unbelievers.

But the Kalmucks became involved in war with China and were almost exterminated. The Chinese then conquered East Turkestan by means of horrible bloodshed.

The Khojas fled over the western frontier and took refuge in Khokand, whence they made several attempts to wrest their kingdom from the Chinese, but any success they may have achieved by these efforts was but short-lived.

Unfortunately A. von Schlagintweit chanced to come to Kashgar just while the rebellion of Wali Khan Tura was taking place, and was put to death by order of this bloodthirsty fanatic.

Then followed the revolt of the Tungans, and the increasing confusion, combined with the frequent defeats of the Chinese, induced the Khoja Buzurg in 1864 to leave Khokand to hasten to Kashgar with a following of barely fifty men. But one of his followers was a remarkable man, named Yakub Beg, who had fought against the Russians and given proof of his capability.

Although as a youth he had been obliged by poverty to struggle for existence as a public dancer and comedian, he succeeded by bravery, energy, and cunning, after the conquest of the country, in disposing of the Khoja and his adherents, and became the sole ruler of Eastern Turkestan. He established a certain degree of order in the exhausted land, but in the end could not successfully withstand the superior strength of the Chinese, who in 1877 carried out a well-prepared attack on Yakub Beg's worn-out army and routed it. Yakub died suddenly, his followers dispersed, and Eastern Turkestan once more came under Chinese rule.

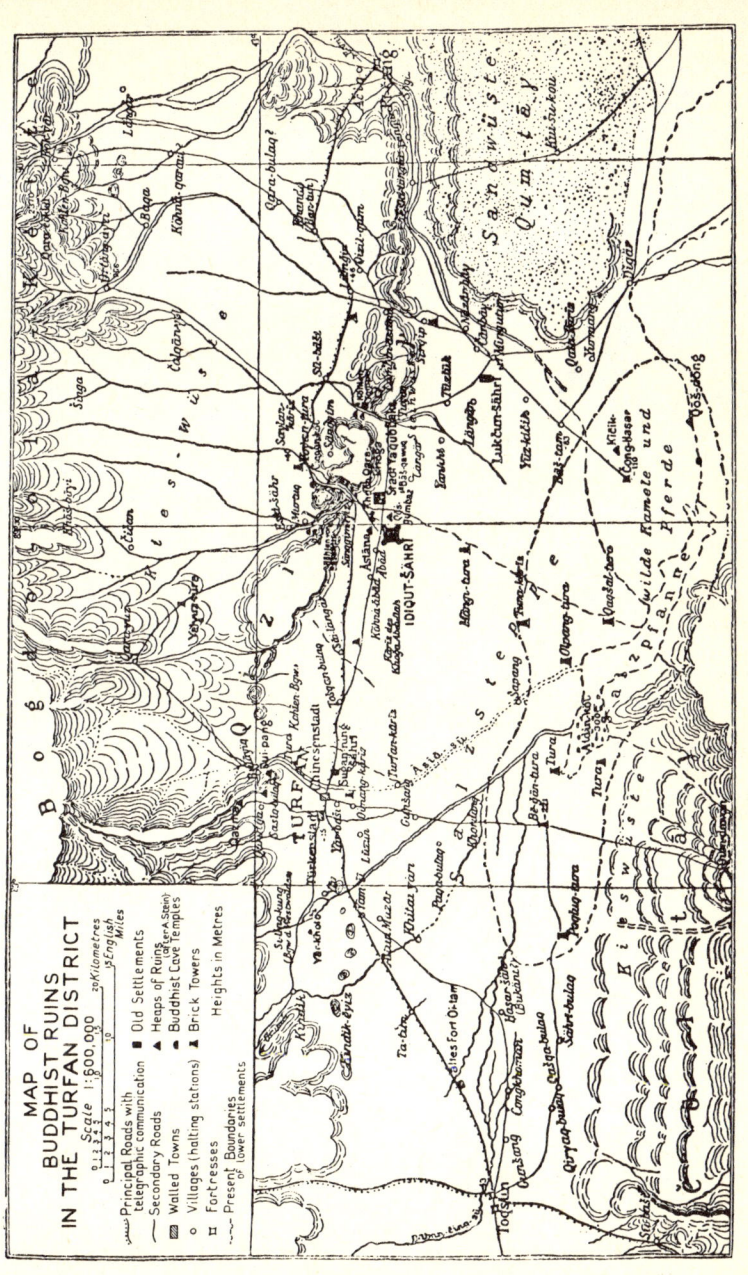

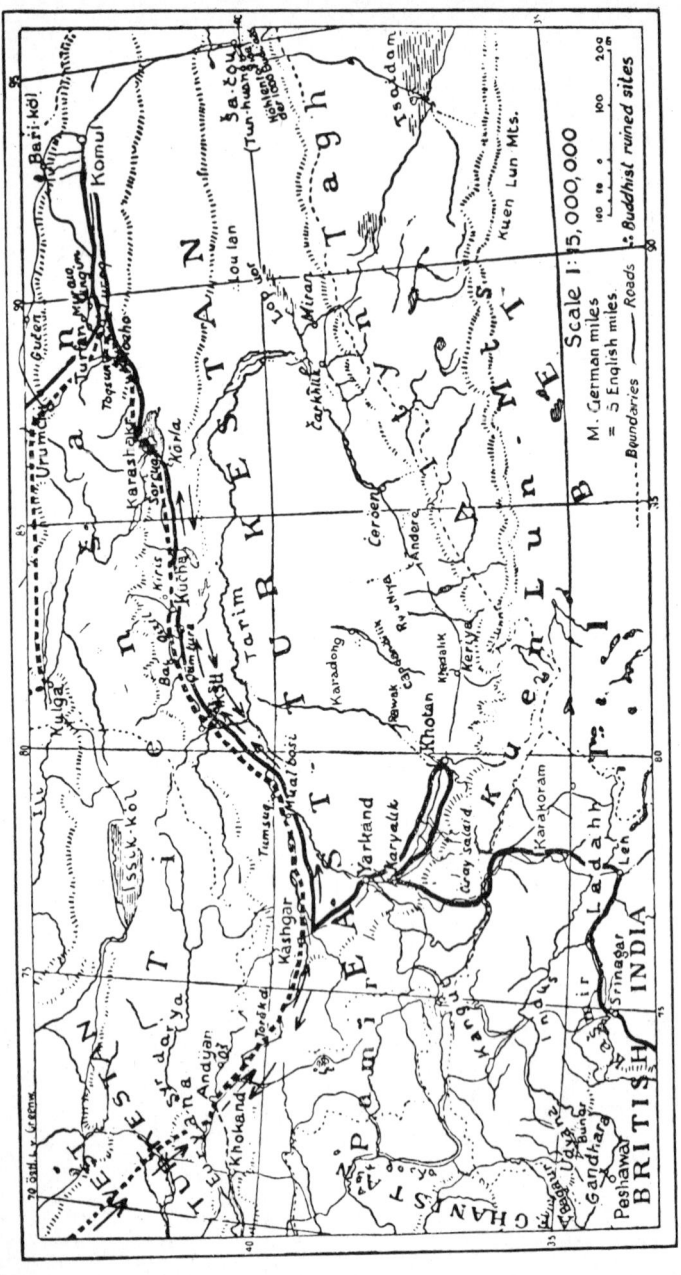

Remarks on the Expeditions

A Record of the Journeys and their Results.

We will begin with a few dry remarks.

Four expeditions have been dispatched to Central Asia by the Berlin Ethnological Museum. The first went to Turfan under the leadership of Professor A. Grünwedel and Dr. G. Huth. Their sphere of operations was the oasis of Turfan, where they worked from November 1902 to March 1903, for the journey there and back took up the greater part of the year devoted to this expedition. The result was 46 chests, each about $37\frac{1}{2}$ kilogrammes ($82\frac{3}{4}$ lb.) in weight.

I took charge of the second expedition, which lasted from September 1904 to December 1905. Our field of investigation was the oasis of Turfan and the neighbourhood of Komul, and resulted in 103 cases weighing from 100 to 160 kilogrammes ($220\frac{1}{2}$ to 331 lb.).

For the third expedition the members of the second were joined by Professor A. Grünwedel and his companion Referendar, H. Pohrt, both of whom we met in Kashgar. This expedition lasted from December 1905 to June 1907. I was compelled, at the end of June 1906, to leave Grünwedel in Karashahr, and to return home by way of India, reaching Berlin in January 1907; whilst Grünwedel came back in June of the same year. Our investigations were carried on in the oases of Kucha, Karashahr, Turfan, and Komul, and our cases amounted to 128 of 70 to 80 kilogrammes ($154\frac{1}{2}$ to $176\frac{1}{2}$ lb.).

The fourth expedition lasted from January 1913 to the end of February 1914 and was again under my direction. It resulted in 156 cases of 70 to 80 kilogrammes in weight.

Our excellent engineer, Mr. Theodor Bartus, accompanied the fourth expedition—as well as the first three—and its work was the exploration of the oases of Kucha and Maralbashi.

The results of these expeditions must be compared with those of explorers sent out by Russia, England, France, and Japan.

Of the Russians Dr. A. Regel, a German-Russian, was the very first European after Benedict Goes (1604) to visit Turfan in 1878. He was a botanist, but brought back the first information concerning the old town near Turfan, which he considered as a late Roman settlement. After him came Sven Hedin, who by his exceptionally daring and successful journeys showed the way to all later expeditions.

The Russians sent D. Klements in 1898 to Turfan, where, it is true, he only met with partial success; but he pointed out that this neighbourhood, the meeting-place of the old trade roads, was less affected by treasure-seekers than the westerly oases, where a prince of the Jagatai dynasty had, as early as the sixteenth century, instituted excavations on a grand scale which met with much success. We had learnt this fact from Denison Ross's *Tarikh-i-Rashidi*, and had, therefore, decided not to go to the south-west, but rather to the little-known north-east of the country. Two Russians, the brothers Grum-Gržimailo, also explored these districts, and published their experiences in a large book.

The Frenchmen Grenard and Dutreuil de Rhins also undertook a great journey through the country, which, however, was ended for both by the death, at a murderer's hand, of the last mentioned of the two comrades.

Very great success crowned the various journeys undertaken under the auspices of the Anglo-Indian Government by Sir Aurel Stein, the English explorer, distinguished both as a geographer and philologist, who undertook several expeditions, especially to the south and east of Chinese Turkestan. He was successful in discovering a great part of the literary and art treasures contained in an immured library of the Mongol period in Tung-hwang.

The expedition of 1906-9, under the leadership of the Frenchman Paul Pelliot, was also rich in results, for he, too, was fortunate enough to be able to get a large number of the manuscripts and pictures of the same library.

The Russian Berezowsky was working in the oasis of Kucha at about the same time as our third expedition. Later on Councillor Sergius von Oldenburg undertook his great journeys, which have borne fruit in his excellent book, dealing especially with the oases of Karashahr and Turfan.

Nor have the Japanese been idle. Count Otani and Mr. Tachibana —both members of the Japanese Buddhist priesthood—especially have brought great numbers of artistic and literary treasures to Japan. Mr. Yoschikawa also spent to good purpose a considerable time in these districts.

The results of all these expeditions supplement each other in the most gratifying way. Yet it must be recognized that the Berlin collection is the best adapted for the study of the developments shown by Buddhist art on its way through Central Asia to China; for the German expeditions alone took with them a man who thoroughly understood how to accomplish the difficult work of sawing off the mural paintings and packing them in such a way as to reach Berlin uninjured.

Since the exploration of the ruins of Nineveh by Sir Austen Henry Layard, no expedition has yielded results that can be compared in importance with those achieved by these researches in Central Asia; for here a *New Land* was found. Instead of a land of the Turks, which the name Turkestan led us to expect, we discovered that, up to the middle of the eighth century, everywhere along the silk-roads there had been nations of Indo-European speech, Iranians, Indians, and even Europeans. Their languages, some only known by name and others not at all, were found in numbers of manuscripts. They were all deciphered in Berlin, translated, and dealt with in a scientific way. The number of such manuscripts is exceedingly great, and there are no less than seventeen different languages in twenty-four different scripts amongst them.

Numerous Sanskrit manuscripts throw much fresh light on the knowledge of Buddhism; great quantities of liturgical works of the Nestorian-Syrian Church in the Syrian tongue were found, and also many manuscripts dealing with Nestorian Christianity in the Sogdian tongue as well.

It was not until the rainless district of the Turfan oasis was explored that a great part of the Manichæan literature, which had entirely disappeared, was at last brought to light. It is generally written in wonderful calligraphy on excellent paper, often in various coloured inks in the beautiful Manichæan script, and contains important information concerning their remarkable religion. We also found pages of books of this religious sect, adorned with surprisingly beautiful miniatures. Credit is due to Professor F. W. K. Müller for discovering the character of the writing and its meaning. The languages in which this literature is written are Middle Persian and other Iranian dialects, especially the Sogdian. Later, Turkish translations of this literature make their appearance in late Sogdian script—a script which, moreover, had been used by the Sogdians at an early date in a *ductus* of a former time.

These Manichæan finds are the more valuable, since in the whole of North Africa, South Europe, and Western Asia, where the Manichæan religion was in earlier times very widely spread, owing to the hatred of Christians and Mohammedans alike, not the slightest trace of this literature has survived.

Of very special importance, too, is the knowledge that the Indo-European inhabitants of the country brought to the Far East not only Buddhism but Buddhist art as well. But this art, coming from Bactria and North-West India, is founded on late classical Grecian art, and our investigations have succeeded in proving that the celebrated Buddhist art of the Far East is, after all, dependent on Greek art in just the same way as are the expressions of art in Western nations.

The Different Styles of the Paintings

A. Grünwedel endeavoured some time ago to classify the different styles of paintings found in the oasis of Kucha—i.e. in the *ming-öi* of Kyzyl, Kumtura, and Kirish—in the oasis of Korla-Karashahr-Shorchuk—and in the oasis of Turfan-Khocho, Tuyoq, Sangim, Bazaklik, and Chikkan Kol.

But this classification is only provisional; we still know too little of the origin of the pictures, and certain differences in the style of painting, which Grünwedel thinks must be accepted as the result of the immigration of another nation into the country, may owe their origin to other causes.

For instance, it is probable that at various times, but often, too, at one and the same time, monks from the most diverse parts of India and the Buddhist districts of Iran were living in the monasteries of Eastern Turkestan. These strangers may very well have brought with them and continued to use the characteristic style of painting with portrayal of the arms, dress, etc., of their own native places, whilst the population of the country was in no way supplanted by another.

Then, too, all studies based on *style-criticism* must be taken up with the very greatest caution, especially where they alone are allowed to determine the date of a picture without confirmation of any other nature; we know that frescoes have been executed by stencils and an old stencil may very easily have been used again at a later period.

The confirmation or alteration of Grünwedel's list must be deferred to a future time possessing more expert knowledge of accessory circumstances. We reproduce it here unaltered, in Grünwedel's own words.

I. GANDHARA STYLE.—Under this term I include, to begin with, several variations of style which show most distinctly elements of a late classical character as they appear in the plainest way in the Gandhara sculpture. The variations are the predominance of the antique element in certain cave-temples, whilst others are marked by a strong admixture of Persian or Indian influences, so that in some of these temples we find compositions that are familiar from the Gandhara sculpture, whilst others suggest as their prototypes antique paintings (pictures on vases). Unless we are mistaken, we must explain these variations by different points of origin whence they reached Kucha and its immediate neighbourhood.

II. THE STYLE OF "THE KNIGHTS WITH THE LONG SWORDS"—which, indeed, ought to be called only an extension of the preceding style, if for no other reason than that we might take the same Benefactors' pictures as belonging to Style I. The coincidence of various details of these pictures with representations on Indo-Scythian coins suggests the grouping together—with due caution—of Styles I and II as the Indo-Scythian (= the Tocharist) Style. Style II has, moreover, variants which, unless we are mistaken, we may ascribe to different epochs and their fashions—for most of them are costume pictures.

III. EARLIER TURKISH STYLE.—This displays, indeed, a somewhat mixed character, since it embodies latent traces of Style I and even more of Style II, which from time to time, under the influence of the nature of the subjects represented, become quite evident. In addition to these, Chinese elements are plainly discernible, viz. as a special instance, the framing of the pictures on walls and ceilings by a rich floral ornamentation of unusual charm, with flowers which—if we are not in error—do not grow in the country. The Benefactors' pictures show a dress entirely different from that of the former styles, whilst the inscriptions appear in Chinese and Central Asiatic Brahmi.

IV. LATER TURKISH STYLE, i.e. the real Uighur style, represented by the great majority of the pictures in the neighbourhood of Turfan, especially in the temple precincts of Bazaklik near Murtuk, may be designated as the faded conglomerate of the foregoing styles.

V. THE LAMAISTIC STYLE, with evident leanings to the Tibetan.

I have given a more detailed treatment of this subject in *Buddhistische Spätantike*, vol. iii, pub. D. Reimer, Berlin, 1924.

MANES AND HIS TEACHING

As our excavations in Khocho brought to light extensive remains of the religion of Manes—a religion which, until then, had utterly and entirely disappeared—and as these have all been submitted to renewed research, it is necessary to devote a few words to the description of this religious leader and of the chief features of his teaching as far as we know them.

Manes was born about A.D. 215 or 216 near Ctesiphon, in the province of Babylon, at that time belonging to the Persians. His father was the descendant of a Persian family of position in Hamadan, his mother's family being Parthian—therefore Persian—and apparently of royal rank. Thus Manes, born of Persian parents in a Persian province, was a Persian.

His father, inclined to mysticism by temperament, devoted much attention to studying the views of the sects that, at this period, were especially flourishing in South Babylonia, and also initiated into their mysteries his son, who, as the result of his mother's visions, seems to have been destined to a prophetic calling.

And the exceptionally gifted child, even as a boy, showed signs of union with the spirit-world. Communications of a supernatural character came to him from "The King of the Paradise of Light," and he seems, when barely twelve years old, to have already thought out to a certain degree the religion he was afterwards to teach. When he had reached the age of twenty-four, an angel or heavenly messenger again appeared to him and commanded him to proclaim his teaching. Accordingly he preached his religion for the first time at Ctesiphon on the occasion of the coronation of the Sassanian king, Shapur I—March 24, A.D. 247. He does not seem to have

INTRODUCTORY

achieved great success—indeed, we find the young man, directly after this event, devoting long periods to travel for study and missionary work, during which he visited Turkestan (Čīn), India, East Iran, and in every district he is said to have left a disciple behind him to carry on his work.

After forty years he returned with his reputation so greatly increased that he was emboldened to invite Peroz, Shapur's brother, to accept his teaching. The prince was favourably impressed, and even brought about a second audience with the king, which resulted in Manes receiving permission to use his disciples to spread his doctrine in Persia.

But the Zoroastrian priesthood, enraged at such favour being shown to a heretic, incited the king against Manes, so that he had to go into hiding, but was captured during the rule of Bahram, the son of Shapur's successor. After a debate with the priests, in which he was defeated, he was crucified, and his body, cut in two parts and stuffed with straw, was hung up at the gates of the capital, Djundisabur. According to our manuscripts the date of his death must have been A.D. 273.

Manes was a zealous supporter of the liberal arts, and was himself a painter of such renown that his enemies, the Mohammedan Arabs and Persians, remember him less as the founder of a hostile religion than as the prototype of a great artist. His wisdom, too, won favourable comment.

For the religious writings in which he recorded his doctrines he used a special variant of the Syrian script with simple and clear characters of great beauty. According to some critics this was a secret script of his own invention, whilst others maintain that it was the variant of the Syrian script used in a small district of Babylonia. His books were written with the best ink on the best white paper, and often illuminated with wonderfully beautiful miniatures—a fact that greatly angered Christians as well as Mohammedans.

He is also said to have adorned temples with mural paintings.

His religion, no less than Manes himself, was of a purely Persian nature. It was a strange combination of Christian and—in Turkestan —of Buddhist ideas on the basis of the Persian dualism maintained with unswerving insistence. Manes also introduced into this combination certain portions of the ancient Babylonian religion and of the Gnostic teachings.

It was an independent religion, but it was easy for Manichæans, living amongst Christians or Buddhists, by emphasizing its Christian or Buddhist leanings, to appear as a sect of these respective faiths.

The basis of its teaching is the opposition between the principle of Good, of Light, with that of Evil, of Darkness. In the contest which develops from such opposition the Light suffers defeat and the Darkness takes possession of some portions of Light and intermingles with them. Darkness is compared to all that is material and to save the portions of Light from their union with Darkness, a fresh contest is waged by emanations from the God of Light in which Darkness is now defeated. From the Light elements mingled with Darkness arises the creation of the heavens, our earth, and the first human man and woman.

But Darkness, in order to prevent the salvation of the Light elements from the material, awakens man's lust. Through the subdivision of the Light elements existing in each human being, that results in the offspring at every birth, so little Light is left at last in human bodies that it can no longer be separated from the material with which it has become intermingled.

Manichæism was a religion of strict asceticism. All sexual union, the consumption of meat or wine, the possession of worldly goods of every kind, was most emphatically forbidden to the "perfect disciples," since all these things bound man to that demonic world in which they had their origin.

Hence only a part of the community could accept the obligations in their entirety. Enthusiastic spirits took the vows and devoted their lives entirely to the teaching of the religion, which, as travelling missionaries, it was their work to spread. They lived on alms which the other Manichæans offered them—that is, then, on bread and fruits and, curiously enough, the portions of Light contained in such foods were on their way through the bodies of these *electi* (*perfecti*) set free from the material world and restored to the realms of Light.

The majority of the Manichæans, the more lukewarm spirits, were to a certain degree the lay-brothers of this remarkable body. They married, traded, tended the land, etc., and owned worldly possessions of every description. But this class which bore the name of "listeners" (*auditori*) had to submit to strict religious rules, contained in ten commandments and in rules of abstinence. The ten commandments forbade worship of idols, lying, avarice, murder, adultery, theft, the utterance of false excuses, want of singleness of thought which betrayed religious doubt, and slackness in good deeds. In addition, they were commanded to pray four or seven times daily.

Whoever wished to become *electus* must in addition submit to seven other obligations and take upon himself three "seals." The complete acceptance and fulfilment of these rules was an indispensable condition of acceptance amongst the *perfecti*.

The rules prohibited (1) Lust and covetousness; (2) All flesh food; (3) Drinking of wine; (4) Marriage; (5) All occupations that required the use of fire and water; (6) Magic of every kind; (7) Hypocrisy.

The three seals were those of the mouth, the hands, and the bosom. The first forbade all objectionable speech and the enjoyment of all unlawful foods. The seal of the hands forbade all occupations involving fire and water, all actions which might injure the preservation of the Light portions in the world of plants or animals, all violent or wrong deeds, everything that might be instrumental in the entanglement of Light by Darkness.

The seal on the bosom forbade all sensual thoughts, especially those of sexual enjoyment, also hypocrisy and similar evil thoughts.

It is evident that the ethical standard of the Manichæans was by no means a low one.

A strictly defined hierarchy maintained the integrity of the communities. These consisted of "listeners," above them the "chosen" or "perfect," then followed three orders, viz. the *Presbyteri*, the *Episcopi*, and over these the *Magistri*.

The head of all the Manichæan communities, whose Latin title was *Princeps*, had to live in the town of Babel. But in time of persecution he fled to some other town offering safety. Samarkand was for a long period a sure place of refuge.

Nor was there any lack of persecution. In the West, where the Manichæans had more actively opposed Christianity, in North Africa, South Europe, and Western Asia, winning more proselytes than any other rival religion, they were persecuted and exterminated by the Christians to such a degree that not the slightest traces of Manichæan writings have survived anywhere. Sects originating in Manichæism survived for a considerable time in the Paulicians,

Bogomils, Cathari, and Albigenses; the horrible destruction of the last-named in flourishing Provence is too well known to need more than passing mention.

Similar views continued to be held in Bosnia, where the invading Turks were hailed with delight as saviours of the sectarians oppressed by the Church.

The Arabian book *Fihrist of An-Nadim*, excellently translated by Flügel in a very illuminating work, *Mani*, gives some information concerning the wanderings of the Eastern Manichæans: "Fragments of the History of the Manichæans, their Emigration to Various Countries, and Information concerning their Leaders."

The first who, apart from the Samanas (Buddhists), entered the towns on the other side of the Oxus were members of the religious sect of the Manichæans. The reason of this was as follows: After Chosroes (Bahram ben Hurmuz, *circa* 272–5) had had Manes crucified and forbidden the inhabitants of his empire to take part in religious contests, he began to kill[1] the followers of Manes wherever he could find them. They were, therefore, constantly fleeing from before him until they had crossed the river of Balkh (Jehun or Oxus) and reached the country of the *Khan*, in whose States they settled. "Khan" is, in the tongue of that country, a title by which the natives designate the princes of the Turks. After the Manichæans settled in Transoxiana (they remained there), until the time when the Persian power was scattered to the four winds of heaven and the Arabs gained supremacy (after 642). In consequence of this they returned into the cities of 'Irak, principally at the time of the dispersal of the Persians and during the rule of Bani Umayya (Ommayades, 661–760). For Châlid ben 'Abdallah al-Kasrî (ruler of the two 'Irâks 724–38) protected them, except that their leader in these districts had to reside exclusively in Babylon. Later on he went to towns where he was the safest. A second time they emigrated during the rule of Mokhtar (18 Abbassid-Caliph, 908–32). They then went to Khorasan in fear of their lives, and whoever remained behind concealed his opinions as he wandered from city to city. About five hundred of them had gathered in Samarkand. Their religion was known and the ruler of Khorasan (the Samanid Abû'l

[1] The persecutions were cruel. Al-Makin (Hottinger, *Hist. Orient.*, ed. ii, p. 166) reports: He (Bahram I) also had two hundred captured and planted head downwards in the ground and their legs crucified to a stake. "That is," he says, "a garden which the King of the Persians, Bahram, son of Hurmuz, planted."

INTRODUCTORY

Hasan Nasr, 913–42) wished to kill them. Then the ruler of Chin (Čīn = Eastern Turkestan) sent to him a messenger—I believe he was the prince of Tagazgaz (*toyuz oyur* = nine tribes = Uighurs) with the message: "In my country there are three times more Moslems than there are adherents of my religion in your country," and he swore to him that if he killed one of these he would in return kill the whole community for him, destroy the mosques, and put people in all countries who would keep a watch for Moslems and kill them. Then the ruler of Khorasan left them alone and made them pay a poll-tax. In the Islam States there are but few of them (Flügel, *Mani*, p. 105). The Abbassid-Caliphs, Al-Hādī and Al-Mahdi, began fresh persecutions between A.D. 785 and 809.

The district of Tocharistan in Khorasan, in the neighbourhood of Balkh, was for a long time a stronghold of Manichæism. Manichæan ambassadors from here succeeded, as early as the eighth century, in crossing China to the Court of the King of the Uighurs and in converting this powerful prince to their religion.

The power of the Uighurs was still so great in the tenth century that they could venture to threaten the warlike prince of the Samanids, on behalf of the Manichæans, as described in the foregoing quotation.

It is to the conversion of these ruling princes in a land as rainless as Egypt that we owe the preservation of the numerous Manichæan texts found there by our expeditions.

The Country and the People in Our Time

The country lies between 36° and 43° northern latitude and 73° to 92° longitude east of Greenwich; the neighbouring countries are in the north and north-west Siberia, north-east Dzungaria, west Russia (Ferghana) and Afghanistan; south Kashmir with Ladakh and Tibet; on the east it adjoins the Chinese Empire.

Eastern Turkestan is like a gigantic bowl filled in the centre with moving sand—a terrible and in many places, owing to lack of water, an impassable desert.

It is surrounded by enormous mountain ranges, viz. in the north the Tien-shan, in the west the Pamir, in the south-west the Karakorum, and in the south the Kuen-Lun. The lowest pass which enters the country from the west, the Terek Pass, is as high as Mont Blanc.

It is only in the east that there is comparatively easy access to Karashahr through the Yuldus valley—a road much traversed by nomadic tribes both in ancient and more modern times. It is true the East is free of mountains, but the horrible waterless desert of Gobi forms as great an obstacle to travellers as do the high mountain passes. A special terror of the deserts are the frightful sand-storms, called *buran* by the natives, and even ancient Chinese writings tell of these. Quite suddenly the sky grows dark, the sun becomes a dark-red ball of fire seen through the fast-thickening veil of dust, a muffled howl is followed by a piercing whistle, and a moment after, the storm bursts with appalling violence upon the caravan. Enormous masses of sand, mixed with pebbles, are forcibly lifted up, whirled round, and dashed down on man and beast; the darkness increases and strange, clashing noises mingle with the roar and howl of the storm, caused by the violent contact of great stones as they are whirled up through the air. The whole happening is like hell let loose, and the Chinese tell of the scream of the spirit eagle so confusing men, that they rush madly into the desert wilds and there meet a terrible death far from frequented paths.

Any traveller overwhelmed by such a storm must, in spite of the heat, entirely envelop himself in felts to escape injury from the stones dashing round with such mad force; man and horse must lie down and endure the rage of the hurricane, which often lasts for hours together. And woe to the rider who does not keep a firm hold on his horse's bridle, for the beasts, too, lose their reason from terror of the sand-storm, and rush off to a lingering death in the desert solitudes. In 1905, between Komul and Turfan, such a fate befell the carriers of a consignment of silver ingots on their way from Peking to Turfan. The heavy two-wheeled carts were violently overturned, the sixty Chinese horsemen galloped into the desert, where some of the mummified bodies of man and beast were found later on, whilst the others had utterly and entirely disappeared, for the sand-storm likes to bury its victims.

On the edge of the desert the ground rises, and consists here, as a rule, of fertile loess soil. The life-giver of Eastern Turkestan, the river Tarim, with its tributaries, winds its way in great curves through this loess district and the numberless irrigation channels—

INTRODUCTORY

which the industrious and clever peasants can skilfully construct without any extraneous guidance—transform, as though by magic, hopeless desolation into a rich and wonderful garden. Here we find woods of *elæagnus* trees (oleaster) that in springtime, especially during the night, fill the land for miles around with the sweet heavy scent rising from their pale yellow umbels; and here, too, we find splendid orchards full of plums, apricots, peaches, mulberries, and pomegranates, and in certain districts walnuts and luscious pears as well. Extensive well-cultivated fields bear incredibly rich harvests of millet, maize, rice, excellent wheat, madder, cotton, and occasionally potatoes, side by side with turnips, different kinds of garlic, and onions.

In suitable spots the cultivation of the vine produces many varieties of the most delicious and often gigantic grapes. Owing to very cold winters—although they are but short—the rows of vines are planted in trenches, into which the vines are bent down and covered with earth until warmer weather returns.

But the chief fruit is the melon, of which endless varieties, all alike in sweetness and delicacy of flavour, are grown in enormous quantities with but little labour, and which form a staple article of food for the inhabitants. The water-melon is less attractive but is also cultivated, both in the red and yellow-fleshed variety.

Willows, poplars, and mulberries are the trees most frequently seen, less often the splendid elms growing in spherical form and giving most refreshing shade to the sun-wearied traveller; their beautiful shape is the result of improvement by grafting.

In those marvellous gardens, the oases, lie villages and towns—sometimes, too, the homesteads of individual inhabitants, poor houses for the most part, although the wealthy may have comfortable dwellings built in the Persian architectural style, provided with good fireplaces and often decorated with artistic paintings.

But all these oases are separated from each other by deserts, not only the desolate and dangerous wastes of sand and the usual barren, treeless plains, but by three other kinds as well.

The tamarisk jungle spreads over apparently endless stretches of land; the individual trees often cover the flat or swelling surface of a plain with their foliage like nothing so much as beautiful feathered fans; but when the shifting sands push into such tracts of land they and the loess dust collect in the branches forming cone-shaped hills, with a tree pushing its topmost branch through the top of each one in its desperate struggle for life. In many districts such hills stand in endless succession, and the impossibility of seeing any distance makes it very difficult to get through.

A second kind of waste is the poplar wood, a copse of the slender stems of the *Toghrak* poplar (*P. Euphratica*), a strange tree with leaves of entirely different shapes on different branches. These wooded lands are generally near river courses, but one often rides for hours through dead woods of this kind of tree; the river has changed its course and all vegetation dies.

The third kind is the stony desert extending over wide stretches amongst the mountains on their lower spurs. In certain places, for instance, between Toksun and Karashahr such a waste of stones fills the whole mountain road (see Plate 1). Enormous boulders, smaller masses of rock, and, lastly, shingle mixed with larger stones make travelling difficult in this waste; the horses are very apt to hurt both fetlocks and hoofs, and the briny sand—so the natives maintain—causes swellings and other ills that make their animals useless. Moreover, in many parts of the deserts the *Fata Morgana* is excessively misleading. The inhabitants of Eastern Turkestan call it *azytqa* (misleader), and the deception is so life-like that inexperienced travellers may very easily follow it; the mirage, as a rule, consists of sheets of water with their shores covered by scattered shady trees.

The spurs of the great mountain ranges are covered by desolate waste lands. The rocks are often split asunder by the frequent earthquakes and heaped on one another into the most fantastic shapes; not a tree, not a shrub as far as eye can reach, not a drop of water, and in many places not a single trace of animal life!

The birds most often seen in Eastern Turkestan are magpies, crows, and several kinds of butcher-birds,[1] hawks, falcons, merlins, saker-falcons, sparrow-hawks, and eagles are of frequent occurrence. In many places, e.g. between Kashgar and Ak-su, the poplar woods are alive with sparrows similar to ours. Pheasants are common in Maralbashi, the beautiful plumiped sand-grouse appear in great numbers on the steppes, the rock ptarmigan frequents the edge of the mountains, where large grouse are also to be found fairly often. There are bustards, too, but we never caught sight of this timid bird.

[1] Shrikes.

INTRODUCTORY

The most characteristic animal of the plain is the gazelle, a rather small, graceful creature with horns like a lyre; great herds of them occur in all parts of the land. Specimens of the lynx tribe, smaller wild cats, foxes, and martens are also common, but instead of the hare we only saw rabbits.

Especially in the districts near Maralbashi, Shikho, and Manas, also by Lop-nor, there are extensive reed thickets, the hiding-places of pheasants and the shy tiger. In the same districts, too, the ground often looks as though it had been broken up by a ploughshare; this is the work of the wild pigs, which also, although quite able to defend themselves, serve as the food of the tigers and the numberless wolves, which, however, are too cowardly to be a source of danger.

It is most striking that for a long period, i.e. since the terrible wars of Yakub Beg, when the inhabitants of whole districts were exterminated, scarcely a human being has been killed by wolves or tigers. These beasts of prey are here as harmless as the men of the country, who, although they are the descendants of the invincible warriors of Jenghiz Khan and Timur, of the men with whom the great Mogul Baber won India from the valiant Afghans and natives of Rajputana, are to-day more gentle and amiable than any other race I know. This gentleness is all the stranger since they do not happen to be Buddhists but give their allegiance to warlike Islam. Perhaps one and the same reason is responsible both for the harmlessness of the beasts and the change in character of the inhabitants, viz. that life is easy here. Another contributory cause may also be that the Chinese since their reconquest of the country (1877) have put in force a complete disarmament of the subjugated population and broken their resistance by corporal punishment.

This population consists in the oases of East Turks, Tungani, and Dolani, of some West Mongolians or Kalmucks in the Ili valley and near Karashahr, as well as of a residue of Iranian tribes in Sarighkol and the Pamir (Wakhi and Pakhpo).

Kirghiz wander amongst the mountains in the west and southwest and also in the neighbourhood of Barkol; Kazak-kirghiz are found chiefly in the district round Ak-su and Uch-Turfan. Here and there, for example, near Khotan, Keria, and Kashgar there are settlements of people called the *Abdal* race who speak East Turkish, but also use some words of unknown origin. In many places they take a poor position socially. In addition, there are numerous colonies of foreign merchants in the large towns, where they are under the watchful eye of a consular agent (*aqsaqal*). They are Afghans (mostly from Swat and Bajaur, but also Shiite Pathans from Multan), natives of Ladakh and Kashmir, as well as Baltis, Arghuns (descendants of East Turks and Ladakhis), Turks from Tashkent, Andijan, Samarkand, etc., all known under the common designation of Andijani (*Andijanlyk*), as well as Hindus from Shikarpur. These are the most repulsive usurers that can be imagined.

There are also a few Jews from Bokhara. They are nice-looking people whose appearance and character distinguish them in a favourable way from many Ashkenaz Jews; they are, nevertheless, despised by the Mohammedans.

The rulers of the land, the Chinese, every one of them from Hu-Nan or Hu-Pe, fill all the offices of the civil and military government; a few great merchants and very many shopkeepers, some mechanics, drivers, etc., as well as soldiers, are also of the same nationality. Unfortunately there are also some very unpleasant, and at times dangerous, people amongst the otherwise very estimable Chinese; these are criminals (*champan*), banished for all sorts of crimes to great distances, who lead a vagrant life in the cities as thieves, gamblers, procurers, and the like.

The natives of Eastern Turkestan are a mixed race, and the European touch in many of them has been noticed by all travellers. Some have light or even blue eyes, and many of the men, if dressed in European clothes, would not be conspicuous in any European city. Side by side with this rarer European type another is to be seen —a Persian type distinguished by a tall slim figure, an unclipped beard, aquiline features, large expressive eyes, and a somewhat yellow complexion. The third element is the Eastern Asiatic, and besides these three types there are innumerable mixtures; the majority of the population might be characterized as mountain Iranians with a pronounced Turkish modification. Their speech is a beautiful and, in the east, a fairly pure form of Turkish with wonderful possibilities of expressing shades of meaning. Anyone who has anything to do with it must acknowledge the truth of that East Turkish proverb which says: "Arabic is knowledge, Persian is sugar, Hindu is salt, but Turkish is art."

Greater attention should be given to the study of Turkish languages. They are of great interest to the student of languages, and the

Plate I

Rest-House to the North of Urumchi

A dangerous pass near Aighyr Bulak

v. Le Coq, Turfan.

Plate 2

Mosque of Anim Khoja

A street in Urumchi, with execution apparatus

Plate 3

A street in the ruined city of Yar-khoto

Cave temples near Yar-khoto

Plate 4

Mahommedan tomb with Buddhist wheel symbol, near Turfan

Buddhist terraced pyramid in the ruined town of Khocho

View of Khocho ruins

INTRODUCTORY

traveller who is conversant with the modifications of the different dialects will, with his knowledge of Turkish, be able easily to make himself understood through the whole of Central Asia, starting, let us say, from Bosnia, until he reaches Peking.

When travelling through Russia I found even in the great Moscow hotels that all the waiters were Turks—the Russian waiter would scarcely be able to keep his lips from any drinks that were ordered—to whom I could easily make my wishes known, although I knew no Russian.

In the west of Turkestan, owing to the influence of the Mohammedan religion, Arabic is being used more and more, and there, too, many words are borrowed from the Persian, which are much less frequent in the East, where instead, however, we find some, if not very many, Chinese expressions for articles in daily use.

The civilization of this gentle, industrious, intelligent, and amiable people is, as in olden times, of an entirely Western character. The Islam civilization, which was late in reaching the country (tenth century), and which destroyed the flourishing Buddhistic civilization with its innate possibilities of development, itself mainly originated in that of Ancient Greece. Unfortunately contact with Europe and the natural intercourse with the neighbouring State of Russia are gradually destroying those beautiful arts and crafts which had been preserved here from earlier times. Thus the carpets, many with very beautiful patterns, known as Samarkand carpets, which were a special product of Khotan and the surrounding country, are now slowly disappearing. In the same way the art of making felt with various colours stamped in to form exceedingly remarkable patterns, almost reminiscent of Mycenæan prototypes, has almost completely died out.

The embroidery, often of a very artistic nature, and the silken goods, too, are deteriorating. The celebrated copper and bronze vessels, at one time made with great artistic skill in Yarkand and Khotan, no longer exist. The plank-weaving, once capable of producing really beautiful patterned belts, etc., is to-day satisfied with turning out simple white cotton strips for horses' reins and other parts of their harness.

The architecture of the private houses copies Iranian patterns, whilst the mosques resemble those of East Persia.

The intellectual education is slight and chiefly confined to a certain knowledge of writing. But nearly all the people know some arithmetic, using the copper coins to help them in their calculations. There is to-day not a single printing office left through the length and breadth of the land.

But, on the other hand, most of the natives are born traders and diligent, clever husbandmen. If good schools were available, these people would most certainly make quick progress, for they possess exceptionally good mental ability. The chief national failing is a very pronounced sensuality, prevalent in all classes, and greed, mixed with a certain habit of untruthfulness so commonly found in conquered races.

Moreover, despite the habitual gentleness of this small nation (for it does but number a million souls), the people can, when roused, be capable of appalling cruelty. Thus I was informed that the landlord in one of the desert rest-houses between Komul and Gu-čeng, on the road to Urumchi, made a practice of robbing and murdering travellers. Public suspicion grew more and more intense and a number of people combined to investigate the matter. The landlord was taken by surprise and thrown into chains. In the loess soil of the courtyard, holes were found filled with the mummified bodies of those he had murdered.

The revenge was terrible. The murderer was stripped naked and crucified by wooden nails to the hard-trodden ground of the yard. Then the avengers took a pot and a live rat and fastened the pot with the rat under it on to the murderer's belly. There he lay in the merciless rays of the sun with the rat eating its way through his flesh until loss of blood and sun together slowly killed him. It is true that this might also have been an instance of Chinese justice.

THE JOURNEY OF THE SECOND EXPEDITION TO TURFAN-KARAKHOJA

The German "Turfan" expeditions, so called from their first field of operations, originated in the Berlin Ethnological Museum; they could, indeed, only have originated in this institution, for none other has at its disposition the special knowledge required in planning out such a task. Due credit must always be accorded to Albert Grünwedel, Director of the Indian Section, and to his assistant, F. W. K. Müller,[1] for having recognized the connection between the Buddhist Art of Eastern Asia and that of Ancient Greece and Rome, and for having discovered the way in which such connection has been formed.

Grünwedel's book, entitled *Buddhist Art in India*, is a work of fundamental importance. He shows how the types of Grecian Art in N.E. Afghanistan, the Bactria of former days, and in N.W. India (Gandhāra) had, about the beginning of the Christian Era, been utilized by the Buddhists with some modification in the creation of the representations of their gods and saints. Buddhism then passed on over Pamir, and afterwards over the Karakorum Pass to Eastern Turkestan, thus gradually reaching China, Korea, and Japan.

Grünwedel quite rightly concluded that the connecting links between the Hellenistic and Eastern Asiatic types must be sought in Chinese Turkestan, and such a conclusion resulted in his planning an expedition into these regions, remote and inaccessible as they undoubtedly were. The inhabitants were said to be hostile, and their Chinese rulers wished to keep Europeans at a distance. The tribes on the frontiers are all cruel and treacherous. Quite a number of the few Europeans who have visited the country have met their death at a murderer's hand, either within or on its boundaries. Thus Adolf von Schlagintweit was killed at Kashgar in 1857, whilst the Scotsman Dalgleish, the Englishman Hayward, and the Frenchman Dutreuil de Rhins met the same fate, the last-named no earlier

---

[1] Later on, Director of the Eastern Asiatic Section of the Museum, and well known for the recognition and translation of the Manichæan and Sogdian literature and for his no less gifted work in that of ancient Turkey.

44 BURIED TREASURES OF CHINESE TURKESTAN

than the end of the nineteenth century. For these reasons it was decided to defer carrying out such an expedition.

It was Sven Hedin who proved by his intrepid and epoch-making journeys in Eastern Turkestan that it was possible to cross the country uninjured, and after the English traveller Marc Aurel Stein, in 1901, at the instance of the Anglo-Indian Government, had carried out his successful exploration in Khotan (in the south-west of Eastern Turkestan) and given an account of his discoveries at the Oriental Congress in Hamburg, Berlin decided to send out the expedition. Grünwedel and Dr. George Huth, F. W. Müller's assistant, procured the necessary means from private sources. A great part was provided by Herr Friedrich Krupp, one of those who looked with most favour on our expeditions. Dr. G. Huth did estimable service in obtaining these funds and, later on, also by his endeavours to persuade Grünwedel not to give up the fulfilment of his plan. It is much to be regretted that this young savant fell a victim to his own zeal; he died shortly after his return home, in consequence of the over-exertion and hardships he had endured. After a suitable travelling-companion had been found in Herr Theodor Bartus, the expedition started. And here a few words must be given to the personality of Herr Bartus.

He was the son of a master-weaver and born in Lassan (Pomerania). He went to sea in a sailing-vessel and passed his pilot's examination after many years of nautical life. For a time he was a squatter in the Australian bush, where he learnt to ride exceedingly well, whilst his many years as a sailor had made him most familiar with all the arts of tailoring, sail-making, cobbling, forging, and carpentery—in a word, with all the handicrafts needed by a capable worker on a sailing-vessel. During a visit to Germany he had to take a post in the Museum, as the collapse of his Melbourne bank suddenly deprived him of all his savings. The presence of this man with his ingenuity and exceptional strength and courage contributed in no slight measure to the success, not only of the first expedition, but of the three following explorations as well. Special praise is due to the zeal and self-sacrificing devotion shown in his arduous work, by which, however, he was fascinated in no less a degree than were the savants taking part in the explorations.

In all the many months which we spent in the scenes of our labours we always worked from dawn to sunset without any off-days

SECOND EXPEDITION TO TURFAN-KARAKHOJA

at all. Our holidays were only those days—and weeks—which we had to spend on horseback to cover the great distances between our different centres of activity.

On Grünwedel's return in July 1903, his finds, which consisted mainly of a large number of valuable manuscripts and a collection of wall-paintings, sculpture, etc., not very many, it is true, but all of excellent quality, excited the greatest interest (Plate 12). It was clearly shown that Eastern Turkestan until the eighth century A.D. was in no sense a Turkish country, but rather that Iranian tribes, and even a people of European speech, the Tochari, had lived in the north, whilst the south-west had been occupied by other Iranians, and the whole of the southern border as far as Lop-nor by an Indian tribe. In spite of its remote situation it had been the centre of endless traffic; the silk-roads used for the interchange of Chinese goods with those of India, Persia, and the Eastern Roman Empire, passed through the north and south of the country, and there was not a town but had its colony of industrious traders from all Eastern lands.

This explains how it was that our expeditions brought to Berlin a sum-total of seventeen different languages in twenty-four different varieties of script. All these writings have been deciphered in Berlin, and nearly all, after such deciphering, were studied, their nature determined, and a translation made of the contents of the manuscripts.

These contents were nearly all of a religious character, and it is evident that the chief religion of the country was Buddhism, with here and there small communities of Syrian (Nestorian) Christians, and in the east of Manichæans too.

The remarkable religion of Manichæism, which, in spite of its great spread for a time through Southern Europe, Western Asia, and Northern Africa, was utterly and entirely exterminated in these countries by the hatred of Christians and Mohammedans alike, survived in Eastern Turkestan. For the Turkish Uighurs about the middle of the eighth century conquered the eastern districts (Turfan), their kings embraced Manichæism, and in the temples of the Turfan oasis we found very many remains of Manichæan religious literature, both in Persian dialects and in early Turkish as well.

In consequence of the importance of these discoveries a committee was created with the object of sending a fresh expedition into this archæological land of promise. Its chief members were

Pischel, the Sanskrit scholar, and Eduard Meyer, the historian of the Berlin University, as well as Professors F. W. K. Müller, Sachau, and others. In a short time they succeeded in getting together the 32,000 marks required for another journey, and again Herr Friedrich Krupp gave a substantial contribution, whilst about a third of the total was provided through the interest which His Majesty the Emperor had always shown in our efforts. The second expedition was put under my guidance, and after short preparations I left Berlin, accompanied by Engineer Bartus, to proceed to St. Petersburg, our first destination. There we made the acquaintance of the savants of the Russian Academy, who assisted us with passes and letters of recommendation, after which we went on with our baggage to Moscow, intending to proceed from there by the Siberian Railway to Omsk.

In Moscow difficulties began. When Herr Bartus and I arrived at the station with our many cases—84 poods in all (a pood = 36 lb.) —and wished to travel by the *train de luxe* for Peking and the East, the weight of my luggage aroused the indignation of the station-master. "You come here with two first class tickets and 84 poods of luggage. You may take such and such a number of kilos with your tickets and the rest stops here; otherwise I would have to put on another luggage van, and that is impossible, so it must stay here." I saw what this meant, and holding a 50-rouble note[1] behind my back, I passed up and down before the Cerberus, gently waving the paper. When I had passed him three or four times the note disappeared and the station-master said: "Well, we'll manage." And sure enough they did manage and our luggage was secured. The train was entirely filled by Russian officers of all descriptions who were going to the Japanese seat of war, but only in a few individual cases did they come up to our idea of officers. After five days we arrived in Omsk.

Luckily enough we had arrived just in time to catch the Irtysh boat which took us to Semipalatinsk. Here—it is an appalling hole—we made the acquaintance of two typical Russian means of conveyance, viz. the *tarantass* and the *telega*. The *tarantass* consists of two pairs of wheels connected by a number of slender, springy stems of young birch-wood. The clumsy coach is placed on these slender stems, the luggage stowed away in it, and mattresses

[1] About five guineas.

SECOND EXPEDITION TO TURFAN-KARAKHOJA 47

spread on the top, so that travellers accomplish the journey lying down. The *telega* is a flat, somewhat bowl-shaped cart for heavy loads, a very unpractical vehicle in my opinion and one which often caused us great annoyance. We bought one *tarantass* and four *telegas* and started on our way. The drivers were, one and all, Kirghiz, and had the unpleasant habit, whenever we came to a posting stage, of beating up the worn-out horses into a gallop, so that we never failed to drive into the station with a great hallooing and smothered with dust.

One particularly unpleasant feature of the journey was that the axles of the *telegas* frequently caught fire and began to burn, so that we were forced to stop and put out the fire with sand—since no water was available—an operation in which the Kirghiz were remarkably skilful.

It is important on such journeys to take spare axles, and iron ones are specially to be recommended since they do not break; but they, too, have the drawback of getting hot and causing an axle fire even more quickly than the wooden ones.

We drove day and night, and consequently accomplished the journey to the Chinese frontier in eight days' time.

It was October and the cold was distinctly perceptible at night, but it did not now trouble us, since we had provided ourselves in Semipalatinsk with Russian furs. On the contrary, our first waking in the *tarantass* was very amusing. Herr Bartus looked at me and I looked at him, and, as with one voice, came the mutual inquiry: "Good heavens! what on earth do you look like?" For the dye had come off these furs and our morning greeting was that of two veritable niggers. Moreover, the colour on our faces and hands was distinctly faster than it had been on the furs.

The Siberian landscape is intensely sad and unattractive: wide plains, only broken here and there by poor little birch-woods, and slow, unlovely river-courses; but, on the other hand, great fertility, so that flour and meat can be sold at incredibly low prices.

One strange feature was the unusually frequent appearance of large birds of prey at various points of the steppe. Even from a distance we could see bare patches covered with great brown moving objects whose nature we could not at first understand, but, as we got nearer, they flew into the air and were seen to be large birds of prey—eagles, so the Kirghiz said.

The Russian posting-stations, at which we changed horses so that we might drive on without delay, are of the most primitive kind. Nothing can be obtained there but bread, tea, and sugar, so that, as we did not dare, on account of the customs, to open our expedition chests in Russian territory, we were forced to live on this simple diet.

At last we reached the last Russian station of Bakhty, and crossed the Chinese frontier, where we were welcomed in the border town of Chuguchak by the Russian consul and offered hospitality in the consulate.

Here the Chinese passports had to be shown and the caravan hired for the further stage on to Urumchi. All these preparations took considerable time, so that we began to fear the weather would no longer permit us to cross the mountain passes to Turfan. At last we got the horses; they were dear, much dearer, I fancy, than if we ourselves had managed the buying, but finally we went on our way to the mountains in our *tarantass* with four *telegas* and a number of baggage ponies as well.

Scarcely had we reached the mountains, however, than our *tarantass* wheel broke. The drivers got out of the difficulty by a simple expedient; they cut down the first birch-tree they could find, stripped it of its branches, and fastened it to the axle-tree, slanting to the back. It bent in such a way that it formed a sort of sleigh-runner.

Thus we went on until the roads grew worse and worse, and our *telegas*, fairly heavily laden as they were, kept continually falling over. When that happened we had to call a halt, fish our cases out of ground that was often swampy, and load up again.

When this had occurred for the fifth time I felt I had had enough of such incidents, so, as we had just arrived at the station of Dorbuljin, a stopping-place for many Mongols, we bought a couple of splendid Mongolian saddle-horses, lightened the *telegas* by packing a part of the baggage in the *tarantass*, and accompanied the caravan on horseback.

And now a most uncomfortable time began for me, for the consul had told us we must travel with great caution, as the Mongols and Kirghiz were fighting one another and making the country unsafe with their wandering companies; and, as a matter of fact, at one station, Yamatu, we found a Kirghiz woman with her children as

Plate 5

A ruin with Iranian arches, Khocho

The old city walls at Khocho with our baggage camels

v. Le Coq, Turfan.

Plate 6

The visit of the *Wang* of Lukchun

Our quarters in Karakhoja, 1905

SECOND EXPEDITION TO TURFAN-KARAKHOJA 49

sole survivors of a whole settlement that had been attacked by Mongols. Thinking, then, that the journey might not be entirely free from danger, I had been foolish enough to carry 12,000 roubles in gold in leather bags on my chest. They were a considerable weight even in the *tarantass*, but when I began to ride—my grey steed being a high stepper—the pressure became so unbearable that I had to give up riding after the third day. So the money, packed into a box, was placed on the *telega*, and I sat on the top with my Mauser carbine. It is impossible to imagine the discomfort of the journey over bad roads in that rough, springless conveyance.

Our path went through a wild mountain district, where we often caught sight of wolves and sometimes of great horned sheep as well, quite close to the road. Magpies chattered on all sides, for this bird, that we scarcely ever saw in Turfan, was exceedingly common amongst these mountains.

It was a strange sight to look up to the mountains and see the Kalmucks and Kirghiz, driving their flocks or galloping on horseback along the paths, that traverse the giddy heights above.

The dogs of these pastoral people often constitute a real danger, for they are great wild beasts with a distinct aversion to the European. In approaching a settlement it is wise to call out: "*Nokhoi! nokhoi!*" (Dog! dog!); then someone will come out of a *yurt*[1] and drive off the furious pack of snappy curs with heavy lashes of their knouts.

It was sad to pass whole districts that had dropped out of cultivation, and again and again to ride through the ruins of what had once been large places, the villages with Chinese or Turkish inhabitants destroyed by the Tungans in the wars of Yakub Beg—or vice versa—for at that time every man's hand was against his neighbour.

Thus we reached Urumchi in sixteen days. This town is called in Chinese *Di-hwa* and sometimes *Khung-meao-dze*, from a little Chinese temple situated in a wonderfully romantic spot on a neighbouring rock. Urumchi is a great trading-place and the seat of the viceroy (*fu-tai, sung-fu*); it used to be one of the three national mints, the two others being Ak-su and Kashgar, but in 1913 coins were only being minted in the last-named town. Urumchi is inhabited to some extent by Eastern Turks, but mainly by Tungans (Chinese-

[1] *Yurt* = a Kirghiz felt hut.

speaking Mohammedans) and by Chinese. The Tungans are even less pleasant here than they are in other places.

There were many Chinese troops in Urumchi just then, when the Japanese were continually routing the Russians; a very little more and the Chinese would have invaded Russia. They would undoubtedly have been able to occupy all Siberia without more ado.

The Russians in Urumchi made no effort to conciliate the Chinese. On the contrary, when the consul took his drive he did so in an open carriage with an escort of twenty Cossacks in front and twenty more behind; whoever crossed his path and did not jump to one side with all imaginable speed got the whip on his face, his shoulders, or wherever it so happened, in the most inconsiderate fashion. After I had become acquainted with the consul I made some modest protests, but only to be met with the response that I did not know how these people had to be treated.

In the town there are a few fine Chinese buildings belonging to secret societies.

The fortifications are those usual in China, and the streets, on the whole, are representative of a Chinese town. The sight of a Chinese execution-apparatus, set up in the principal street, made a very unpleasant impression on me. It was a cage in which a condemned man was standing on a movable foot-board. His head was firmly fixed between planks and every day the foot-board was moved down a little so that the unhappy man's neck was slowly dragged out more and more until in the end—eight days it was said to last—death occurred. My Turkish servant called the apparatus simply *kapas* (cage), from Arabic *kafas*. Radloff names it *khokhanjan*, a term I could not verify (see Plate 2). The traffic went on as usual past this barbaric apparatus, and a melon-dealer was selling his juicy fruit with no concern for his neighbour's misery.

We visited the Russian Consulate, where we met with a very kindly reception, especially from Dr. Kochanowsky. The Chinese passports had to be produced, and we also had to pay our respects to the viceroy. He invited us to the *Yamen* (Government buildings), where we had to submit to a dinner of eighty-six courses. But before that began the viceroy held a levee—a general march past—of the Manchurian officials. All these dignitaries in a long row trotted past the viceroy, and when they were exactly in front of his raised

SECOND EXPEDITION TO TURFAN-KARAKHOJA

seat, they bent one knee and extended their right hand to touch the ground.

This first experience of the punctilious ceremonial, costly garments, and dignified bearing of the natives gave me a vivid picture of the ancient Chinese civilization and much impressed me.

Not so the food, which I never learnt to appreciate. My Turki servant stood behind me and called out continually: "*Yēmanglar, tūram, yēmanglar!*" (Do not eat, my prince, do not eat!). I found that the dishes against which he warned me were always either pork or duck, of which bird the Turks show a holy terror when it is cooked by the Chinese. We appeared in top-hats and dress-coats—not at all suitable attire in the terrible dust with which the air is always heavy. But the Chinese looked upon it as a polite attention. We brought, however, so much dust home with us that we might have grown a small plantation on our festive garments.

After a few days we took our leave and proceeded on our way to Turfan.

When the mountain range had been crossed we descended into the remarkable depression of Turfan, which, according to the American geographer, Ellsworth Huntington, lies in part more than three hundred feet below sea-level. It is surrounded by bare, red hills, strangely rent and torn; the names of these ranges (Kum-tagh, or Sand Mountains, and Chol-tagh, or Desert Heights) plainly show the nature of this mountain district.

The pitiless sun of Central Asia pours its rays into this depression, where they are absorbed by the red rocks that radiate the heat out again at sundown. No wonder, then, that a tropical heat prevails here—our thermometer often registered 130° F.—and that the natives designate this oasis as *Turkistan ning Hindustani*, the Hindustan of Turkestan.

As a means of escape from the heat, the well-to-do inhabitants of Turfan have underground rooms where the temperature is certainly considerably lower than in the rest of the house. But, for my part at any rate, I always found it unbearable to stay in these apartments, for not only was the air somewhat oppressive but the numerous mosquitoes and sandflies tormented everyone who tried to rest there. Insect pests are very much in evidence here. There are scorpions whose sting is a very serious matter, and, in addition, a kind of great spider that, in spite of a hairy body the size of a pigeon's egg, can take mighty jumps with its long, hairy legs. It makes a crunching noise with its jaws and is said to be poisonous, although I have never known any bitten by it.

Another spider, very much smaller and black but hairy too, lives in holes in the ground. It is very greatly feared and its bite is said to be, if not deadly, at any rate extremely weakening and dangerous. The cockroaches, too, are a repulsive pest, in size quite as long as a man's thumb, with big red eyes and formidable feelers. It was enough to make a man uncontrollably sick to wake in the morning with such a creature sitting on his nose, its big eyes staring down at him and its long feelers trying to attack its victim's eyes. We used to seize the creature in terror and crush it, when it gave off an extremely disagreeable smell. Fortunately there were no bugs, although fleas abounded everywhere, but were not very obtrusive. The louse, on the contrary, is *the* domestic animal of all Turkestan and Tibet. We, however, never had to suffer from this vermin, for I had provided myself with grey ointment. This mercurial ointment was spread between two pieces of blotting-paper, and this ointment sandwich cut into long strips, which were distributed in our outer pockets. The mercury evaporates in the heat and kills lice and nits. Every fresh servant that joined our camp had, before entrance, to wash himself with mercurial soap. During this proceeding his clothes were rolled up with similar strips of mercurial blotting-paper and laid in the sun. By the time he had finished washing, all the lice had been killed by the combined action of mercury and the fiery rays of the sun.

Wherever the rich loess soil of the Turfan oasis is sufficiently watered, it produces the most luxuriant harvests, the most renowned of which are the melons, grapes, and pomegranates.

Maize, millet, and particularly good wheat are produced in abundance; the wheat is said to ripen twice in the year, producing, so it is stated, forty to forty-six grains for each one sown. Cotton, too, of exceptional quality is cultivated here.

But the one chief essential for all agriculture in this country is water. It is true a few lesser rivers come down to the valley from the northern mountain heights, but this amount of water, since it scarcely ever rains, can only supply a portion of the fields with the precious liquid they require, although the natives, without any kind of apparatus

SECOND EXPEDITION TO TURFAN-KARAKHOJA

for measuring and with nothing but their broad, heavy pickaxe (*ketman*), know so well how to arrange the water-courses with the most intelligent calculation of the fall of the land, that the very utmost use is made of the amount available.

These astonishing feats are a consequence of the practice and experience of thousands of years. This is shown, too, in a very practical contrivance used by these people to guide the mountain springs into the plain. These water-courses, called *kariz* (Persian), are made as follows. After the exact position of the spring is fixed a large number of shafts, often very deep, are sunk in a long, straight line on the rising ground. When they are finished they are joined to one another by tunnels, the spring is directed into the topmost hole, flows through the tunnel, and since this slopes less steeply than the rising land, the water issues at the desired spot in the plain. All this difficult work is carried out by the people without any scientific help.

The whole district between the mountains and the oasis is intersected by such *kariz*, and at night they form a danger to any stranger on horseback, since their crater-like mouths are never closed.

The distribution of the water supply is the work of the Mīrāb (Ar.—Persian: king of the water). He is also called *su nung bāgī* (Turkish), which has the same meaning; or again, in Persian, *bārāndād* (giver of rain). He has to keep proper registers, and, as a rule, only the most intelligent, honest, and prosperous natives are appointed to this office.

Whether the *kariz* were in use during the Buddhist period or have been introduced in more modern times, I would not venture to decide. At any rate, such water-courses are still made, and at the time of our visit in Komul a *water-engineer* from Turfan was making a few *kariz* for the *Wang* (king) of Komul.

How remunerative such *kariz* can be is seen from a case with which I was personally acquainted. The *Wang* of Lukchun had some made at the cost of seventy yambu (a yambu = roughly £19). The amount they brought him in the first year was sixty yambu, but in the second, eighty.

Coming down from the mountain we reached a remarkable valley called, from its great steep loess cliff (*yār*), the Yār ravine. Here two small streams unite in swampy land, and, on their shores, rise high cliffs in whose steep sides there are cave temples, but on the

54 BURIED TREASURES OF CHINESE TURKESTAN

horizontal surface at the top we find the ruins of a fortified town. This town, where the arrangement of the streets can still be easily recognized in certain parts, was, for a time, the capital of the Uighur realm. To-day it is often called by the half-Turkish, half-Mongolian name of Yar-khoto (the cliff town), whilst its Chinese name is Kiao-ho (see Plate 3).

From here the next place to be reached is the Mohammedan city of Turfan. As is the case in many of the larger towns in this country, we find at a greater or less distance from the older city, fortified by walls and towers and inhabited by natives, the *Yanghi-shahr*, or new city, generally even more strongly fortified, the dwelling-place of the Chinese garrison, and formerly also a place of refuge—not, however, one that was always quite reliable.

All these towns have a marked family resemblance. The streets pass between high walls enclosing either gardens or courtyards; often, too, they are bounded by windowless houses—or they widen out to form a *bazar* street. In these we find shop-buildings—poor little mud-houses with a mud platform on each side of the door for the exhibition of their wares (cf. Plate 30).

As a protection against the excessive strength of the sun's rays, on both sides of the street poplar-stems or little willow-trees are fixed in the ground to support a framework of strong reeds or thin branches; on this framework bundles of rushes and the like are laid, so that business activities can be carried on in the shade.

After traversing the twelve miles or so between Yarkhoto and the Old Town we rode into the latter, much to the interest of the inhabitants. Women and children crowded on to every roof and on all sides rose the cry of *"Uruss! Uruss! Uruss käldī!"* (Russians! Russians! Russians have come!).

But the scene soon changed. As we were driving through the *bazar* Bartus was recognized by a butcher, an enormous man who remembered him from the first expedition and now greeted him with joyous cries of *"Bātúr! Bātúr!"*

His name, Bartus, in East Turkestan is pronounced *bātúr*—a title which the Great Moguls, in the form of *Bahādur*, carried to India, where it is still conferred on people of distinction. In Turfan it has almost the significance of "hero," and this occurrence contributed not a little to our reputation. And now the cry was *"Parang käldī!"*

SECOND EXPEDITION TO TURFAN-KARAKHOJA

(Franks have come!). Since the Russians are greatly hated, we found this explanation of the circumstances very agreeable.

The king of Lukchun had already sent to meet us a delegation of notables (an *istikbāl*), who received us with the usual meal (*dastarkhan*), consisting of many kinds of food, tea, and fruit. We found special refreshment in the delicious melons, grapes, and pomegranates after the very strenuous days of our mountain journey.

From the Mohammedan town of Turfan the road leads through a frightful desert to Karakhoja.

Outside the New Town of Turfan rises a mosque with a high minaret. This tower is, in places, inlaid with patterned perforated tiles, but is built, like the mosque, only of the tough, air-dried bricks (Spanish: *adobe*) common to the country. The style of its architecture is that of buildings of the same nature in Samarkand, Bokhara, and Khiva (Plate 2).

Former travellers have looked upon this minaret as the bell-tower of an ancient Nestorian Christian community. It is not so, however, but rather a building of comparatively modern construction. The building inscription to be found on a pedestal in the mosque states that the building was erected or restored about 1760 by the famous Amin Khojam Khanlyk, founder of the Royal family of Turfan-Lukchun.

In the neighbourhood there are extensive Mohammedan cemeteries with some domed tombs. The largest of these tombs has a walled-in entrance court. The wall is crowned with graduated battlements, and at the junctions of the wall with the tomb-building itself it bears the representation of a wheel, a Buddhist symbol. Here, too, Buddhism has left a trace behind (see Plate 4A).

OUR LIFE AND WORK IN KARAKHOJA. I

At last, on November 18th, we arrived at the scene of our excavations, the old ruined town of Khocho, to-day called Karakhoja. By native tongues it is called *Apsūs* (Ephesus), also the city of *Dakianus* (after the Roman Emperor, Decius, the persecutor of the Christians) and *Idikuchahrī*. The old Chinese name was *Kao-chang*. The name of *Dakianus* finds its explanation in the circumstance that in the immediate neighbourhood, in the valley of Tuyoq, there is a sacred shrine of the Seven Sleepers, which, even at the present day, has the reputation of great sanctity, and is visited by Mohammedan pilgrims from such distant lands as Arabia and India. But the Mohammedans were not the first to bring the legend there—Islam did not reach these districts before the thirteenth or fourteenth century—for it dates from Buddhist times, as I shall show later on.

The old town is an enormous square, covering about a square kilometre or 256 acres (Plate 4). The massive old wall in many places is still in good preservation. It is almost twenty-two yards high and made out of stamped mud in the fashion common even at the present time from Persia to China. Numerous towers—there are still seventy of them existing—strengthen this wall, which diminishes in solidity towards the top, but which in the lower part is so massive that the builders could have arranged whole suites of rooms within its bulk, especially near the gates.

The masonry of the gates is destroyed, but there appears to have been a fortified gate in the middle of each of the four walls enclosing the town, and apparently there was a fifth gate in the north-west corner of the wall.

The buildings are too much destroyed to allow the course of the streets to be plainly traced, but two wide main streets, one running from north to south and the other from east to west, seem to have crossed each other in the centre of the town by that Ruin *K* which we recognized as the shrine of the Manichæan kings of the Uighur Turks (Plate 8). The ground plan of the town, therefore, doubtless follows the pattern of the Roman *castrum*.

The buildings of the city are, without exception, temples, monasteries, tombs—in short, nothing but religious buildings (Plate 4),

Plate 7

Hellenistic heads, Khocho

v Le Coq, Turfan

Plate 8

The corpse hall, Ruin K, Khocho

Manichaean vaulted building, Khocho

Plate 9

Christian fresco (Palm Sunday?) Khocho

Painting of Manes, Ruin K, Khocho

Plate 10

A page of a Turkish-Manichaean book, illuminated, Khocho

Hellenistic Buddha torso, Khocho

OUR LIFE AND WORK IN KARAKHOJA

for we did not succeed in finding a single exception to this class. The architecture in every case is either Iranian (with dome-shaped roof, Plate 5) or Indian (*stūpa*, Plate 26). No Chinese buildings are to be found either in the Turfan oasis or in any other of the old settlements visited by us.[1]

It was a city of temples, and a necropolis whose strong fortifications in time of war formed a refuge for the inhabitants living in simple mud-houses outside the gates. These mud-houses, probably of the same kind still used as dwellings to-day, have disappeared without leaving a single trace. Some of the present inhabitants, native Eastern Turkestan tillers of the soil, have their modest homes outside the city wall, the houses of others are built in a long street. The sum-total of about 1,100 dwellings form three small settlements, viz. Abād, Astāna, and Karakhoja.

We dismounted at the *sarai* of the peasant Saut (Sābit), in whose house the first expedition had lived and who received us with unfeigned joy. He was an exceedingly artful fellow, whom we cannot call anything but a great rogue, but his rogueries were accomplished so cleverly and gracefully that it was not easy to be angry with him for long. His family were quartered out elsewhere, and we were given the best room—a little over five yards square—that communicated with old passages and apartments constructed in the city wall. This was to be our home for eleven months (Plate 6).

From the very first day our relations with the natives were exceedingly friendly, although an accident had happened immediately after our entry. One of our landlord's sons had been playing with a Browning pistol and unfortunately hurt himself with it. The bullet passed through his left arm between the two bones of the forearm, without, however, inflicting any injury on a single blood-vessel, nerve, or bone. So great is this nation's power of resistance that in a few days the wound was perfectly healed.

[1] The Persian domed edifice, in its simplest form, consists of a square building roofed by a cupola formed of two hemispherical sections. The uncovered corners are closed in by small shell-shaped arches.

The Indian *stūpa* is generally a building cut across into many polygonal divisions, and as a rule provided with a small room in which are preserved relics of the saints with a few manuscripts and valuables such as coins and jewels or the ashes of distinguished people who have been cremated.

Many of the temples are a combination of the two styles of building, only in this case the *stūpa* is a simple rectangular or square pillar, in front of which a square *cella* with a domed roof is built, and from this narrow corridors, covered with cylindrical roofs, surround the pillar.

In a short time we received a visit from Amin Khoja, King of Lukchun, the last descendant of the kings of Turfan, who invited us to move into his palace (*orda*). We were obliged to decline this invitation, since the old town was our field of operations, and we had no wish to ride the thirteen miles to Lukchun twice daily. Our refusal, however, in no way interfered with the good relations existing between us and the Prince. We hastened, however, to pay our ceremonial visit to him immediately in Lukchun.

On the following day work began. A few beautiful heads modelled on classical lines out of clay (Plate 7) were brought to us at once, and soon after some peasants led me into the centre of the town, where they had torn down a thin wall of more recent erection in a great hall-like building. Behind this wall, on the more ancient wall, appeared the remains of a great mural painting, representing a man over life-size in the dress of a Manichæan priest, surrounded by Manichæan monks (*electi*) and nuns (*electæ*) also dressed in the white garb of their order. All these figures, painted on a smaller scale, bore on their breasts their beautiful Persian names written in Sogdian script. We have reason to think that we had there a traditional representation of Manes, the founder of the Manichæan religion.[1] The picture forms one of the principal objects of our collection (Plate 9). The discovery of this picture puts an end to the view that the Manichæans had no churches (nor religious buildings) adorned with paintings; this hall, which was but one of several similar rooms comprising the building, was probably one of the "fasting halls" of this remarkable religion.

Our expeditions arrived too late at Karakhoja. Had they come earlier, more of these remarkable Sassanian-Hellenistic paintings would certainly have been secured. We should have saved, too, very much more of the literature of the religious community, important as it is to the history of religions and languages alike; one of the peasants told me that five years before the arrival of the first expedition he had, in the ruins of one of the temples, which were pulled down to turn their site into fields, found great cart-loads (*araba*) of those manuscripts "with the little writing" (i.e. Manichæan) for which we were making such diligent search. Many

---

[1] For Manichæan religion and art, as well as details of Mani or Manes, the reader is referred to A. Le Coq's *Die Buddhistische Spätantike Mittelasiens*. Band II, "Die Manichäischen Miniaturen" (Dietrich Reimer, publishers, Berlin, 1923).

OUR LIFE AND WORK IN KARAKHOJA

had been ornamented with pictures in gold and colours. But he was afraid, to begin with, of the unholy nature of the writings and, secondly, that the Chinese might use the discovery as a pretext for fresh extortions, so he straightway threw the whole library into the river!

The Manichæan manuscripts appear in different kinds of books, viz. (1) the ancient book-roll; (2) the folding book—a long sheet of paper folded concertina-wise; (3) the Indian book; and (4) the European bound book. The *pothi*, or Indian book, is a pile of long, narrow, square-cut leaves, pierced on one side in one or two places. Two somewhat larger pieces of wood, pierced to match and often beautifully modelled on one side, are placed outside the leaves to protect them. A long cord is drawn through the pierced holes and wound several times round the bundle of loose papers. The Manichæan writings are found on paper, parchment, soft glove-leather, and silk. We found remains of beautiful book-covers reminiscent of Egyptian art; they are made of punched, stamped leather, sometimes in perforated work and often with gold ornamentation. Very splendid one book-cover must have been, which was made of finely cut tortoiseshell lined with gold leaf, of which we found a fragment. But whether this fragment was part of a Western or a Chinese book we do not know.

The Manichæan manuscripts are distinguished by that masterly calligraphy, that love of artistic adornment of everything, which must be recognized as the peculiar endowment of the Iranians, the first civilized nation of Asia. They are written in Manichæan script, a clear, legible, and very beautiful form of the Syrian script; or again, in the bold characters of the Sogdian alphabet, a script which, with some modifications, has been adopted by the Uighurs, the Western Mongolians (or Kalmucks), and the Manchus from the Uighurs. This script is derived from a Semitic form of writing not yet discovered.

The Indians in Turkestan mainly used the national form of book, the *pothi*, the roll, and the folding-book, as well as wooden tablets. They sometimes overlaid the paper with a paste (wheaten flour and chalk).

The Manichæan Turks occasionally used as well the remarkable Turkish "runic" script, so called from a certain outward resemblance to the runes of the Germanic peoples. This Turkish style of writing bears witness to deep insight into the phonetics of the Turkish language and can only have been invented by people of a scientific turn of mind. It is a striking proof of the advanced civilization of the ancient Turks!

The great Danish philologist, Professor Vilhelm Thomsen, of Copenhagen, some time ago succeeded in deciphering this singular and very difficult script, of which hitherto the only specimen known was from the Orkhon stone monuments. When, later on, I found manuscripts in this style of writing, I immediately put the best page on one side, intending to offer it on my return to Berlin to the consideration of the gifted decipherer as a little mark of my homage.

Grünwedel had commissioned me to devote particular care to the exploration of three special groups of ruins. We carried out this commission, but unfortunately with the utter want of success which Bartus had already foretold; and, moreover, in the time that had elapsed since the first expedition, the natives had destroyed a very great deal by their constant digging; for the city ruins contain various things that are of use to the present inhabitants. To begin with, there is the loess dust which the spring storms in the course of centuries have heaped up amongst the ruins, and which, mixed as it is with the fragments of statues, etc., that have been crushed and trodden underfoot, forms a valuable fertilizer.

And another, still more valuable, is found in the paintings on the clay coating of the walls; these paintings are, in any case, an abomination to Moslems, and hence wherever they are found they are damaged—at all events on their faces.

For the belief still exists that painted men and animals, unless their eyes and mouths at least have been destroyed, come to life at night, descend from their places, and do all sorts of mischief to men, beasts, and harvests! But in the neighbourhood of the villages they also knock down these bright water-colour paintings to get fertilizers for their exhausted fields. The Chinese, acting as officials in the country, pay no attention to this destruction; they are all Confucians, and despise Buddhism as the religion of the "small folk." (It was only when we found stones with Chinese inscriptions that the interest of these officials was aroused; we were only allowed to keep such as were Buddhistic in character.)

The beams of the doors, etc., were also especially sought after

OUR LIFE AND WORK IN KARAKHOJA

in the old temples, as fuel and wood for building is scarce in the lowland round Turfan. The beautiful fired tiles which covered the floors of many temples were much coveted as well. In earlier days the natives used to look for treasures, and they are said to have often made valuable discoveries of coins, gold, and silver statuettes, etc.

Finally, with the increase of population came the peasants' craving for land. Whole districts of the town had a clearance made by the gradual carrying off of the ruins, then the old sites and ground were levelled, water canals brought in to the ruined town, and with them the damp that worked such havoc. In many places the water had risen in the loess walls and done terrible harm to the ancient relics they contained.

Thus I had the grief of discovering in the Manichæan shrine *K* a library which was utterly destroyed by water. When I had unearthed the door from the heaped-up loess dust and sand we found on the threshold the dried-up corpse of a murdered Buddhist monk, his ritual robe all stained with blood. The whole room, into which this door led, was covered to a depth of about two feet with a mass of what, on closer inspection, proved to be remains of Manichæan manuscripts. The loess water had penetrated the papers, stuck everything together, and in the terrible heat of the usual summer there all these valuable books had turned into loess. I took specimens of them and dried them carefully in the hope of saving some of these manuscripts; but the separate pages crumbled off and dropped into small fragments, on which the remains of beautifully written lines, intermingled with traces of miniatures executed in gold, blue, red, green, and yellow, were still to be seen. An enormous treasure has been lost here. On the walls we found exceedingly well-executed frescoes, but they, too, were much damaged. In a narrow passage near this library a tremendous quantity of textile materials, some Persian and some Chinese in character, was discovered, amongst other things Manichæan hanging pictures on cloth, depicting a man or a woman in the full canonicals of the Manichæan priesthood.

These temple and votive pictures have the form of the Chinese and Japanese hanging pictures (*kakemono*); they are common to both the Manichæan and Buddhistic religion and appear to be of Western origin.

In the north-east of this same building we found a collection of four dome-covered buildings in the Persian style. In one of these Herr Bartus was fortunate enough to make the first of the more important discoveries of Manichæan manuscripts, amongst them a splendid miniature showing on one side Manichæan priests in full canonicals and a few lines in the Sogdian and Uighur languages, and on the other a row of musicians, as well as a beautiful ornamental scroll and a few red lines in late Sogdian script, containing the name and title of an Uighur king but which were unfortunately destroyed in places (Plate 10).

In one of the southern domed buildings, which we named "the corpse hall," we made a horrible discovery. The outer door of this building was walled up. The dome had partly fallen in, but a new arched floor had been laid above it, and on this had been built a late Buddhist temple, the walls of which had only survived to a very low elevation. We recognized, however, the remains of Buddhist mural paintings on these walls, representing mainly demons of the Lamaistic period (Plate 8).

After we had examined everything we broke open the floor, found the remains of the old domed roof, and then came suddenly upon confused heaps of the piled-up corpses of at least some hundred murdered men. Judging from their clothing they were Buddhist monks. The top layer was all intact—skin, hair, the dried-up eyes, and the frightful wounds which had caused their death, were in many cases intact and recognizable. One skull especially had been split from the top of the head to the teeth with a frightful sabre cut.

It is probable that the date of the terrible fate which apparently destroyed the old town must be assigned to the middle of the ninth century, for at that time the Chinese Government, in order to keep the monks in check, had issued an order that all monks, whether Christians, Manichæans, or Buddhists, were to return to civil life, do practical work, marry, have children, pay taxes, and become soldiers in accordance with the State regulation; any case of disobedience was threatened with death.

Here, as always, the same result was produced: pious men preferred death to conformity, and thus the tragedy to which the terrible destruction is mainly due must have happened.

Our work was carried on under the most difficult of all conditions, for in winter an incredibly cold, piercing wind from the north-east

OUR LIFE AND WORK IN KARAKHOJA

used to sweep through the town, whilst in summer the heat in low-lying Turfan was so intense that even the very lightest clothing was too heavy. Yet as a rule we had to work in shadeless places, exposed to the full rays of the sun.

It was interesting to see how Herr Bartus, a native of Pomerania, grew redder and redder, whilst I, of French extraction, burnt quite black in the sunshine.

The loess dust was especially tiresome. It filled the air frequently without our noticing the slight haze of dust, but often, when the spring storms were raging from March to May, it came flying along in dark-brown clouds. As it only rains in Turfan at most once every ten years, and the traffic of the native carts (*araba*), whose two iron-bound wheels are higher than a man's head, is very great, the roads were intersected by very deep cart-ruts and the loess was ground in them to the fineness of powder.

During our excavations this dust always rose in very suffocating clouds, and in the evening we often used to cough up solid streams of loess from our bronchial tubes.

This dust-fog absorbs the heat-rays, but the rays of light also lose some of their power under its dominance. Thus all my first photographs were under-exposed; it was not until after the first six weeks of our stay there, when, going out of doors, I suddenly for the first time saw the snow-covered mountains, that I understood that the whole time there had been a haze of dust which had veiled the mountains from our sight.

The food was exceedingly simple, consisting of rice mixed with mutton-fat, or of mutton-fat mixed with rice!

In summer the mutton-fat was very soon rancid, and although *palao*, the steamed rice mixed with this fat, is in itself a nourishing and tasty dish, in the great heat we always grew weary to the very last degree of this food, somewhat rancid as it never failed to be.

There were melons and grapes all the year round and dried fruits as well; the bread was excellent and baked by our landlady in the native stove called a *tonur* (or *tanur*). This stove, a most ancient invention, undoubtedly comes, like its name, from Mesopotamia. It is a crater-shaped opening inside a round stove, which is heated from outside. The women climb on to the top of the stove when the crater is hot enough, mould the dough into the required shape, and clap it with their hands on to the hot inner side, where the flat cake remains hanging until it is baked through. Then it falls off, is taken out, rubbed clear of any dust sticking to it, and eaten as very excellent bread (Plate 14).

Without our bread and tea we should certainly have come to grief, for the excessive consumption of fruit, especially of apricots and peaches, is very apt to cause upsets of stomach and intestines which, in the great heat, are difficult to cure and often assume dangerous forms. Of preserved foods we had only brought with us a couple of dozen tins of sardines and some pease-pudding.

Of alcohol we had four bottles of arac and rum, which we scarcely ever felt any inclination to drink; later on I handed over three bottles to the third expedition. On the other hand my sisters had given me, as a parting present, a dozen bottles of Veuve Cliquot Ponsardin, which, when cooled in native fashion, proved an extraordinarily refreshing drink after exhaustive work. The bottle, wrapped in a wet piece of felt, is hung in a draught, and if the felt is kept wet, evaporation keeps the contents beautifully cool.

Our working hours lasted from sunrise, often even before 4 a.m., till 7 in the evening. Then the workmen were paid, the discoveries registered and packed, the expenses put down, letters written, and the simple supper eaten.

Unfortunately the whole courtyard would then fill with sick folk who came from long distances to be cured of their sufferings by the foreign gentleman. They were mostly cases of rheumatism and malaria that presented themselves, and as quinine and salicylic worked veritable miracles, the applications gradually became extremely inconvenient. It was sad, indeed, to meet some with incurable diseases, but they were sent home with some harmless remedy and always comforted in spite of everything.

One evening I was acting as physician when a bird of prey suddenly passed over the courtyard. I jumped up to see what bird it was, rushed out on to the street, and ran straight against a little old woman who stood crying at the gate. In astonishment I asked her: "Why are you crying so bitterly, Grannie?" Then she said: "Sir, I haven't the five cash, you know." I asked again: "What five cash, Grannie?" And she answered: "O sir, don't you know that your landlord always takes five cash from each of us sick folk before

Plate 11

Stupa, temple *Gamma*, Khocho

Surroundings of ruin *Gamma*, Khocho

Plate 12

Splendid floor in fresco style, Khocho

OUR LIFE AND WORK IN KARAKHOJA

we can come in to you?" I was much annoyed, led the old woman in, and made her repeat her statement, which was then confirmed by the other patients.

This trick of Saut's angered me to such an extent that I gave him a couple of good cuts with the whip I always carried in my belt—the only time I had ever struck a native. I told him, too, I would complain of him to the King of Lukchun, and he would see he got a proper dose with the "big stick." Saut disappeared and we went to bed, but had scarcely fallen asleep when a loud wailing of many voices arose outside the door. The sly old dog had sent his grandmother, mother, wife, his beautiful daughter, Zuwīde Khan (Plate 13), his nieces, and all his other female relations; each had a little handful of raisins, two lumps of sugar, a little tea, and such-like valuable gifts, which they offered me amid loud sobs, whilst with one accord they begged me to pardon once again their grandson, son, husband, father, etc.

It was such a comic and yet so touching a sight, that I allowed myself to be persuaded, and promised freedom from punishment on condition of better behaviour in the future.

The women's terror was not without foundation. It is true that the king, in former times all-powerful, has since the restoration of power to the Chinese come under their control. A Chinese official lives in Turfan, and the real power lies in his hands, somewhat as is the case with an English resident at the Court of an Indian prince. Yet, although the king is not allowed to execute anyone, he has the power to order culprits to be beaten. The beating is done either with the "little" or the "big stick." This big stick is a long bamboo cane, the top end of which is somewhat flattened out like our racing oars. The culprit, condemned to a beating, is put on the ground, his back bared, and so mercilessly beaten with this stick that the blood gushes out at the first stroke, and twenty-five are enough to kill the man.

This king, or *wang*, of Lukchun is a handsome Turkish youth, the seventh in the direct line of descent from the founder of the Turfan kingdom, Amin Khoja Khan, the ruler of Turfan in 1760. We possess in the Berlin Museum a life-sized portrait of this prince, painted at that time for the Emperor Kien-Lung; it is remarkable in that the nose is long, narrow, and straight, but the eyes blue. Thus, in this man there survived the characteristics of the Tocharian race, even one thousand years after their disappearance. Our young patron bore the name of his more important ancestor.

At the Chaghan feast, in the beginning of December, we were invited to his palace; and a great festivity it was. In the pillared hall of the palace there sat in two long rows the dignitaries of Amin Khoja in their State garments, the *wang* himself at the upper end of the hall, and Bartus and I respectively on his right and left hand.

An enormous charcoal-brazier stood near us, but the charcoal had not burnt up properly and the fumes made me very uncomfortable.

A festive meal was given, beginning with fruit—grapes, melons, nuts, pistachios—Russian bonbons, and excellent tea, into which the king, by way of honouring us, unfortunately threw sugar by the handful. Later came soup with mutton, delicate boiled mutton chops, and, lastly, an enormous *palao*, rice stewed in mutton-fat with fowl, raisins, sliced carrots, and quinces—an excellent, tasty, and nourishing dish as long as the fat is not rancid.

This meal passed, with due observance of strict etiquette, in dignified silence, and somewhat tedious I found it. At last the worthy gentlemen stroked their beards, said their *Allahu akbar!* and after many salaams filed out of the hall.

The *wang* then invited us into inner rooms, where, after a little time, his singers, tall, well-grown women, sang songs to us. They were accompanied by a single musician, who, with a horse-hair bow, drew forth extremely pleasing airs from his *si-tār*, a long-necked instrument of the violin type. The singing of these stately women— they were past their first youth—was quite different from the nasal bawl of the Arabians and the shrill songs of the Chinese, which I always found absolutely unendurable.

I begged the *wang* to send these singing ladies to me at Karakhoja, so that I might record their songs on my phonograph.

He kept his word to do so, and soon after our return to Karakhoja the ladies arrived in a gaily decorated coach (it is called a *ma-pa* there) with their servants, and were received by our landlord with many profound bows. Two apartments were emptied for them in which they washed and adorned themselves, and we then received them in our room, hung in festive fashion for the occasion with our red counterpanes, and they were served with the usual light refreshment (*dastarkhan*).

OUR LIFE AND WORK IN KARAKHOJA

They were very nervous at first, but soon regained their composure, especially as they enjoyed the French champagne exceedingly.

I then produced the "song-box" (*nāghma sandūq*), set up the receiver, and begged the leading lady to sing into the apparatus. She was a little frightened, but quickly pulled herself together and sang into the phonograph with a resounding voice—so loud, indeed, that the vibrations of the metal receiver were transferred with her notes on to the wax roll.

In vain I begged the second lady to sing more gently; both women were, no doubt, a little nervous, and they seemed to wish to dissipate their fear by an exceedingly loud performance. After I had taken down several songs, I thanked them and let them go, highly delighted with the Russian *tila* (gold coin) that each had received. The same afternoon they drove back to Lukchun.

The rolls are now in the Berlin Institute of Psychology, to which I unfortunately gave them. No one has studied these documents of such striking and melodious beauty—people think they are listening to European airs!

This occurrence had tiresome results. With the strange speed, with which all possible news is spread in the country by the *bazar* gossip, the *zamīndārs* (landowners) of the neighbourhood heard that the *wang's* singers, celebrated for their beauty, had sung into a magic song-box belonging to the foreign gentleman.

On the second day after that visit I found, to my annoyance, that, in addition to the numerous patients, quite a number of worthy, well-dressed old gentlemen were waiting for me in the courtyard of our *sarai*. They rose with great politeness, salaamed, and asked if I would not play those ladies' songs to them.

As they were quite unusually polite, I agreed. But more people came every day, so that these visits wasted a vast amount of our time.

When, therefore, the number of visitors was particularly large, I invited the three oldest gentlemen into my room, gave them tea, etc., and made the following speech:

"*Ai dūstlarim ā!* O my friends! You know that there are two kinds of magic—white magic, that has to do with Allah, and black, that has to do with *Schaitan* (Satan)."

Chorus: "*Balī turam!* Yes, indeed, great sir!"

"Well, then, you know that Allah has given to us Franks a greater *hikmat* (understanding) than to you" (Chorus: "*Balī turam!*"), "and that we are allowed to practise both kinds, but you only the white!" (Chorus: *Balī turam!*) "Good! I am anxious for your welfare; the song-box belongs to black magic; in it there sits a little *Schaitan*, who writes down the words and sings them afterwards. Now, go tell that to the other gentlemen. If, in spite of this, you wish to hear the songs again, I will play them, but you must know all this first."

They stroked their beards seriously, uttering pious exclamations the while, went away, and spoke to the others. In barely three minutes they were back again. "*Taksir turam!* you only want to get rid of us. There is no *Schaitan* in it; it is only a *makina* (machine) which you Franks have invented, and, if you please, let us hear the songs."

I was delighted with this answer, plainly testifying, as it did, to the ancient civilization of the people, and gave them a song-box performance. The old gentlemen rocked themselves with delight and went away satisfied.

But from then on, one of our landlord's sons, christened "Sheep's Head" by Bartus, a lad of incredible ability, was taught how to work the apparatus. He managed capitally and relieved me greatly.

To give an idea of the style of native songs I will now reproduce three of them:—

Three Love-Songs sung by Zuwīde (Zubeïde) Khan of Karakhoja.[1]

Our landlord's beautiful daughter had, when she was fifteen years old, married a peasant landowner of Turfan (Plate 13). But he treated her badly, so that Saut fetched his daughter home again.

Soon after our arrival her baby came, and it was astonishing to see how this young creature, with a skin as fair as any Northerner, could give birth to a little dark-skinned Mongolian.

When she nursed the child she used to sing all kinds of little songs, and as we were on very confidential terms, she allowed me to make a note of the words. Two of these songs have been composed

---

[1] These songs have been published in *Sprichwörter und Lieder aus der Gegend von Turfan*, by A. Le Coq. Baessler Archiv, Beiheft I, publisher B. G. Teubner, Leipzig, 1911.

OUR LIFE AND WORK IN KARAKHOJA 69

by a young Karakhojan, who afterwards died of mental disease, and lives in the memory of his fellow-countrymen as "the love-sick one" (Arabic: *maǧnūn*).

The third little poem sings of the love of one of the warriors of Yakub Beg for the most beautiful woman of the East, Ambar Khan of Dabančing. It was here at Dabančing that Yakub Beg's army made their last desperate attempt to drive back the superior forces of the Chinese. It failed, however, and the two lovers were parted for ever.

1

Bārisan bir bir bēsip	Step by step thou leavest me
daryā suiyidak airilip	Parted are we like the waters of the stream!
wāi!	Woe is me!
munčima baɣring qaturmu	And is thy heart in truth so hard?
baqmiding bir qairilip	Not once hast thou looked back at me!
wāi!	Woe is me!
bārɣica bāɣ bīla bardim	As through a garden fair I passed to be with thee!
yanɣiča tāšliq bīlan	As through a desert drear I passed to go from thee!
nai!	Woe is me!
χōšmoɣu bandam kotardim	And yet, O black-browed lady, I, thy slave,
san qara qāšliq bīlan	Found favour once with thee!
nai!	Woe is me!
yāri ning yāri tōlá	My lady fair has many loves
mandin bolak, mandin bolak	Other than I, other than I!
wāi!	Woe is me!
amdi yār tutmai man—a!	But never again shall I have a love
sandin bolak, sandin bolak	Other than thee, other than thee!
yāi!	Woe is me!

2

ú kōčada san bolsáng	In that street where thou art found
bú kōčada man bolái	In that street fain would I be!
ánār gúli san bolsáng	And wert thou the bloom of the pomegranate
yŭpurmāqi man bolái	Oh, would that I were the leaf!
ičimdiki rangimni	Beloved, the pain within my heart
yārim san bilalmaisan	Thou canst not ever measure!
man koidum bū otlarɣa	It burns me up, that flame
san bolsang čidalmaisan	Which, in my place, thou ne'er couldst bear!

qara χōğaning suyī	The little stream of Karakhoja
qarangγō bāγlardin āqur	Flows through gardens of dark shade;
qara qāš qāwil ğugan	The lovely black-browed lady there
yurakka ōtlarni yaqur	Lights flames of love within the heart.

korgali kaldingmo yar	And didst thou come to see me, loved one,
koidurgali kaldingmo yar	Didst thou come to kindle me?
koyup očkan otini	And didst thou come to light the flame
yandurγali kaldingmo yar	That once had been put out by thee!

3

Dāban čing ning yari qatiq	Hard is the earth of Dabančing
tāwūzi tatliq	But sweet the water-melons!
Dāban čing da bir yarim bar	I have a love in Dabančing
Ambar χān ātliq	Her name is Princess Ambar.

Ambar χān ning sēči uzún	Long is the hair of Ambar Khan
yarga tagamdō	Does it touch the ground?
Ambar χāndin sōrap baqing	Cautiously question Ambar Khan
arga tagamdō	Will she, I wonder, take a man?[1]

ūšaqqinâ ūncalarim čečilip katti	My tiny pearls bestrew the ground,
terip barsang čō	Wilt thou gather and give them back to me?
soyai dasam boyum yatmas	To kiss thee I am not tall enough,
ēgilip barsang čo	Wilt thou perchance bend down to me?

ātlaringni haidait ikan	To be obliged to drive thy steeds
mus dāwán birlan	Over the glacier pass
bir yáχsinī qinait īkan	Is like a good woman
bír yāmán birlan	Chained for life to an evil man.

qārisam koranmaidō	And if I look, ne'er can I see
Dāban čing dikī qōrγán	Aught of the fortress of Dabančing;
—ağap bir yaman īkan	An evil strange it is to be
Ambar χan din airilγan	Parted for aye from Ambar Khan!

Explanation of Transliterations

γ (Gk. gamma) = gutteral gh (Northumbrian burr).
χ (Gk. chi) = ch in Scottish "loch."
q = hard guttural k.
š = sh in "shame."
č = ch in "quench."
ğ = j in "jump."

[1] Ambar Khan was married.

Plate 13

Mamasit Mirab, a frequent male type, Karakhoja

Zuwida Khan, a finer female type, Karakhoja

Plate 14

An oven (*tanur*, *tonur*) with women making bread, Karakhoja

A plank-weaver, Karakhoja

Plate 15

Burial monuments, Persian vaulted buildings, east of Khocho

Large *stupa*, Surkup

Plate 16

Fortified temple, Sangim Ravine

Rock temple in the curve of the Sangim Ravine

OUR LIFE AND WORK IN KARAKHOJA. II

I MUST add the following notes concerning our life in Karakhoja.

Our room was very spacious and had, as is the Persian custom, raised mud benches running round its walls. In some places these were hollow and could be heated from outside. But we avoided this kind of heating, for charcoal fumes are easily produced, and we preferred to keep a coal fire going in the good fireplace. In Turfan the coal is found at no great depth. The Turks also call it mineral coal (*tash komur*). But the coal-fields at Komul are still more abundant; there the people go out at night with picks and buckets to the field where it comes to the surface; the coal belongs to the king, but all Komul runs off at night and steals it.

In spite of fires, however, it was often unbearably cold during the winter.

I arranged my photographic dark room in the old passages in the city wall. When the scraps of paper had accumulated there I often heard a suspicious rustling. I crept in cautiously and found that hedgehogs were making a home there. They were caught and brought to Berlin, where Professor Matschie recognized them as belonging to a species extinct in other parts.

Another charming visitor was a little jerboa that moved about in kangaroo fashion, and, when it peeped out of the corners, used to look at us quite trustfully with its wonderful big black eyes.

One evening when I was doctoring my patients in our courtyard—it must have been April by then—we heard a loud whirring sound, almost like a covey of partridges rising, and the next moment a violent hail of heavy dark-brown bodies fell upon us with great force—a hail of living creatures! In a second the courtyard was filled with them, but no less quickly the landlord's family and all the patients attacked the ugly intruders, whose crushed bodies soon covered the stamped clay surface of the yard in hundreds and hundreds.

It was no wonder that these peasants made every effort to destroy such unpleasant insects; they were great mole-crickets, certainly four to six inches long, whose habits make them destructive enemies of the farmer.

Housekeeping was difficult; for a time we lived only on tea, bread, *palao*, and different kinds of fruit. But with increasing heat the mutton-fat soon turned rancid, and then we had to give up eating this main dish of our bill of fare. The fruits, too, especially the apricots, proved treacherous, and were often the cause of quite serious illness.

In order to be able to associate with the natives I had to exert myself to learn their language. I had a certain knowledge of the Osmanli tongue which proved very useful to me, for before starting on the expedition it had enabled me, under the guidance of Professor M. Hartmann, to become quickly conversant with the general rules of the much easier E. Turki language.

In Karakhoja I engaged a peasant who was able to write, Obul Makhdi (*Abu'l Mahdī*) by name, to come every evening after our supper and give me a lesson. This chiefly consisted of taking down at his dictation the text of the bilingual (Chinese and Turkish) Government edicts (that the people had torn down from the walls on which they were stuck, although such action was strictly forbidden) and all Turkish letters that arrived. Soon I received from the king a Turkish translation of the Chinese Criminal Code, the so-called *Li kitābī*, and from a Turfan physician a handbook of medicine, the *Tibb kitābī*; I spent many hours at a time making a written translation of both of these books.

Later on, I got my teacher to dictate songs, and thereby learnt that scarcely any of their songs are of a martial character. The few that I discovered were satires on unsuccessful leaders of the time of Yakub Beg. All others took as their theme nothing else but love, which certainly plays an all-too-important part in the life of these people.

In this way my ear grew accustomed to the sounds of the language, and after persistent efforts I learnt to speak and, what is far more difficult, to understand.

Bartus had quite a good knowledge of the most important words, and, for the rest, he spoke in Low-German dialect (*plattdeutsch*) to the workmen, and, far-travelled as he was, he managed to make himself understood everywhere. When we left the town, in the middle of August, all the young men spoke a species of remarkable but quite comprehensible Low-German dialect.

At the end of February the cold weather ceased, and it soon grew

OUR LIFE AND WORK IN KARAKHOJA

warm. The children threw off their little wadded coats and ran about, the boys without any garment but dirt—they are not washed as a protection against the evil eye—the girls in little red garments, cut after the fashion of our pyjamas.

Then we could see that many of the children had snow-white skins, others again were the colour of corn, and some, even at that young age, almost chocolate; the fairer types were European, the darker ones East Asiatic.

We always had great fun with the children. My pockets were kept full of raisins and lumps of sugar, and wherever I went I was besieged by these often charming little creatures clamouring for sweets. I made a cocked hat out of the Berlin newspapers, which in course of time had grown into a great pile, stuck a cock's feather in it, and put it on the head of one of my little favourites. Then, as they all wanted to have hats like that, I instructed one of the boys in the art of making them, and soon the young folk, boys and girls alike, were all proudly strutting about in these head-coverings.

When we had been living there some time we were visited one day by the Kasi and the "great *Achund*," a priestly dignitary, and a conversation took place much as follows: "Sir, it is not good that you two should live alone. You must marry." I answered: "We *are* married." "Yes, but your wives are many thousand *li* [Chinese miles] away from this place; you must take wives here. My daughter and the Kasi's are ready to enter into matrimony with you." This was an unpleasant revelation. How were we to get rid of these respected people without hurting their feelings? I began by thanking them, and then said: "Friends, you know that the Chinese have spies [*sinchi*] here who, every week, send to Peking a report which is given to our ambassador [*ilchi*]. He sends the report to the great emperor *Gillehallim* in the great land *Ba-lin* [Berlin]. According to our law we may only marry one wife. If the great emperor hears that we have married here, what do you suppose would happen to us?" They stroked their beards, and answered that they certainly did not know, whereupon I explained to them that we should doubtless get twenty-five with the "big stick" dealt out to us. They were horrified at our barbarity, and took their leave with many expressions of pity and friendship. In Karakhoja we passed as a kind of higher grade Mohammedans, and were always acknowledged by the Arabic greeting, "Peace be with you." We took care, too, to avoid any more serious breaking of the law.

The natives knew little of their prophet's teaching, and, strangely enough, they showed much less fanaticism in their attitude to the Chinese than to the Chinese-speaking members of their own faith, the Tungans (Chinese: *Khui-khui*). Thus they sometimes permit a daughter to marry a *Khitai* (Chinaman) but never a Tungan; also they will never enter a Tungan house of prayer. Great mutual contempt prevails without exception between both Turks and Tungans. But even for Mohammedans it is not very easy in Turkestan to marry several wives, although their religion permits polygamy.

Just at this time Mamasit (*Mahammad Sayid*), the *mirab* of Lukchun, returned from Kashgar (Plate 13), to which place he, at the king's request, had accompanied Abdu-s-Sa'id Khojam, the last descendant of the Khojam family—the former princes of Eastern Turkestan. This harmless scion of a bloodthirsty race had been brought up as a prisoner in Peking and did not know Turkish. He only spoke Chinese, but could recite the Koran. The Government had recognized his harmlessness, and given him permission to make a begging expedition through the land of his fathers, when he is said to have received about 20,000 Sar (approximately £3,500) from the faithful. On his homeward journey I met him in Karakhoja escorted by the *mirab*.

Now the *mirab* had married two young girls in Kashgar, as permitted by the custom of the country, and had parted with them when he left. But when he arrived in Karakhoja, where his family lived, his wife Āi-en-nissā (moon of wives) would not let him enter his own home. She struck him with the whip, saying: "Just go to your Kashgar women!" and banged the door in his face. He came to me in the evening in great distress and told his sad experience. I said to him, however: "But, my friend, you have brought back so many rolls of beautiful silk from Andijan and Khotan, lovely muslins, fine red cloth, and other beautiful things. Choose some and take them to your wife." This prescription worked wonders, and on the following day peace was restored.

But the incident shows how great is the influence exercised on their husbands by the women here, who, besides, always appear in public unveiled.

OUR LIFE AND WORK IN KARAKHOJA

As we have before remarked, Bartus was a great favourite everywhere. His natural gaiety, his Herculean strength, and his abounding good nature pleased the people, and many a good laugh we have had together.

One day I said to him: "Herr Bartus, here is the tin of dried bilberries that we brought as a cure for diarrhœa. But beetles have got into them so you may throw away the contents, but we will keep the tin for packing manuscripts and such things."

On the following day Bartus came with a bundle of fine old manuscripts. When I asked him where he had got the *kaghaz*[1] he said: "Well, doctor, as I was going to throw away the stuff yesterday a few of the old gentlemen came, asking me what I had got there. So I told them it was a medicine to make old folk young again. Then they all wanted to have some. But I told them not until they had brought a nice lot of papers, and you see they brought me the whole bundle at once. Then I gave them some, and this morning they were back again for more. They have eaten it, berries, beetles, and all, and say it works splendidly."

Another amusing incident happened the day before we left for Komul. I was still sitting in my room, trying to get my accounts in order for the upper Finance Committee. It was a terrible task, for I had before me Russian money in paper, gold, and silver, Chinese in silver and copper coins, State paper money and local paper, or, more correctly speaking, silk money. The notes (Chinese: *tī-zā*) were printed pieces of oil silk about six by four inches in area, and the Government seals were stamped in vermilion on the printing. I also had silver bars from which pieces are cut and weighed. The rate of exchange for all this money varies almost daily.

I was sitting in a somewhat irritated frame of mind, busy with this work and Bartus was still hammering away in the courtyard when the town notabilities, dignified old gentlemen, paid me a visit and delivered themselves somewhat as follows: "Sir, you are going away, you have been here a long time, and we have all grown rich. You have cured many of their infirmities for nothing; unfortunately you have not wished to marry our daughters. But we have found you well-disposed men. We regret your going, and now we have only one more wish and that is that when such dis-

[1] The Turks call the old writings either by the Arabic word *chatt* (a writing) or by the Persian *kaghaz* (paper).

tinguished people come again from the court of the great emperor *Gillehallim*—their pronunciation of William—we would like to greet them, as etiquette requires at the court of the great land of *Ba-lin*." I groaned a little, but answered in well-turned phrases, thanked them for the attention, and said I was still busy, for we were anxious to make a start. As regarded the greeting, my "hero" (*batur*) would teach them the way in which the king and nobles greeted each other.

I bowed them out and called to Bartus: "Herr Bartus, these gentlemen wish to know the ceremonial greeting usual in Berlin." Bartus replied: "I'll soon teach 'em that." So I returned to my work, and when it was finished I still heard from outside all kinds of words of command, and, lo and behold! Bartus had marshalled the fifteen old gentlemen, five deep in rows of three, and there they were making their bows, first to the right as they said quite distinctly, "Good morning, old fat-head," and then, turning to the left, repeated the bow, this time with a "Good morning, old tippler."

It was so comical that I could scarcely keep from laughing. But they took their leave in a state of great delight, and, when Grünwedel arrived six years later, out they came to make their most formal bows and greet him in the courtly fashion of *Ba-lin*!

We explored many more ruins in the old town, amongst others the mighty terraced pyramid, south-west of the eastern gate (Plate 4). It has a frontage of more than twenty yards, and in earlier times the many niches were filled by large figures of Buddha, either gilded or painted. Gilding was put on extravagantly in the form of thick gold-leaf, and even walls, many square yards in area, were inlaid with it. Those who destroyed the building scraped off the precious metal with their sabres, but in several places it escaped their notice. There is another monument quite similar, only with less sharply defined terraces, to be found close by in Āstāna, and is probably responsible for the place being so called, since the Persian word *astana* bears, amongst other meanings, that of "place of rest, of sleep," also a saint's tomb. Another similar building, but not terraced, stands near the little place of Syrkyp, N.N.E. of Lukchun. In the niches of this monument there still survive remnants of painted Buddha figures (Plate 15).

In Syrkyp, moreover, vessels of a remarkable kind are made out of black mountain sand.

In other ruins of the old town we found enormous quantities

OUR LIFE AND WORK IN KARAKHOJA

of ruined Indian documents, more or less destroyed. The pages were often so torn that each scrap showed no more than one letter of Indian Nagari; in any case, the destruction was mainly aimed at Buddhism.

It must also be mentioned that documents belonging to all four of the religions practised in the country were discovered in the same shrine; hence Buddhists, Christians, Manichæans, with isolated Zoroastrians, appear to have used the same places of worship—a fact which points, if our assumption is correct, to great tolerance and . . . to the great political power of the Uighur Turkish kings.

The ruins of the church to which Grünwedel gave the designation of *gamma* (Γ) were very attractive. The high *stūpa* tower, with its wonderful moulding, was still in good preservation, and very possibly contained votive-writings as well. But we could not make up our minds to demolish this beautiful building. Other ruins showed the high narrow arches that resemble those of the great Sassanian palace in Ctesiphon. I still do not understand the object of these arches (Plate 5).

But—and the statement cannot be over-emphasized—all surviving buildings are either Persian or Indian, whilst every trace of Chinese architecture is wanting, even here in Khocho, where, however, the Chinese were the rulers for a long period.

We also succeeded in making some noteworthy finds in the temples outside the city. A small building on the east side of the river, south of the bridge and north of the ford, aroused our curiosity by the water-colour representation, almost effaced by time and weather, of a knight on horseback carrying a labarum, decorated with a cross. Only the outlines were intact, and the foundation so decayed that all idea of securing it had to be renounced. The walls showed one peculiarity, viz. inner walls only one stone thick had been built in front of the original walls enclosing the building, thus hiding the old frescoes. This pious style of renovation—in our country the old picture would simply have been covered with a coat of colour wash—was used, so it seems, not only when a temple was to be dedicated to another god of the same religion, but also when a Manichæan or Christian Church was to be used for the worship of followers of another creed.

We have already described how the picture of Manes has been

found walled up in this way. This other little temple, apparently a Christian place of worship, a Nestorian house of prayer, or the like, had lost its Christian character by the erection of new inside walls. But when the fresh walls were torn down there were traces of the old mural paintings to be found only here and there, for much destruction had been caused by melted snow dripping from above through a crack in the wall. The figure was, however, preserved of a priest of a marked Byzantine character, apparently with an incense thurible and a vessel of holy water. He is standing before a row of three people, drawn on a smaller scale than he is, and carrying branches of green leaves in their hands (Plate 9).

Behind the group we catch sight of the foreleg of a horse; evidently his rider had approached whilst the priest was officiating.

This priest is neither a Buddhist monk nor a Manichæan, for both these can be recognized by their officiating garments. Perhaps it is a representation of the celebration of Palm Sunday. In any case, the style of painting shows Western influences, which are more recent than the time of the Gandhara art.

On the road to Tuyoq there are still standing two ruins designated by Grünwedel with the Russian letters Z and B respectively.

The first contained several chapels with figures of Buddha seated, some of them on a gigantic scale. A few beautiful mural paintings in the Uighur style were still extant on these walls, but also later renovations, in the same style, as imitated by the Chinese.

In the chapel turned towards the east we found the great plinth of a destroyed Nirvana Buddha.

In front of the plinth a thin layer of stucco had been placed to hide the old paintings on it. When the stucco was removed they came to light in a fair state of preservation; they were representations of monks in a style of painting very decidedly reminiscent of Romanesque art.

We made an important discovery in ruin Russian B. Here, too, the old paintings, etc., had been overlaid by a wall decoration of later date; apparently in the late Lamaistic period (perhaps thirteenth century?). At any rate, the renovation had been made more ruthlessly than was customary when the power of the Uighurs was at its zenith.

On the eastern side of the wall containing the door, to the right of the entrance, we found in a recess behind a wall of

Plate 17

Southern buildings of temples at Bazaklik

Northern end of the main terrace, Bazaklik

v. Le Coq, Turfan.

Plate 18

Main terrace from the east, Bazaklik

Southern end of main terrace, Bazaklik

OUR LIFE AND WORK IN KARAKHOJA

more recent construction a magnificent torso (Plate 10) almost five feet high.

The upper part of the statue, which was fastened to the wall by strong wooden pegs, had suffered considerably. Not only had the head and shoulders disappeared, but the abundant snow that had fallen at times, or the downpouring of the rain—very rare, it is true, but at the same time very violent when it comes—had carried a solution of earth and water in little streams over the upper part of the body, and destroyed the colour of the clothing to a certain extent.

The statue stands on a semi-circular throne formed of a lotus plant, the leaves of which were probably red with white edges. The fruit foundation had perhaps been painted green, but to-day only shows traces of the white grounding—the border that appears under the leaves is of plaster—it is a feature that had been added as an essential for the erection of the figure. The feet are not very well modelled, and have, moreover, suffered from the walling up of the statue; the unfired tiles had simply been placed upon them. An ugly feature, too, is the way in which the toes project over the edge of the foundation.

The figure itself is very reminiscent of types in the Gandhara art. The drapery falls in noble lines, not yet degraded by Eastern Asiatic misunderstanding of classic forms. Very characteristic, too, are the heavy side-folds which fall from the shoulders or from the lower part of the arm, which is now missing but which had undoubtedly been raised as though in teaching. They show abundant traces of green colouring and are apparently part of an outer cloak. The flowing mantle beneath clings to the body in graceful folds; the painting has been destroyed as far as the knees so that the brownish colour of the composition used is here seen. From the knees to the edge of the beautiful folds the ever-increasing richness of colour is preserved. Two undergarments are worn—all that is seen of the first of these is a triangular piece of red on the left side between the folds of the outer cloak, of the mantle beneath, and the narrow strip of a second blue undergarment which is visible under the red tip.[1]

This beautiful statue, a Buddha in almost pure Gandhara style,

---

[1] For further details the reader is referred to the Plate "*Chotscho*," Dietrich Reimer, Verlag, Berlin, 1913, from which I have taken this description.

proved a great enigma to us; for we could not help wondering why the modelling of antique art had survived in sculpture, whilst in painting the Greek elements already showed signs of Eastern Asiatic influence. The statue is by no means the only sculpture which has preserved the Hellenistic character. The first expedition had also found heads of a very Greek type, and a whole number of such examples of sculpture fell into our hands as well. The Buddhas on all the mural paintings already showed the same misunderstanding of the draping of the folds, and the Eastern Asiatic faces of the later Chinese period. The sculpture most undoubtedly belonged to the same period as the paintings—why had not it, too, been affected in the same way?

At the time of the discovery we did not yet know that the sculpture of Eastern Turkestan is a casting art and that they used moulds for making all statues.

It was not until the third expedition that we found some specimens of casts made of stucco in the monastery workshops of Kyzyl; and, in Shorchuk, Herr Bartus succeeded in excavating thirty such moulds out of a similar workshop.

This discovery solved our riddle, for the old type was just cast again in these moulds, and if a mould happened to get either broken or was worn out, a new one was moulded by a mechanical process over the original type, and then fresh ones were cast as before.[1]

[1] Since no suitable stone existed in Eastern Turkestan, the casts were made out of mud, mixed with the hair of animals, fibres of plants, or chopped straw—sometimes, too, but less often and principally in the western districts, stucco was used. Faces, ears with their earrings, arms, legs, hands, feet, and all other parts were cast, each separately in the moulds.

The large statues were thus formed in many separate parts, the not very thick portions filled with the same material and with bundles of reeds and dried in the sun. Then the separate pieces were fixed together by rough little wooden pegs, or sometimes, too, only tied together by straw ropes; the hands, etc., were put on and the whole statue— they are always only in half-relief—was smoothed over at the back with a coating of loam and fastened to the temple wall with tamarisk pegs. After this the front was smoothed off, the joints filled in, the whole gone over carefully with a wash of clay, covered with a thin layer of stucco, painted in water-colours and gilded with thick gold-leaf. The gold-leaf was cut in little square pieces, stuck on and picked out by black paint or beautiful transparent carmine (the latter especially in book miniatures). In order that the gold decoration might stand out in bold relief on many specially valuable statues, they, first of all, formed the ornaments in a very firm white paste (perhaps stucco), then the little squares of gold-leaf and its painting were applied to this, any rough corners of the gold were painted over, and the gold ornament, now in relief, was given a brilliant polish by a jade point or something similar. We found evidence of this technical process only in the very beautiful mural paintings of Ruin B in Khocho. A similar process was used later in the painting of miniatures on paper, but on our paper miniatures it does not yet occur.

OUR LIFE AND WORK IN KARAKHOJA

During the Turkish period, owing to the increasing admixture of foreign blood, a gradual change took place in the national ideals of beauty, and the heads plainly show how, after a comparatively short space of time, in about the ninth century, the casts had been deliberately changed to a more E. Asiatic type. The eyes are more projecting, the eyebrows and also the lines of the upper and lower eyelids become more slanting, the nose is shortened, the typically Greek arrangement of the hair is misunderstood and stereotyped. Finally, the artist gives his cast the stiff coarse hair of the E. Asiatic race and . . . the head of Greek art has become typically Chinese. It is easy to understand how in painting there is far less persistence of type. Even the Sassanids had already barred the way to the Hellenist East, and out of Iran and India but few people came, and these, with the exception of rich merchants, only monks who gave their homage to the celibate. But the way to Eastern Asia was always open, and Eastern Asiatics, Turks and Chinese came to the country in increasing numbers, and thus the admixture of foreign blood became more and more pronounced.

If, then, a master accepted a pupil of mixed race, he thereby introduced into his studio an alien eye, an alien hand, and thus the change of type proceeded much more quickly in painting than in sculpture. Painting, too, no less than sculpture, did not disdain mechanical means. We have found stencils made out of paper, and even some on thin paper for paintings on linen, *bœhmeria*,[1] silk and paper, and some of a kind of pasteboard for the frescoes. The painting was sketched in contour drawing on the stencil paper. Then the lines were perforated and the stencil laid either on the smoothed and whitened wall or on the delicate materials mentioned above, and a porous bag of fine charcoal passed over it. The faint outlines so produced were then lined in and finally covered with paint. The painters had such practice that they scarcely needed the tracing—as many pictures plainly show—and did not keep to it exactly; to a certain degree they jotted down each of the gods, saints, etc., with which they were so entirely familiar, much as a Chinese writes down his complicated letters, each of which is, moreover, a work of art in itself.

To the south of these two temples (Russian Z and Russian B) there are two groups of tomb monuments. These are Persian domed

[1] *Bœhmeria* = material woven of ramie threads (*bœhmeria nivea*).

buildings, still called there by the Persian term of *gumbaz* (*gunbaz*). On many of these buildings the cupola consists of two domes placed one above another[1] (Plate 15).

In one of these graves we found a little cap such as the girls in Eastern Turkestan wear to this present day. It had been saturated with blood, so that evidently its owner had taken refuge in the tomb and been murdered there. It is evident from the embroidery that the cap belonged to the Buddhist period, for it represents a fabulous creature (*garuda*) of the Buddhist mythology.

[1] Cf. U. Monneret de Villard, "Sull' Origine della doppia Cupola persiana," in *Architettura e Arti decorative*, fasc. iv, Anno I, Milan, 1921.

THE TEMPLE-SETTLEMENTS OF SANGIM AGHYZ, BAZAKLIK, CHIKKAN KOL, AND TUYOQ

The Sangim Ravine

IN several temples of Khocho old town we succeeded in discovering mural paintings which Bartus, with his usual masterly skill, sawed out of the walls, no matter in what heat, cold, or dust.

Close by small finds were made every day of coins—chiefly Chinese of the period of the T'ang emperors, but older ones as well, Sassanian and later, also Mohammedan of the time of the renegade princes of Kashgar; in addition to these, valuable woven materials of silk, linen, and ramie, and finally large quantities of manuscript fragments in the twenty-four different styles of writing that are to be met with there.

In spite of this, however, the results by no means came up to my expectations, and as the discoveries in Khocho old town seemed to be exhausted and the weather became warmer, which it did in Turfan as early as the end of February, we transferred our activity into the gloomy ravine of Sangim, situated to the north of Karakhoja. It is called in Turkish the mouth (*ayïz*; colloquial, *eyïz*) of Sangim, after a small place situated at the northern end.

The river of Karakhoja forces its somewhat tumultuous way through the loess rocks of this valley. It is a dark, mysterious gorge with steep hills, raising their threatening heights along the western bank of the stream, and with frequent torrents of stones and avalanches of mud, during the melting of the mountain snow, crashing down upon its narrow paths. In spite of the forbidding character of the landscape, the left or western side of the ravine is studded with a line of temples (Plate 16), whilst the heights on the right are occupied by many Indian relic memorials (*stūpas*), some of which rise on the very edge of the stream.

These *stūpas* contained the remains of cremation ashes, artificial flowers, votive offerings—pictures of saints on paper—and of very many manuscripts. It is a striking fact that in one of these monuments, at the curve of the river, the almost perfect page of a Manichæan book was found amongst the fragments of many Buddhist Indian manuscripts. How did it get there?

There are twelve buildings on the left bank, the ruins of the Buddhist monasteries, and temples of the early period (eighth to eleventh century). Most are structures of adobe bricks, though some are excavated temples with terraces and buildings in front. The adobe monasteries without exception are, at the same time, strong fortifications with massive doors and towers. The appearance of the ravine is, throughout its whole length, most weird, for the wild gorges in the hills lend a romantic, almost an uncanny, character to the landscape.

In these temples we found two libraries: one was discovered by Herr Bartus in the monks' cells of a large monastery and was large enough to fill several corn-sacks. These manuscripts were nearly all written in the early Turkish and the Uighur script; their subject-matter was religious, being fragments of a kind of drama describing the meeting of the faithful and also of the lost with a Buddhist Messiah, Maitreya (*Maitreya Samiti*). It is indicated in the colophons of the chapters that this was a translation from the Tocharian language into Turkish, and the name of the author is also given.

Later, in another place, we found fragments of the said Tocharian manuscript, which in its turn, so the tail-pieces of the chapters state, is also a translation from the Indian language.

The second discovery fell to my lot in a strange building, the annex of a small temple on the terrace of temple No. 10. It consisted mainly of the Turkish translations of Buddhist fairy tales.

Here and there we discovered Manichæan and Indian manuscripts as well, but the following incident was very annoying. We had worked very hard at excavations in the "Constellation" cave temple (Temple No. 6) situated at the entrance of the ravine, without, however, making the very least discovery. Whilst we were occupied there two old women went to work opposite to us, on the other side of the stream, amongst several shapeless mounds. Some of these were only chance heaps of loess, but one was opened to good purpose, for it was a ruined *stūpa*, and gave these treasure-diggers, before our very eyes, some strange demon-heads and a great quantity of Tocharian and Indian manuscripts in various Indian scripts. We were obliged to buy their booty from these extremely

THE TEMPLE-SETTLEMENTS

disagreeable women at a fairly large price, paying nine shillings for about one hundred fine sheets of manuscript.

Our net gains up till then in the old town at Karakhoja and in the Sangim ravine were not quite unimportant, but they in no degree fulfilled the expectations harboured by those who had commissioned us to come. Frequent letters came from Councillor Pischel in which he expressed his conviction that I had already secured a gigantic mass of manuscripts, sculpture, and mural paintings. His Majesty also had often inquired with interest as to the rich results which the expedition was doubtless achieving. But our discoveries so far in no way fulfilled these exaggerated expectations.

Grünwedel had requested me not to work in the great monastery buildings at Murtuk, but to reserve the untouched temples of this settlement for him. The reports concerning his coming changed, however, with every letter. At one time he was starting, at another he could not make up his mind to the journey, so that I was hampered in all my arrangements. When, then, a letter arrived saying Grünwedel had decided not to come, I determined, in order to secure at any rate one great success for the expedition, to push on to this settlement and dismantle one of the numerous temples of its pictures. We therefore made an exploratory journey to Murtuk.

To get there the traveller follows the Sangim ravine in a northerly direction as far as the point where the Murtuk water-course flows, between steep cliffs, into the stream rushing down the Sangim valley. Then he must climb the high cliffs on the right bank to follow a narrow road winding on the top of these cliffs to the great monastery settlement of Bazaklik, which lies a little to the south of the great village of Murtuk. A visitor to the monastery of Bazaklik [Eastern Turkestani = the place where there are paintings (decorations)] reaches its immediate neighbourhood without once catching sight of the great settlement. Only in one spot is it possible to get a glimpse of the temple, but there the old monks put up a wall—parts of which are still standing—which protected their settlement from the eyes of passing travellers. Evidence is everywhere forthcoming of the endeavours made by monastery dwellers to secure the greatest possible isolation from the busy world and its doings.

The road suddenly widens and ends on a broad, sandy plain, behind which rise high, curiously shaped hills. Even from here the monastery is not to be seen, for it is situated on a terrace, about ten yards above the bed of the stream and the same distance below the precipitous edge of the level expanse, lying in a horse-shoe curve of the high river-bank. It is only when the traveller gets quite close to this edge that he sees the building on its terrace.

Two little domed buildings had once stood here—one at the upper, the other at the lower end of the group of buildings, but only that at the upper end still existed, and, although in a very tumble-down condition, it could be visited. It contained a steep, narrow stairway— also in a very ruinous state—that led down to the terrace. Probably, therefore, the two small buildings were the approaches by which in olden times the settlement was reached from above (Plates 17, 18).

The chief terrace lies to the north of the group of buildings, and at its northerly end there was a great monastery with cells for the monks. Adjoining this, and following the course of the stream to the south, came a whole row of temples that were, one and all, so covered with the sand from the mountain range lying behind and by the loess dust prevalent throughout the whole country, that all to be seen of them was the corner of a wall or the rounded roof of a temple projecting here and there from the great heaps of sand.

The buildings—in earlier times they were doubtless connected with one another by wooden structures—are either stone erections or cave temples cut out in the clay and soft stone; others, again, as in the Sangim ravine, are combinations of the two systems, with a front hall of adobe bricks erected before a rock temple.

A total of some hundred temples are still in existence there. Many of those to the south, however, had been taken as dwellings by the goatherds, and the paintings were spoilt by the smoke of their fires. We could only expect to get a harvest in those temples that were entirely buried under the sand. After ascertaining this we decided to clean out some of the temples spoilt by the goatherds and to instal ourselves in them.

Then we began to work.

A messenger from the Chinese Governor of Turfan just then brought me a letter from Pischel expressing his most joyful expectations. But so far we had found nothing worth mentioning. One day, however, fortune smiled upon us. We had begun to work at a great temple building, and had got as far as the entrance hall in front of

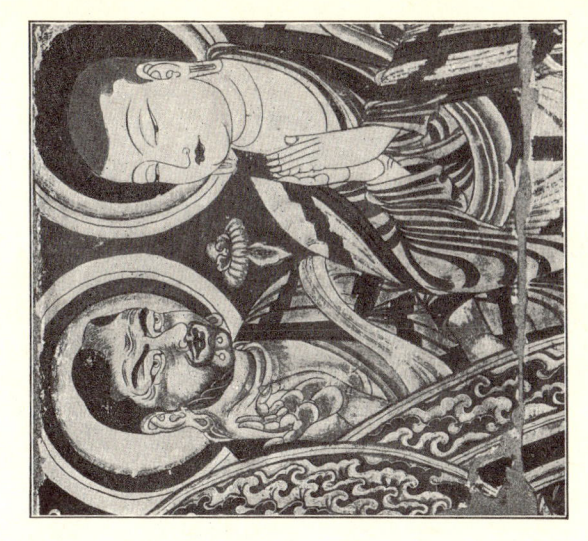

Plate 19

Types of early inhabitants on the frescoes, Bazaklik
a) Syrians b) Tochari and Eastern Asiatics

v. Le Coq, Turfan.

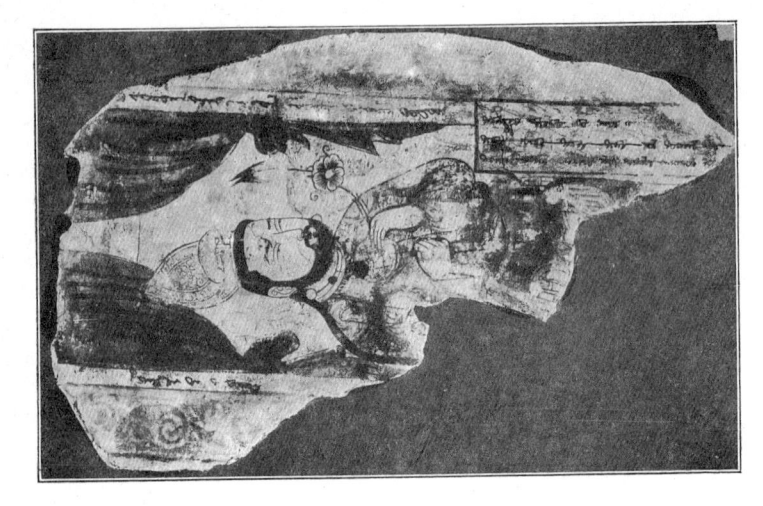

Plate 20

Types of the early inhabitants on the frescoes, Bazaklik
b) Turkish Prince
a) Persians

Plate 21

Types of early inhabitants on the frescoes, Bazaklik
a) East Asiatic monks
b) Indian monks

Plate 22

Exhibition of Bazaklik frescoes in the Ethnological Museum, Berlin

THE TEMPLE-SETTLEMENTS

the cella. Unfortunately the frescoes in this hall proved to be entirely destroyed; all that could be seen of them was a faint outline.

The narrow corridors, which in these temples often encircle the cella, existed here, too, but were filled from the floor to the top of the walls with fairly compact mountain sand. With some difficulty I got on to these heaps of sand in the left corridor, and as I clambered up the sand slipped down under the weight of my body, so that by constantly lifting my feet high and stamping to get foothold I dislodged many hundredweights of the heap lying there.

Suddenly, as if by magic, I saw on the walls bared in this way, to my right and left, splendid paintings in colours as fresh as if the artist had only just finished them.

How delighted I was! I waved my hat and called to Bartus, who was working on the other side; he came up and we shook hands in our joy. If we could secure these pictures the success of the expedition was assured.

We pressed on slowly, clearing away the masses of sand, with the result that we saw in the entrances of the corridors, on each side, a painting of three monks more than life-size.

They were portraits, and, indeed, on both sides of the left corridor there were paintings of Indian monks in yellow robes with their Indian names in the Brahmi script of Central Asia, whilst on the right side of the right-hand corridor there was a painting of three Eastern Asiatic monks in violet, and on the left side of the same corridor a similar painting of three Indian monks in yellow robes.

These people, too, bore at their heads little name-plates, and, again, the names of the Indians were written in Indian, whilst those of the Eastern Asiatics were in both Chinese and Uighur characters.

It was interesting to notice that the Turks, who erected these temples at the zenith of their power (ninth century), were not satisfied with only stencil-work for the faces, but there is plain evidence of an attempt to individualize the face of each of those represented—in other words, to paint portraits (Plate 20).

This attempt was never made in the older Indo-Aryan work; the same stencils were used for all faces and then the inscription was added: this is Knight X, Y, or Z, as the case might be.

This indifference as regards portraits is the more striking since the paintings of the older period are of a distinctly better quality compared with these later pictures, marked as the latter are with evident signs of being a more mixed art.

As we continued to open up the corridors we found on the walls, which were thirteen feet high, fifteen gigantic paintings of Buddhas of different periods—three on each of the longer outer walls and two on each of the shorter inner walls of the corridors. Before these Buddhas there are kneeling either Indian princes in garments of Indian mythology or Brahmans with tiger-skins and gaiters, or, again—and this increases the value of these pictures—men dressed in native costume, bearing gifts in their hands.

Quite different types are to be seen, some plainly Persians with caps of eagle's wing feathers, curious hats, or turbans. They have aquiline features with dark or sometimes red hair, in which case their eyes are painted green or blue.

Still more striking are representations of red-haired, blue-eyed men with faces of a pronounced European type. We connect these people with the Aryan language found in these parts in so many manuscripts, which were, as we proved later, Tocharian. These red-haired people wear suspenders from their belts to keep up the long tops of their soft leather boots—a remarkable ethnographical peculiarity which is only found elsewhere, as far as I know, on the stone figures adorning the Scythian grave-mounds of South Russia and the Crimea, and which are to be seen in exactly the same form on numerous grave-mounds all along the Celestial Mountains right into the depths of Mongolia.

These grave-mounds belong to a bronze age which is identical with that of the *kurgans* (Russian: *kyrgan* = barrow) or grave-mounds of South Russia. I am of opinion that these grave-mounds in south Siberia and Mongolia mark out the road which these Indo-Europeans took in pre-Christian times to get to China.

Another type only occurs once; it is of a pronounced Semitic character, and must represent one belonging to the Syrians, of whom a fair number, as Nestorian Christians, had built their monasteries on the spurs of the mountains north of the Chinese town of Turfan. The man depicted must, accordingly, have been a convert to Buddhism.

The cella of the cleared temple measured about two and one-fourth yards square. Here, however, the storm had so often whirled the sand round the walls that it was only to a height of one and

THE TEMPLE-SETTLEMENTS

one-half yards, where the force of the storm could not reach, that there had been a stationary layer of sand which had protected the pictures.

They were remarkable representations. Opposite the door there was a picture of a pond, out of which rose a curious conventional tree protected by dragons and which once bore the throne of an *Avalokitesvara (Kwannon)*.

The throne was no longer there, but to the right and left of the pond there are still two frightful demons who, with their six hands each, are threatening two little imps with pigs' and elephants' heads kneeling at their feet. On the left, near the pond, appears the form of a Brahman, provided with a crutch, stamping angrily with his foot and supported by his frowning disciple, likewise dressed in a tiger-skin.

It gives one the impression that this Brahman has been disputing with this god and come off second best.

A row of fantastic Indian divinities follow on at the top, but above these Brahman gods the picture is completely destroyed. On the left side of the cella a king is seen on a splendidly painted white horse going to hunt, followed by armour-bearers and courtiers. In one corner stands the scribe with ink-slab and pen.

On the right side of the cella we see a very strange scene, viz. the pursuit of *garudas*—fabulous creatures with human bodies, but the claws, wings, and heads of birds—that have carried off a child. One child that they had taken is already in safety; the *garudas* are followed by archers and lasso-bearers and caught.

We have reason to believe that we are here dealing with the latest development of Leochares' Ganymede group in an Eastern Asiatic version.

Finally, in the corners stand the four guardians of the world in suits of armour with their attendant demons.

On the walls, to the right and left of the cella door, there were several rows, one above another, of the portraits of Uighur-Turkish benefactors; on the one side the men, on the other the women, of Royal or noble rank, the names of a few being still visible in Uighur script on the name-plates by the side of each figure. Originally there had been three rows of such figures, one above the other; in the lowest there was a half life-sized painting of the prince on the one side of the door, of the princess on the other, and above them, on each side respectively, two men and two women, whilst above them again appeared a row of three men and of three women. Only the top row, containing three figures, remained of the men, and of the women no more than the two figures of the middle row. By dint of long and arduous work we succeeded in cutting away all these pictures. After twenty months of travelling they arrived safely at Berlin, where they fill an entire room of the museum. This is one of the few temples whose sum-total of paintings has been brought to Berlin (Plate 22).

Here in the mountains the air was less oppressive than in Turfan, and here, too, we worked from sunrise to sunset and were less troubled by visitors. Yet twice we did have some of an unpleasant kind, as I will show.

The mountain, rising behind the monastery settlement, is snow-white in colour, but regularly flooded with crimson under the rays of the rising and setting sun. In front of this mountain there lies a sharply outlined accumulation of black mountain sand; below this stretches the plain, covered, like the ruins themselves, with the golden hue of the yellow loess.

But when we saw the moon rise enormous in the heavens, the colour of mountains and the loess changed in a surprising manner. The mountain peak became a violet blue, the heap of black sand green with golden shadows, but the loess assumed the most marvellous and magical colours that varied with the brightness or shadow in which it lay; here crimson, there violet, now blue, then deepest black—in short, I have never seen such a fantastic and wondrous colour symphony as we enjoyed on every bright moonlight night.

And on such nights, when we went to bed, sleep would not come at first in spite of all fatigue; the impressions and experiences of the day were too strong to let our minds find rest at once.

In the death-like silence that always reigns there, the splashing of the rushing stream, as it fell over the rocks at the foot of the gorge in the mountain-side, sounded like scornful laughter. Even though the landscape was one of incredible, indescribable beauty, it did not lack with this note of demoniacal laughter a certain suggestion of something weird and uncanny, and one understood why, in all these temples, the ugly demons appeared on the walls.

On such a night, when all was still as death, ghastly noises suddenly resounded as though a hundred devils had been let loose. We sprang

THE TEMPLE-SETTLEMENTS

up in terror, seized our rifles, and rushed out on to the terrace. There, to our horror, we saw the whole horse-shoe gorge filled with wolves that, head in air, were baying the moon with long-drawn-out howls.

Our servants hurried up to reassure us with: "Sir, sir, you needn't be afraid, they'll not hurt you." And that was true, too. After a few shots, one of which hit one of the visitors, the animals left us after they had eaten their dead comrade. This scene occurred once again, but in no way discomposed us on the second occasion.

The wolf, like the tiger in the northerly and westerly inhabited regions, especially near Shikho and Manas, near Maralbashi and also in Lop-nor, is in this country a relatively harmless creature.

I only heard of one case where a human being had been killed by wolves. This was in the tragic history of a pretty twelve-year-old little girl of Karakhoja—we knew the child—who was to be married, against her will, to an old man of sixty. She ran away to Lukchun across the desert, but only got half-way to a spot where an enormous elm-tree on the banks of a spring provides a resting-place amid the sandy wastes. Here she lay down to rest, and was attacked by wolves in her sleep. All that was found later were blood-stained fragments of her clothing and her long top-boots with her legs still inside.

At the end of the work in Bazaklik I got a violent kick from my horse on the knee, and was so much hurt that I could do no riding for ten days, as I had to use crutches during that time. But in the evenings, after I had finished my Turkish study, I used to decorate the walls of our room with proverbs and verses in Arabic, Persian, German, Latin, Greek, and the European languages, with which I was thoroughly conversant, and over the entrance I wrote in huge letters "ROBBERS' DEN."

These mural decorations proved a source of profit to our landlord, who, later on, used to show them for money. They were even displayed as a wonder to a German vice-admiral who had escaped from Japanese captivity!

The King of Lukchun, hearing of my misfortune, came and begged me to give him the horse, which was very strong and handsome, for his State coach, since it was not comfortable to ride, and he would give me a good nag in exchange. I was delighted to be rid of the animal and to get in exchange a horse from the stud of Pi-chang, so I agreed to his proposal. The king then sent me a very big horse—it was known later throughout the land as *chong at* (the big horse), a bay with a magnificent action. It was an ambler, but at such a pace as other horses could only manage at a gallop. After my high-stepping grey this new horse was a veritable rocking-chair, and I began to enjoy the long rides we had to take daily. I used this horse every day during the whole of my stay in Turkestan, and finished up by riding him over the Himalayas and finally selling him in Kashmir for 150 rupees.

The treatment of horses in Eastern Turkestan differs from ours. When a posting-station is reached the horse is at first led round the courtyard of the station for at least an hour by a little boy; then after the saddle has been somewhat eased his head is tied to a beam, so that he cannot drop it. At midnight he gets water and some lucerne hay, and then a feed of corn, chiefly black millet. I considered these arrangements ridiculous, but was forced to acquiesce in them by my attendants, who maintained that if the horse got water any sooner his hoofs would swell and he would be useless. To cure horses of over-fatigue, when they cannot go any farther the natives cut a piece of cartilage out of the nose. Whether this treatment is of any use and has been proved by experience, I cannot say.

In the neighbourhood of Murtuk, between the village of Bazaklik and the upper part of the Sangim ravine, to the west of the range of hills, there lies another little settlement, called Chikkan Kol. We discovered it on our first exploratory expedition to Murtuk, and worked there some days in the most bitter cold. The settlement consists of a number of cave-temples in a ravine near a large lake, and there, on the shores of the lake and on an island in shallow water, we found Buddhist ruins. Our excavations showed that the water had done much damage, yet we secured some fine heads (of the *kwannon* type), as well as some manuscripts and embroideries. Out of the temples in the ravine we took pictures and frescoes, which, although they were fairly badly damaged, showed us that we were dealing with a settlement of about the seventh century. They resembled the mural paintings of Tuyoq in style, and, like these, are the oldest paintings obtained from the Turfan oasis. In the vaulted roofs we found the interesting "lantern" roofs, not cut in the rock as in Kyzyl and Korish, but only painted on the dome; the same lantern roofs are found in the religious foundations of

Plate 23

Mosque of the Seven Sleepers (*ashābu 'l kahf*) Tuyoq

Plate 24

Monastery on the right bank, Tuyoq (destroyed by earthquake, 1916)

Cave-temple in the bend of the left bank, Tuyoq — Find of manuscripts here —

Bamian (Afghanistan), and in Kashmir in the beautiful stone temples, which show so plainly the influence of Greek art (Plate 39).

The lantern roof dates back to a construction of wooden beams, which is still used by peasants in Armenia, Afghanistan, Kashmir, and Little Tibet (Plate 40). Transferred into rock-temples, they came by way of Turkestan to China and Korea; in the former country they have been changed as a rule into no more than a painted decoration, but in the latter they are still found in many temples cut into the rock as in the West.

Tuyoq

To the east of Karakhoja, about thirteen miles from the old town, a wonderful valley, very wide at its lower end, but quickly narrowing as it continues, leads into a frightfully rocky waste amid bare and awe-inspiring mountain heights—a range of hills that are, indeed, terribly wild and rugged. The little valley winds northward into the mountains, makes a sharp turn to the west, and then goes to the north once more, becoming at last too narrow for a vehicle to pass, even if driven in the actual bed of the stream.

This district is called Tuyoq (carved out), a very appropriate name! In the broader part of the valley the little stream is divided into innumerable canals, and with its water makes the rich loess soil almost incredibly fertile. The small village of Tuyoq lives on its vineyards, for here they grow the "Turfan" grapes, little oval fruit (*kishmish*), but seedless and so sweet that, when dried, they make the best raisins of the world, and are a highly prized commodity even in Peking, at a distance 115 days' journey to the east.

Besides grapes the district also produces an enormous quantity of apricots, peaches, melons, and a remarkably hard pear that can only be eaten when dead-ripe, but then has a delicious flavour.

On the right bank there rises a modern mosque, the "Shrine of the Seven Sleepers" (Plate 23). I visited this mosque, and was told that behind the modern Mohammedan portion there was an ancient temple hewn out in the rock.

Here, as in many other places, we see how Islam, when it came into the country, took possession of the old native sanctuaries. In this case it was easy for the Mohammedans, for the legend of the Seven Sleepers is very familiar to them. Unfortunately I was not allowed to enter the old cave-temple, since its entrance was covered by a number of flags which Yakub Beg's troops had taken from the rebellious Tungans in the 'sixties and 'seventies of last century.

This sanctuary is, even to the present day, visited by pilgrims from the whole country, and also from India and Arabia; indeed, one Indian pilgrim worried me to such an extent with his foolish fanaticism that at last I had to get the king of Lukchun to help me to send him off from the district.

Since the "Seven Sleepers" mosque lies close to Karakhoja, the name of Ephesus in its Arabic-Turkish form of *Apsūs* was given to the Old Town.

Farther up the stream there are a number of cave-temples, and on its right bank some large *stūpas* (Plate 24); and quite at the very end, on the giddy heights of a terrace, there used to be a very large monastery that, like similar buildings in Tibet, clung, as might a swallow's nest, on to the almost perpendicular slope of the mountain-side. In 1916 this monastery fell, owing to an earthquake, and utterly disappeared.

On the left side, almost opposite the mosque, rises a steep hill crowned with a few ruins, but at its foot we found one of the houses for drying the grapes. It is a building with numberless square openings at regular intervals in the walls to allow free entrance to the air. The bunches are hung in rows on fixed horizontal poles, and, in consequence of the entire lack of moisture in the air and the great heat, they dry in a short time without any loss of flavour.

Farther up the stream there are many more temples, all unfortunately in a very ruinous condition, but the chief building lies at the very top of the valley, where both mountains and streams made a sudden sharp turn to the west.

I had entrusted Bartus with some excavations in the Sangim ravine. As there were no more discoveries to be expected there and the excavation was only to lay bare the foundations, I took up my quarters with the Imaum of the Seven Sleepers mosque and visited a ruin that promised to repay excavation.

And this repayment I found in the large building in the bend of the valley (Plate 24). An enormous block of conglomerate had fallen from above into a monk's cell, broken down the walls to a certain extent, and was now fixed like a stopper in the room.

THE TEMPLE-SETTLEMENTS

I succeeded in clearing out this soft, crumbling rock, and to my joy I found the whole cell, which, moreover, was built after the pattern of an Iranian room,[1] filled with great heaps of old manuscripts. An attempt had been made to destroy this great store of documents by fire, but the old fact that books burn badly had proved true again in this case, for only the edges, especially of the Chinese roll-manuscripts, were charred. In spite of everything, we found about two sackfuls of eighth and ninth century manuscripts, mixed, it is true, with some of later date.

Whilst I was busy clearing out these treasures Bartus rode over and shared in my pleasure at this valuable addition to our collection.

Wonderful embroideries were found here, too, and a little reliquary of turned wood, circular in shape, with a lid on the top (Plate 39), tastefully painted in rich tones of red, yellow, and blue.

The Imaum was one of the very few people that I met in Turkestan who could not only read and recite Arabic but understand it as well.

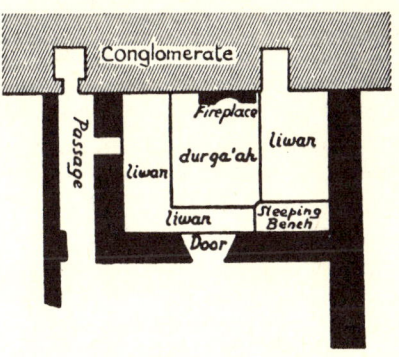

GROUND PLAN OF MONK'S CELL

I had with me the Egyptian (*Bulaq*) edition of the *Arabian Nights*, but had, so far, found no one who would have been worthy to possess such a book. But now I handed it over to my host, who was most highly delighted with the gift.

Every evening I held a grand reception, when the important people of the little place came to visit me and were served with tea, whilst I chatted to them all quite informally for a short time.

Delightful refreshment in this valley is afforded by a spring of excellent pure water, flowing from a rock below the mosque. The

---

[1] This monk's cell consisted of a rectangular apartment with a fireplace and stone sleeping-bench. All round the walls there were broad stone platforms corresponding to the platforms—(called *liwan*) of the modern Egyptian house—the somewhat sunken part in the middle corresponds to the Egyptian *durqa'ah*. The style of building is Persian, and has also been borrowed by the Arabians from the Persians.
Cf. Lane, *Modern Egyptians*, fifth edition, London, 1860, pp 11 *sqq.*

heat in this neighbourhood was fairly great, and a cool drink from this spring was a treat that far surpassed other pleasures.

Bartus soon moved over into my quarters, and we explored the remaining temples, with but poor results however. Only in the *stūpas* close to the mosque we chanced to find strange gifts buried with the dead, amongst others a great roll of white material which I thought was linen, but which, on closer inspection, proved to be made from the fibres of the *bœhmeria nivea*.

It so seldom rains in the Turfan oasis that a downpour is a great rarity, and not one that the natives by any means desire. The rains, when they do come, are generally so violent that the corn is laid, the streams and canals overflow at an inconvenient time and their waters cause widespread destruction, whilst mould and fungus develop on both fruit and grain.

During our stay in Tuyoq, one afternoon the sky darkened without the least warning, a terrible storm broke, and the rain came down in torrents. In a few moments the brook began to swell, in half an hour it overflowed its banks, and in an hour a red-brown, roaring torrent was sweeping all before it through the bed and over the banks of the former stream.

We had already arranged our manuscripts and packed them away in a box; but suddenly the flat mud roof of our room began to leak, and streams of dirty, muddy water poured on all sides into our dwelling. We had to keep on moving everything likely to be spoilt by water round the room, whilst the Imaum's sons and the mosque attendants did their best to patch up the roof a little. But it was no good, and if the downpour had not ceased as suddenly as it began, our things would certainly have been injured.

Unfortunately, short as the storm had been, its results were very regrettable. The stream had done damage everywhere, and the flooded fields had been covered with mountain sand and stones.

About ten miles to the south of Karakhoja there are two monastery settlements—*Chong-* (Great) and *Kichik-* (Little) *Hasar Shahri* (fortified town; *hasar* = Arabic *hisar*), in a very wild dune district where wild horses and camels were to be found, so it was said.

An old treasure-seeker, Radil by name, who was an even greater rogue than our landlord, but just as humorous and witty, too, but far coarser in his fun, had told us marvellous tales of the valuable finds that had been made in these desolate regions.

THE TEMPLE-SETTLEMENTS

So, although it was June, we marched with ten men through the shifting sands and encamped in the old temples, where unfortunately many scorpions had made their home as well.

Water had to be brought from a distant *kariz* (it is fetched in wooden vessels slung on either side of a donkey's baggage-saddle) and the *mirab's* young son was entrusted with this errand.

We worked about half the day, and discovered that the Buddhist religion had been practised here at a comparatively recent date. At one o'clock a frightful sandstorm blew up and the heat grew very great. We had no water, however, for the boy had started but a short time before with his donkey. Whilst the storm lasted we could not get on with our work, and all of us began to suffer from dreadful thirst. The storm, although of unusual violence, soon subsided, and shortly after the water-boy reappeared; the donkey had fallen and broken a leg!

The servants went off at once. They killed the donkey, and I am convinced they ate it at home. At any rate, horse-flesh is so much liked that strayed horses seldom come back unless the natives happen to know that they belong to some distinguished person.

Bartus followed the column to Lukchun, whilst I rode through the desert back to Karakhoja. After that, what an excellent flavour there was about the cool water from the depths of Saut's eighty-foot well!

The ruins of Little Hasar consist of Persian domed buildings and Indian *stūpas* with some very ruined walls. Great Hasar we did not visit; it is best to go to such places in winter when water can be carried as ice.

Bartus afterwards dug here for Grünwedel with some success, but not as much as was expected.

In June we again had a great number of cases ready to be sent off. But to make certain of a safe journey I was obliged to treat with the Russian consul in Urumchi to secure his mediation to get the viceroy to provide me with a trustworthy caravan leader. As the German-Russian servant,[1] whom we had hired in Semipalatinsk,

---

[1] If this man was a fair specimen of the German-Russians, they would not make a very favourable impression. It is true he looked down on the Russians with great contempt, but was himself nothing but a *moujik*. He was a Catholic; his family belonged to the Oppenheim district, and his German, in spite of the one hundred and fifty years that the colonists had spent apparently at Samara, still kept its native dialect. When he caught sight of the first camel as we entered the Karakhoja part of the country, he showed

could by no means get used to the certainly somewhat rough conditions under which we lived in Karakhoja and wished to return to Siberia, I took him with me. The *mirab*, too, joined my party.

After the posting-station of Kindik we had to stop a little as all kinds of repairs were needed to the vehicles. I wandered about the adjacent country, and was pleased, in the immediate neighbourhood of the *sarai*, to come upon a number of gazelles that, in the twinkling of an eye, gracefully bounded out of sight. On a steep wall I saw several charming birds, black with touches of red and white and long beaks—wall-runners they were.

At this station we experienced the only unpleasant adventure of all our stay in Eastern Turkestan. It was as follows: I noticed that a fine, tall young man, very respectably dressed and, by his speech, a native of Andijan, kept trying to finger my carbines and silver-mounted dagger that were hanging on one of the *sarai* pillars. He was so obtrusive that I told my servants to warn him from me to keep away from these things.

In the *sarai* at Dabanching we had three large rooms; two of these I gave up to the servants, and in the third, a smaller room, I slept myself and kept under my pillow a small box, in which I had six thousand roubles[1] in gold that I intended to change in Urumchi into Chinese money. In the night, when I was sleeping quietly, I was roughly awakened by Iwan, the young German, who was standing, trembling, by my bed with a little lamp in his hand. He stammered: "Shoot, sir, shoot, sir; thieves, thieves!"

I sprang up immediately, and with my Browning in my hand I followed Iwan into the servants' room. All was excitement there, for saddles, saddle-cloths, their clothes, and mine as well, had disappeared! We could not discover where the thief had forced his way in, so we ran to wake the landlord, and found that the gate was locked, our horses standing in the stable, and not a trace of his entrance anywhere to be seen. Nor were any of the horses belonging to the other travellers missing.

But on our return to the servants' room we saw on the wall next to the street a great hole through which the thieves had forced an entrance. After wetting the mud wall and boring holes, a broad

his appreciation of Russian artistic skill as follows: "Sir, sir, just look at that creature. What it looks like! Look at its neck, and its head! Why, they don't match! And what a hump! And the legs are put on all wrong! God Almighty never made that beast—a Russian did it." [1] About £650.

THE TEMPLE-SETTLEMENTS

Chinese sword had been used to cut it away, and through this opening the robber (or robbers) had made good their entrance. The clang of stirrups on the flagged floor as they stole the saddles had awakened the Mirab, but the thieves were so quick that they had disappeared through the hole before anyone could catch sight of them in the pitch-dark room. I crept through the hole on to the street, and at once found the cardboard box with my army helmet, and, a little farther on, the parcel containing my khaki uniform. The thieves had simply left these things when they saw they were of no use to them, but with these exceptions there was no trace of them whatever.

If they had come back whilst we were looking for them, they could easily have carried off my little money-box, which very possibly they had been aiming at when they came. We blocked up the hole at once with a great Chinese table, set a watch by it, and then, with the landlord's help, searched the whole house. Such a *sarai* (called there by its Chinese name, *dan*) is generally surrounded by a great square wall, in the front of which is a large gate that is shut at sundown and secured by great wooden bars. Opposite this gate lie the guest-rooms in a long row: some of them are single rooms with only one door, opening on to the courtyard; others, intended for several travellers, have communicating doors as well. The doors and windows only open as a rule on to the courtyard, none on to the street outside. Against the side walls and by the gate the stables are built with mangers for horses, donkeys, and camels.

The gate was firmly barred, and all the other travellers were awake and helping us to find the thief. It turned out that in one room there were all kinds of women's ornaments in silver, coral, and the less valuable gems, costly silk dresses, etc., such as are worn by ladies of high rank or of doubtful character; this was the room taken by the young man that I described above. His two horses, one a fine bay, were also forthcoming. But he was missing, and the landlord told us that he had left the *sarai* in the afternoon. In all probability this young man was the thief, and he had doubtless meant to steal the things, get a friend to hide them, and then, once the deed was accomplished, come in all innocence to demand admission. After attaching identification labels to the horses, valuable garments, and jewellery, I handed them over to the care of the local *amban*. All efforts to find the thief, however, proved fruitless.

The *amban* took the horses and stolen goods to Urumchi, where they were handed over to the viceroy, from whom I received, as indemnification for the servants' stolen clothes, saddles, etc., the liberal sum of fifty Chinese dollars—about £8 or £9—which was more than sufficient to replace all they had lost.

We quickly received horses for the return journey, and I started.

The stream near the little fortress of Dabanching (Chinese-Turkish = the place by the pass) was much swollen. We managed to cross the ford, which my men found without mishap; but a Turkish woman who, carrying her baby, had tried to cross the water above the ford on her little donkey, got into deep water, and would have been drowned if at my cry a long-legged Tungan, whom the Turfan magistrate had sent to accompany me, had not seized her at the last moment. She had kept her baby tightly clasped in her arms, but the donkey was whirled away a moment after.

Here, close to Dabanching, Yakub Beg's army was defeated in April 1877. Shortly after, the death occurred in Korla of this remarkable man, who had worked his way up from a dancer to king of the enormous country. It is said by some that he was poisoned by the governor of Khotan, by others that he died of apoplexy.

I had asked Herr Bartus during my absence to visit and work at the old settlement of Shui-pang, near the hamlet of Bulayik, north of the Chinese town of Turfan, a settlement that we had visited before. He carried out my request, and dug out of the terribly ruined walls a marvellous booty of Christian manuscripts. Amongst these a complete psalter in Pahlavi inscription script of the fifth century, also middle-Turkish translations of the Georgios legend as well as of a Christian apocrypha, dealing with the visit of the Three Kings to the Infant Christ. But special value attached to great numbers of manuscripts in a variant of the Nestorian Estrangelo script, and in a language which was afterwards found out by F. C. Andreas and F. W. K. Müller in Berlin to be Sogdian. There were also fragments of the Nicene Creed, portions of St. Matthew's Gospel, the legend of the finding of the Holy Cross by the Empress Helena, and other Christian texts. A page among these Greek texts bore a line in the Greek script and language, which, according to U. von Wilamowitz-Moellendorf, belongs to the ninth

Plate 25

Ruins in the bend of the left bank, Tuyoq

Summer castle of Ana-Tam belonging to the *Wang* of Komul

v. Le Coq, Turfan.

Plate 26

Indian *stupa* and Persian domed building
Kichik Hasar Shahri

Buddhist temple ruins, Ara Tam. near Komul

Plate 27

Funeral mosque and tombs of the *Wangs* of Komul

Hall with pillars in the funeral mosque, Komul

Plate 28

Rock temples
on the River Muzart,
Kum Tura

Passage in the
temple buildings,
Kum Tura

THE TEMPLE-SETTLEMENTS

century. So there we have ninth-century Greek in West China. Finally he found numerous liturgical and other Nestorian documents in the Syrian language and script.

I hastened back from Dabanching without a moment's delay, and reached Karakhoja again at dawn on the third day; Herr Bartus arrived there, too, almost at the same hour. So eager had he been that, as his horse was ill, he had driven with his finds in one of the large two-wheeled carts without stopping from Shui-Pang to Karakhoja, and, although we were both very exhausted, we did not go to bed until we had sorted out our valuable finds, numbered and packed them.

THE JOURNEY TO KOMUL, OUR STAY THERE, AND DEPARTURE FOR KASHGAR

AT the beginning of August the heat was so unbearable and we were so tormented by "prickly heat," a tiresome skin affection caused by the sun, that we were obliged to look out for a cooler climate. When we heard that the oasis of Komul, situated amongst the spurs of the Celestial Mountains, enjoyed a comparatively cool climate, we decided to visit the town of Komul, the last Turkish place near the frontier of China proper, and to explore the numerous Buddhist ruins to be found there.

The road to Komul passes through extensions of the Gobi, a waterless desert of stones and sand-dunes, intersected by terribly bare unwooded mountain ranges, where frequent storms often rage with quite extraordinary violence.

Here and there, close to the rest-houses, there are water-springs, and in the neighbourhood thus watered, rhubarb grows in the greatest luxuriance.

A dark rock, situated at a corner of the road, bears eloquent testimony to the force of the storms, for here the masses of sand have been whirled so long against this rock that they have perforated it with an endless number of holes, yards deep. In these holes flocks of ringdoves have made their homes, and fill the air to a long distance with their melancholy cooing. What these birds can find to live on I cannot imagine, but, as they are very strong on the wing, no doubt they visit cultivated lands in the far distance. We found, too, numerous herds of lyre-horned antelopes in these dry deserts and rugged mountain heights.

The halting-stations were exceedingly dirty, and very tumbledown as well; in one of these houses we were, for the first time in Chinese Turkestan, attacked by innumerable swarms of bugs.

We should have had to put up with much more hardship on this journey if the king of Lukchun and his father-in-law, the king of Komul, had not sent in advance for us, to all these halting-stations, eggs, sour cream, mutton, fruit, and other gifts. The journey occupied twelve days, but at one of the last stations we suddenly saw the German flag on a Chinese cart. We galloped up, and read the words

JOURNEY TO KOMUL

"Carlowitz & Co." on the flag. We hoped we were meeting fellow-countrymen, but the travellers were Chinese employees of the great firm who had been sent out to start a branch in Urumchi. They were very courteous and insisted on our dining with them, and accompanied us back to the station, which they had just left as they wished to do us honour with a meal. These people (Tungans) knew as early as August about the Emperor William's speech concerning Morocco, and were greatly delighted that the Germans intended to prevent the downfall of the *Sherif*, the Sultan of Morocco.

Since they came from Shanghai, a journey taking at least 115 days, they could not have received the news there, and I was once again astounded at the speed with which news is spread in these trackless lands.

We reached Komul, the royal seat, in the middle of August, and rode into the town at 4 a.m., when the temperature had dropped very appreciably.

We had letters of introduction to the mayor (*darogha*), who gave us a friendly reception and very abundant hospitality. But we learnt that, in accordance with the old Persian custom, we could not go out until we had been received by the king. Here, too, as in Persia, the rising and setting of the sun are greeted by the Court musicians with kettle-drums and shrill flutes.

On the following morning I sent my Chinese visiting-card—somewhat like a legal document in shape—to the king, who immediately dispatched a guest-receiver (*mihmandar*) to greet us and bring us an invitation for the next day to the palace. After this royal recognition it was possible for us to go into the town, where the chief object of interest for us was the royal mausoleum, built in the eighteenth century (Plate 27). It consists of the tomb, mosque, and monuments. The mosque is a splendid building for this district, built of adobe bricks overlaid with glazed green tiles. The great interior contains seventy-two enormous wooden pillars carved in the Persian style; the walls are painted magnificently with floral decorations that seem to have some affinity in style and colour with the ancient native art. In the entrance hall there are two large granite inscription-stones in Chinese style, one of which sets forth in Persian, the other in Turkish, information concerning the building and pronounces benedictions on the royal family. I had these inscriptions copied at once by a Mullah, and paid the customary fee which every traveller has to give, in proportion to his means, to this burial mosque; in my case it was ten Chinese dollars (about thirty-five shillings).

Near the mosque we see the royal tombs—wooden erections in a curious mixed style which is semi-Chinese. These buildings are called in native dialect the *Altunluk* (gold place) of Komul. A school for priests is connected with the *Altunluk*, a part of the money received going to the upkeep of the tombs, the rest defraying the expenses of the school.

On the next morning we paid our visit to the *orda*, the royal palace. Like the *orda* at Lukchun this building was an enormous square adobe building of large rooms, some furnished with exceptional beauty. We saw on all sides splendid, fast-dyed Chinese and Khotan carpets, beautiful silk embroideries, both in Chinese style and also in that practised in Bokhara; valuable jade carving from Khotan, side by side with Chinese porcelain; French clocks for a mantel-piece and, O horrors! terribly ugly Russian paraffin lamps of the cheapest and commonest kind. A cuckoo-clock, too, adorned one of the walls in the reception-room, and delighted us with its homely note.

The king, Shah Maksûd, an extremely amiable, distinguished, and clever man, received us in most friendly fashion. In passing I may mention that he, like his son-in-law, the *wang* of Lukchun, knew not only Chinese but Manchurian as well. They gave us refreshment three times in the day, and I was astonished to find in the house of a Mohammedan prince an enormous quantity of Russian liqueurs and excellent French champagnes. He was continually drinking our health, and seemed quite hardened against any of the ill-effects of alcohol. But when I asked to be allowed to take a photograph of him and his heir he flatly refused my request, saying: "*Sūrat tārtkan yok*"—(" There are not to be any photographs!").

The dinner was also a mixture of Chinese and Turkish dishes. We ate Chinese macaroni and *mantu*, a kind of turnover filled with minced meat, onions, and garlic; the chopped meat is covered with a paste of wheat-meal and cooked by steaming in sieves over vessels of boiling-water. I had an extraordinary aversion to these steamed turnovers, but Bartus ate them with pleasure. Then came mutton boiled, roasted, and as Irish stew, bouillon, soups, with mincemeat, and, above all, the inevitable *palao*, which here, however, was quite excellent. But, as always, the meal began with tea and fruits, of which the melons and grapes were particularly delicious. A high official of the king squatted on a carpet at our feet—the king and courtiers having taken their places like us on Chinese chairs at a Chinese table. About eighty wonderfully fragrant melons were placed in front of us; he cut into all of them, tasted, and selected ten for final choice. We revelled in the slices handed to us.

The dried Komul melons are well known, and, in spite of the journey of more than a hundred days, they are sent every year as a present to the Imperial Court at Peking. Even in the Komul district, amongst the mountains, the force of the sun, combined with the great dryness of the air, is sufficient to dry the slices, into which these exceedingly juicy melons are cut, so that they can be sent great distances.

With the king's permission we visited his country castle of Ara-Tam, situated about sixteen miles north-east of the town (Plate 25). We reached the castle, which is built in a style of architecture half-Chinese, half-Persian and situated in a wonderful garden, in the evening, after a hot ride, and greatly appreciated the shade of some splendid leafy elms in the castle court. In the middle of the garden there are ruins of some Buddhist temples, and after a steep climb up the bare mountains surrounding this idyllic spot we found two more large Buddhist temples (Plate 26). We immediately set to work, but found, to our regret, that the snow, which frequently falls in these mountains, had made the earth so sodden that the sculpture and other antiquities, which were there in abundance, were sticking out of the ground quite shapeless and spoilt.

Whilst we were deliberating whether we should visit the second of the old settlements, Khotun-Tam, I received a telegram[1] from Berlin to tell me that Grünwedel had decided to revisit Turkestan, and to ask me to meet and help him in Kashgar.

This news placed me in an awkward position for this reason: in Ara-Tam I had been visited by a man from Tashkent (Russian

---

[1] The Chinese Government has had a telegraph-line put up between Peking and Kashgar, but obstinately refused to allow it to be connected with the Russian line in Irkeshtam. The telegraph-poles are excellent guide-posts, but are sometimes laid low by the frightful spring storms. I have been told, too, that in the mountains the posts are sometimes knocked down by bears, who, misled by the audible humming of the wires, imagine that bees have made their homes in these "trees."

Turkestan), Kasim Achond by name, on his way from Sha-chou (in China) to Kashgar. He was a merchant who had passed some time in Su-chou and Sha-chou, and told me that in the old Buddhist rock-temples of Tung-hwang, near Sha-chou, a Chinese temple-servant (*kho-shang*) had, in 1900, discovered an old walled-up library containing many documents that no one could read. A quantity of pictures and little bronze figures had also been found in this same library. The temple attendant had already given away many Tibetan texts and little figures of the gods to the Mongolian kings, and doubtless he would be prepared to give me all I could use of the manuscripts that no one could read.

This communication roused my most lively curiosity, and, although it was seventeen days' journey through horrible deserts to Sha-chou, I determined to visit the place.

But anyone with my experience of having gone a seven days' journey and seven days back to see an inscription-stone (*sgraffito*) promised by a native, only, after great exertions, to find a poor erratic block crossed and recrossed by glacier scores and scratches, accepts such communications with due caution. Kind, well-meaning people have only too often told us similar tales, just by way of saying something pleasant to the foreign gentleman. Bartus, too, was led round amongst the mountains near Turfan for eight or ten days, during which the guide's dog perished from thirst and fatigue, and men and horses very nearly shared the same fate, but the promised old settlement was never found!

I therefore looked upon the news somewhat doubtfully. It was a distance of about 1,250 miles to Kashgar, where Grünwedel was to arrive on October 15th, and we had already reached the end of August. It was difficult to know what to do. Should I undertake the journey to Tung-hwang, seventeen days' there and seventeen days back? We might, of course, ride each way in twelve days, but then the twenty-four days' journey and six days' stay would be a whole month.

If I undertook this journey it would be impossible to meet Grünwedel in Kashgar on October 15th. Kasim Achond's information, however, sounded so improbable that I doubted its accuracy.

So, somewhat in despair, I left the decision to Fate by tossing a Chinese dollar: heads win, tails lose! Tails, i.e. the inscription side, came uppermost, and I had my horse saddled and began our journey

JOURNEY TO KOMUL

to Kashgar. After a very cordial parting with Shah Maksud, the king, we rode in quick marches back to Turfan, whence meantime our caravan with the discovered treasures had already been sent by the Chinese magistrate on to Urumchi. In Turfan we made up our caravan, and went on through the extremely romantic, wild mountain ravines between Turfan, Toksun, and Korla to the last-named place. The ravine near Aighyr Bulak is especially wild and even dangerous, for when it rains there all the water runs immediately into this gorge, and quite suddenly tears with destructive violence, like a solid wall of water, through the narrow pass. All caught in a storm there will inevitably perish, man and beast alike (Plate 1).

In the ravine we met a Chinese telegraph official going to Ak-su with his wife and child. His carriage horses had failed him, and this very cultured man, who understood English well, was in a great dilemma. We came to his help with fresh horses, thereby gaining his gratitude and that of his superior officers.

In Korla we rested in the house of the consular agent (*aksakal*) of the Russian Turks from Ferghana, living in Korla. It was a wretchedly poor dwelling, made of nothing but bundles of reeds, and put up over a hollow space about a yard deep. We were given the usual *palao*, and when it grew dark our host brought us two Chinese candles stuck into bottles. These bottles struck me as familiar, so I asked Bartus to hand me one, and was surprised to see on the label the name of my grandfather's firm, "A. Le Coq & Co., London." They were two stout bottles of the old firm!

My grandfather Le Coq, a descendant of a well-known Berlin Huguenot family, had chosen an officer's career, and in the early twenties of the nineteenth century was in Trèves attached to the Second Rhineland Hussar Regiment, No. 9. The inaction at that period soon made him leave the army; he married a lady of Trèves, and, having ample means, lived as a well-to-do civilian in Eltville, Kempton-on-the-Rhine, and afterwards in Frankfort-on-the-Main.

In April 1833 the "Frankfort Rising" took place; the students from Giessen with their broadswords, and the Vilbel peasants with their hay-forks and flails—about sixty in all—marched to Frankfort, there to set up once more the splendour of the holy German Empire. Unfortunately a somewhat bloody contest took place, the leaders were dispersed, and two young nephews of my grandfather, seventeen and nineteen years old, students at Giessen, took refuge with their uncle, who hid them in wardrobes. The police entered the very room, but did not find the fugitives. They had to endure this captivity for ten days, then my grandfather drove them, disguised as lackeys, on his coach into Switzerland. But rumours began to be spread in Frankfort, and as my grandfather was in any case somewhat tired of the conditions in Germany, he betook himself to London, where he lived for a long time very happily as a private gentleman, gaining many friends in all ranks of society.

One morning, however, he read in the paper that his bank had failed badly; the report was true, and he found himself suddenly without any means whatever.

His English friends at once came to his help. The head of a large porter brewery (his son became a lord later) offered him good financial support, and the representation of all his brewery interests in Russia, if he would undertake the introduction there of a brand of stout specially brewed for that country.

Although my grandfather had had no commercial experience, he accepted the offer and went to Warsaw, where he had, on his mother's side (she was the youngest daughter of the Berlin painter and copper-plate engraver, Daniel Chodowiecki), many Polish relatives belonging to the nobility—some, indeed, of high rank. The Chodowiecki family had originally belonged to the Protestant Polish nobility, but in consequence of the anti-Reformation movement in Poland they had to leave their estates and take refuge in Germany.

My grandfather did not make his appearance as a commercial traveller, but invited all his relations to Warsaw's first hotel, where after the best dinner the house could produce the well-known stout was put before them. The guests thought it so excellent that they all wanted to have some, and the first orders were given.

My grandfather then went to St. Petersburg, where the banker, Jefremew, financed the undertaking so successfully that my grandfather in a few years could retire again as a rich man. The business was carried on by his partners, Messrs. Sillem and Turnbull, under the old name of A. Le Coq & Co. with great success until the war brought it to an end.

My father, however, as a consequence of the bank failure, had to leave the English public school where he was and become a merchant. He went as the first native of Berlin to Canton, where

Plate 29

Mir Safdar Ali, Prince (*tham*) of Hunza. (Descendant of Alexander the Great)

Khalmat Khan, a fine male type from Ferghana

v. Le Coq, Turfan.

Plate 30

A Roofed *bazar* street Bugur

Islam house of prayer Shahyar

JOURNEY TO KOMUL

he worked for five years with his friends, Messrs. von Carlowitz and Harkort, in the firm of Carlowitz & Co., which quickly developed into a business known the world over.

My grandfather's experience is a good instance of the vital force that still persists in Huguenot blood.

But now, dear reader, let us return to our desert.

The prosperous town of Korla lies on the Baghrach Kol, a large lake, through which the Kaidu river pursues its course. The water of the lake is of fabulous transparency, and enlivened by endless numbers of large fish, most of them belonging apparently to the barbel family. There are, however, shad as well—ugly creatures as long as a man and with enormous mouths.

Herr Bartus, as an old sailor, could not resist throwing his line in here. I, too, put my rod together and whipped the water with my artificial flies. I had a bite at once, but, to my regret, the English rod broke just above the handle; evidently some one had sat on it during the journey and done the damage. Bartus was more fortunate. He had flung into the water a pound of meat on a gigantic hook and strong line, and an antediluvian monster had swallowed the bait. With great effort he dragged it out of the water, to the intense delight of the entire population, who were watching the visitors' doings. It weighed about fifty pounds, had a smooth skin—brown spotted with white—and was something like our eel-pout. In spite of my warning—for some of the fish here are dangerous eating—Herr Bartus persisted in having some of it for dinner and found it excellent. But for myself I shared the Turkish aversion to eating fish.

There are only two districts in the whole country where fish are often eaten, viz. round about Maralbashi, where the River Tarim brings down enormous quantities, which are enjoyed by the Dolans living there; and, secondly, in the neighbourhood of Lake Lop-nor, where the whole population, apparently differing in many respects from the other Turks, live chiefly on fish, either fresh or dried. It is remarkable that both the Dolans and the dwellers round Lop-nor are looked upon as people of another race by the Turks.

The lake at Korla is the playground, too, of innumerable flocks of water-birds, and is the breeding-place of swans, whose plumage is much in demand by the Chinese as an edging for valuable robes. Geese and ducks of different kinds frequent the shores and surface of the water in great quantities, and we always saw numbers flying in their hook-shaped flocks across the sky. Herons of every kind are also to be found there, but we could never inspect them closely as they always took to timid flight at the approach of men on horseback.

Close to Korla there lie the *ming-öi* of Shorchuk, which we afterwards visited with Grünwedel, and we saw an ancient fortified city near Kara-shahr. But the houses have disappeared, and the site, which is entirely surrounded by a wall, is covered with a dense thicket of reeds growing several yards high.

From Korla we went on at double speed to Kucha, and allowed ourselves four days' rest in this town, where some art industry is still carried on. It is true we also utilized these rest-days to visit the celebrated ruins in the neighbourhood, the *ming-öi* of Kumtura and of Kyzyl-Kargha. From Kucha we proceeded by way of Bai and Jam to Ak-su, where we had to pay our respects to the local *tao-tai*—that is, we sent him our calling-cards.

But the pace was too slow for me, and I decided to ride on early the next morning with only one personal attendant. In the evening, before I left, a peasant brought us a present of a dish of fifteen or twenty delicious Aikol peaches, snow-white fragrant fruit bigger than a man's fist, so perfect that they are of great repute throughout the country. The stones, too, come true to type, so that anyone planting such a peach-stone can be certain of finding the same fruit on the tree that grows from its kernel.

THE JOURNEY TO KASHGAR AND MEETING WITH GRÜNWEDEL. THE BEGINNING OF THE THIRD JOURNEY

At three o'clock next morning I rode away from Ak-su with my personal attendant, the Mirab, accomplishing the fourteen days' journey to Kashgar in nine only.

In his way the Mirab was an original, and possessed an inexhaustible store of songs and proverbs, which he knew how to produce with wit and humour. In order to learn something at least in this hurried journey, I made him repeat every evening the proverbs I had heard from his lips during the day and then wrote them down. Often, when I had gone to bed and he had made his couch at the foot of my bed, he would giggle and say: "*Turam*, I've got another," and straightway out came the note-book from under my pillow and the fresh addition to the Turkish *vox populi* was included in the collection.

My good bay once got a flint in his hoof and went very lame. But the Mirab knew an excellent remedy, viz. he bought from a travelling beggar, who was swarming with lice, some of these unpleasant domestic animals for a *cash*, and put them in the horse's ears. And sure enough, after I had taken out the stone, the animal no longer limped!

The natives have a strange method, too, of curing sore backs—although, in passing, it may be said that the Turkish saddles cause these far less often than do the fine English saddles which we had brought with us from Berlin, but soon got rid of. They apply to the sore the innocuous urine of some little boy about seven years old, and, lo and behold! the wound is healed. But it is absolutely essential to procure the remedy from a boy only, and from one of tender age, too.

We often covered two days' journey in the space of one, and succeeded in reaching Kashgar just before October 15th. I waited upon Mr. (now Sir) George Macartney, to whom I had obtained letters of introduction both from the German and the British Foreign Office, and was invited by Lady Macartney to become their guest.

[1] I had asked for introductions to the English officials, first, because I know the English language and English customs as well, whilst I neither understand Russian nor

112 BURIED TREASURES OF CHINESE TURKESTAN

Meantime Bartus, having been seized by ambition, did not wish to be behindhand, so he arrived only a few days after us, although he had had to bring all the baggage with him on the slow two-wheeled native carts.

To our very great consternation, however, Grünwedel did not come on October 15th, nor at the end of the month either, but instead we received the news that he had lost his luggage in Russian Turkestan and his arrival would be delayed! Then, indeed, the atmosphere became distincly electric! We were unspeakably annoyed at having lost the opportunity of visiting Tung-hwang.[1]

But there was no help for it, we had to possess our souls in patience, and after the strenuous exertions of our excavations and the journey, it was most refreshing to stay in a European home.

It is true we had at first to reaccustom ourselves to many habits of civilization. When Lady Macartney had installed me on an

am I acquainted with Russian ways. And, moreover, I had heard so many unfavourable reports of the Russian Representative in Kashgar, the well-known Consul-General Pietrowsky, that I had no wish to put myself in the power of such a tyrannical ruler.

Pietrowsky was an extraordinarily gifted man, and was in his time the real ruler of Eastern Turkestan. No one was better acquainted than he with the history, religion, and character both of the Chinese and the Turks, no one knew more than he did of the economic, military, and other resources of the country, and so far, therefore, residence under his roof would have been advantageous. But he was a man of such conceit that he found it very difficult to be just to other people. Captain Younghusband and M. de St. Ives both had reason to complain bitterly of him. Grünwedel and Huth, during their stay at the headquarters of the consul-general, also found themselves terribly at the mercy of his autocratic moods. On one occasion, indeed, when Huth opposed his unjustifiable arrogance, Pietrowsky asked Grünwedel if he would not be within his rights in having this Jew flogged. Grünwedel took up arms for his companion, but mutual relations became strained thereafter. I did not wish to be exposed to such treatment, and therefore preferred to enter into closer relations with the English—a resolution that gained me most pleasant acquaintances.

When I reached Kashgar, Consul-General Pietrowsky had already been recalled, but Turks and Chinese alike told amazing stories of his method of procedure. His successor was an amiable man who showed me much kindness. But, curiously enough, I met with all kinds of unusual behaviour in my relations with him, too. I shall never forget what happened when the Russian officials were invited to the Christmas dinner at the English consulate. They came and were very pleasant and gay, but absolutely refused to touch a single bite of the festive meal as they had dined just before they came! A proceeding which has always remained a mystery to me.

[1] It may be mentioned that the excellent English scholar and explorer, Sir Aurel Stein, on his visit to Tung-hwang, did actually find the library, and was able to buy a part of its contents, consisting of valuable old manuscripts and paintings on silk, from the temple attendant. Following him, the leader of the French expedition, M. Paul Pelliot, also visited this mine of fabulous treasure and bought a great quantity of the manuscripts, etc.

By the dispersion of these important papers, etc., a number of scholars, who otherwise would have been excluded from all participation, were enabled to share in the work. Even though I cannot help regretting that I personally lost these treasures, I console myself with the thought that they have fallen into good hands.

English bed in a well-furnished room, I thought I was in Heaven. But after a short time in bed I felt as if I should suffocate; I got up, took my rug, spread it out on the veranda, used my saddle as a pillow, and, wrapped in a light fur, slept out in the open air. It was some time, too, before I could get accustomed again to the narrow confines of a bedroom.

There we were, then, waiting in Kashgar for Professor Grünwedel, and getting once more splendidly fit physically, thanks to the exceptionally kind attention and care given us in the Macartneys' house. But Grünwedel tarried and tarried, and we were at our wits' end.

I made use of this free time to write a fair copy and a translation of the Mirab's proverbs; this work was afterwards published by Teubner in Leipzig under the title of *Songs and Proverbs of the Turfan Oasis*. Some of the proverbs are identical with those that occur in Afghanistan. The East Turkestan fairy tales, moreover, often embody tales that are still extant in Afghanistan and the Punjab. The influence of the old Buddhist civilization is still evident in these three countries, which it once united.

We tried then to do some excavating near Artush, where our interest had been awakened by three cave-temples, close to the ruins of an ancient town (Uch Murghan), built in the face of the rock. The doors cut in the stone had been provided in earlier times with wooden approaches, which, however, had disappeared, so Bartus let himself down from above by means of a rope and in this perilous way got into the buildings. But they only contained scanty remains of paintings, which were not worth further examination. We abstained from any digging in the ruins as the Chinese official (*tao-tai*) did not look upon it with any approval.

The Beginning of the Third Journey

At last, on December 5, 1905, a messenger came from the Russian frontier with the news that Grünwedel would arrive the following day. We therefore took to the highway and rode to meet him. He came, too, in the afternoon on an old pony at a walking pace, with his caravan and Referendar Pohrt, Professor F. W. K. Müller's assistant, whom Grünwedel had chosen to accompany him as he knew a little Chinese. Unfortunately Grünwedel himself was ill—

so ill that he had to stay three more weeks in Kashgar, confined to his bed, under the care of the Swedish missionaries.

We celebrated an English Christmas at the Macartneys' and started on December 25th for Kucha. As Grünwedel was not able to ride, I had a two-wheeled cart (*araba*) filled with hay, the mattress fixed on the top, and a sun-awning put over the cart. In this cart Grünwedel made the journey with the inevitable discomfort increased by the bad state of the roads, for wherever the road passes through cultivated land it is cut up by endless irrigation canals. The vehicle always went sideways into these canals, which are often a yard deep; first the one wheel—two yards in diameter—went in with a frightful bump, then the second wheel followed with a similar bump, next the first wheel climbed out, followed by the second, and each time the traveller was shaken this way and that.

Such travelling as this, is, of course, very slow, so Bartus and I used to let Grünwedel, accompanied by Herr Pohrt, start about midnight or 1 a.m., whilst we ourselves went on sleeping until four o'clock, and even so we caught up the caravan half-way. Then we rode on in front, and arranged for night quarters, so that Grünwedel found his *palao*, tea, etc., ready for him on his arrival.

On January 8th our expedition reached the old settlement of Tumshuk, near Maralbashi, and there explored the Buddhist ruins, situated to the north-east of the halting-station, without, however, being able to undertake work of any extent. Later on Professor Pelliot, the leader of the expedition, dispatched by the French Government, hearing of our successes, worked in this spot with considerable result, and found some fine groups of clay statuettes, many still in the Gandhara style.

When we rode on my attendant, the Mirab, said that in the mountains near Kyzyl, close to Kucha, there was an enormous collection of ancient cave-temples that no European had ever yet visited, and which, owing to their remote situation, were but little known, even to natives.

The Japanese expedition Otani worked there in 1902 or 1903, but a violent earthquake is said to have driven them away.

On getting this information from the Mirab, Herr Bartus and I rode over at once. We crossed the low but difficult pass, and found a marvellous settlement of many hundreds of temples in the steep cliffs of a mountain range by the River Muzart.

Plate 31

Western part of the temple buildings (*ming oi*), Kyzyl

Continuation of the same buildings, eastward

v. Le Coq, Turfan

Plate 32

Bartus and labourers
on the temples of
the little brook-ravine,
Kyzyl

The "step" cave-temple,
big brook-ravine,
Kyzyl

Plate 33

Lunette on the wall of the "step" temple *cella*. Above: Mara's attack;
Below: scenes from the life of Buddha, Kyzyl

Plate 34

The right bank. Entrance to the little brook-ravine, Kyzyl

North end of big brook-ravine. Junction of both valleys.
Kyzyl. Temples destroyed by an earthquake, 1916

JOURNEY TO KASHGAR

A man, owning land there, had put up a little mud hut consisting of two very wretched rooms; this hut I hired from him immediately, for we had heard that other expeditions were on the way and intended to arrive in about a month's time.

The rest of the journey passed without any special incident. We reached Kucha, paid our respects to the Chinese governor in the citadel,[1] and then went over to Kumtura, a prosperous little place with a great settlement of ancient Buddhist temples close to it; this group of temples is known as the *ming-öi* of Kumtura.

Here we found excellent quarters in the Imaum's house.

It was terribly cold, and the north and north-easterly winds, with their clouds of dust, were anything but pleasant. We set to work, however. The cave-temples are situated on the left bank of the rushing River Muzart. Its shores are dotted with several groups of temples, separated from each other by terribly wild and rugged ravines; the temple, farthest up the stream, is cut out of the steep cliffs towering high above the water.

It consists of a long gallery with windows opening on to the river, and under these windows there is a long, broad bench cut out of the solid rock on which, no doubt, the monks used to sit, to enjoy the cool of the evening and the romantic view over the wild landscape. On the other side of the gallery there were the entrances to the cave-temples, which, although not belonging to the most ancient period, must formerly have been very fine. Unfortunately treasure-seekers and plunderers had been so successful in their activities that we could find nothing of any value to us.

In the temples farther down the stream, on the contrary, we found single buried temples in which the mural paintings were still in fair preservation, and where we could secure countless treasures of sculpture, manuscripts, and other antiquities.

A portion of these temples was cut out of the rock, which, on closer inspection, proved to my astonishment to consist of brushwood—nothing but fossilized brushwood.

A great fossil-bone was embedded in the mass of stony brushwood. I had it chiselled out, and afterwards handed it over to the Palæontological Institute in Berlin.

In contrast to the Turfan settlements, where we only found

[1] In Kucha the fortified Chinese part is in a district of the native town, not as in Turfan, Ak-su, and Kashgar, a few miles from the old town in a special "new" town.

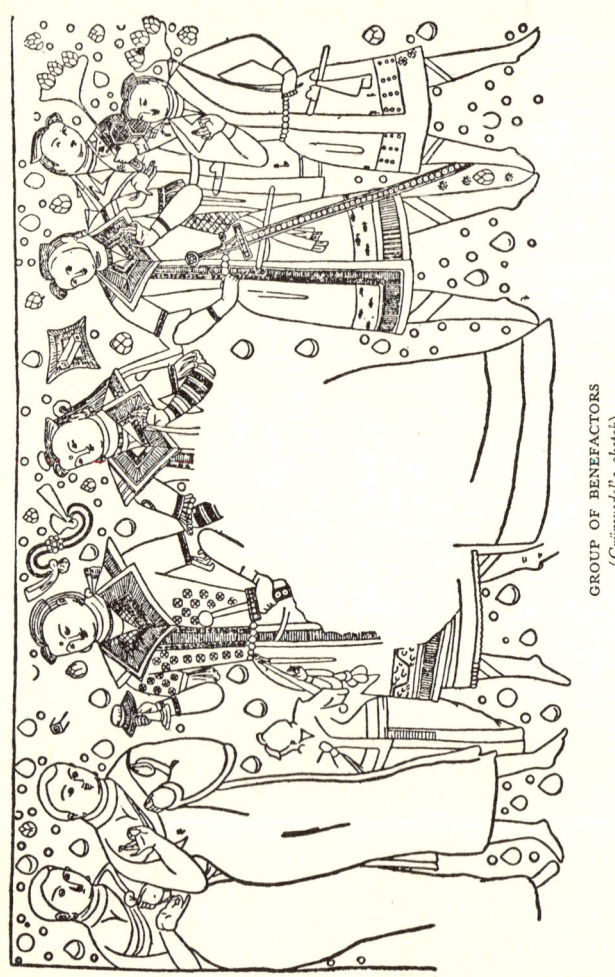

116 BURIED TREASURES OF CHINESE TURKESTAN

GROUP OF BENEFACTORS
(*Grünwedel's sketch*)

JOURNEY TO KASHGAR

pictures, almost exclusively dating from the Turkish period (after A.D. 760), these Kyzyl paintings mainly belonged to a more remote time (up to about A.D. 800) when Aryan peoples still occupied the country. Yet here, too, there were temples where the paintings began to show signs of their Chinese origin.

Here we found for the first time representations of ladies (Plate 36) and knights in what was apparently European dress (cf. p. 116).

I shall describe such representations later on in the account of the Kyzyl *ming-öi*, where they belong to an older period, and also, owing to the greater inaccessibility of the district, are in a state of better preservation.

The stage of civilization, plainly shown by the costumes combined with the artistic worth of the paintings and the beautiful script of the documents, must have been considerably higher than that reached at the same period by the Germanic States of Europe.

We worked here with zeal and delight, for not a day passed without some new and exciting discovery. At first Grünwedel was not fit to take much part in the work, but after the temples had been emptied and made accessible he devoted himself with great zeal to the work of copying the pictures, making plans, and similar occupations.

During our stay in Kumtura I repeatedly left the others to make exploratory journeys to unknown settlements in the Kucha oasis.

At the very beginning of January such an excursion led me through the salt steppe to Shahyar (Plate 30), situated in the south of this oasis. The intervening steppe contains a large number of old settlements, amongst which the most noteworthy is that of *Tongguz Bashi* (= pig's head). This is an enormous square surrounded by a high wall with a fortified gate. In this walled enclosure, however, there were no traces of buildings, and the ground was so saturated with salt and damp that I gave up all idea of excavation there.

The whole country here, and for great distances round, is intersected by the ruins of old canals. It is possible, by using a camera, to view their course, to follow these channels for no little way, and also to see the smaller irrigation runnels that branch out from them to right and left.

We had taken water with us, and had, on the recommendation of the worthy *Aksakal* of the Ferghana Turks in Kucha, Khalmat Khan of Tashkent (Plate 29), engaged a guide, Sharip (Arabic:

šarif) by name, who professed to have an excellent knowledge of all the country. But he was a vain and ignorant man, who was only out to impose upon us. We very soon lost the road, and, as a dust fog obscured the air, we could not get our bearings. On clear days it is possible from all sides to see the peaks of the Tien-Shan range, which runs from west to east and thus provides travellers with an unfailing guide. But the dust wraps everything in a semi-opaque haze, completely veiling distant objects. Most unfortunately, too, my compass, which I used to wear on my watch-chain, had been lost.

So for a long time we rode round in a circle, until at last one of my attendants discovered the right direction and brought us into the rich settlement of Tok-su, where we found hospitable shelter in the village magistrate's house, a splendid building for that part of the world.

During our ride thither I often dismounted to examine the ground. It was thickly strewn with remains of broken pottery, and also of coins, bells, arrow-heads, and bronze and copper seals—all much corroded. Frequently, however, we found broken pieces of wood-carvings, votive *stūpas*, little figures of Buddha, of other gods and similar objects; but, above all, broken pots in such enormous quantities as to bear witness to a settlement of unusual size and duration.

The magistrate's house had several fine rooms in the Persian style, their walls painted with bright pictures in tempera, and a splendid fireplace diffusing a pleasant warmth. The furniture consisted of wonderful padded silk bed-quilts, beautiful mattresses, and red-silk pillows, most tastefully embroidered. Ali Achond, for this was the magistrate's name, had four wives, dignified matrons, who gazed at the stranger with great curiosity, but with the well-bred politeness so characteristic of these people. I fell into conversation with these women, and asked if they happened to have any old-time embroidery in their possession. They immediately opened great portable chests, decorated with carving and paintings, and showed me a great number of those beautiful pieces of embroidery that the women in earlier times used to wear on the lower edge of their white trousers. The women's costume is very simple, consisting of a long cotton or silk long-sleeved chemise and trousers, which, like our pyjamas, are drawn in round the waist with cord

JOURNEY TO KASHGAR

belt fashion. The lower part of the trouser legs, about sixteen inches wide, appears below the hem of the chemise, and is always most tastefully decorated with very beautiful embroidery, generally in red.

This embroidery usually represents a kind of bright flower-bed enclosed by a border of a very pleasing scroll pattern.

The chemises, too, were often embroidered in the same way; a particularly valuable specimen was one of cream silk entirely covered with the tops of fronded palms, embroidered in gold thread. Other chemises were very tastefully ornamented with flowers, which were sometimes combined in bunches. In my opinion it was all in Persian style, for this kind of decoration is found from Bokhara through the whole of Afghanistan up to the northern Punjab, and through all Turkestan up to Komul. I bought from the ladies a great number of these trouser embroideries, which are now no longer worn, for intercourse with Russia has unfortunately pushed out these tasteful things in favour of horrible Russian printed cottons. Thus I saw one woman with a chemise of Russian muslin printed with a pattern of a ballet dancer in short skirts, standing on one leg, and reduplicated over and over again in endless monotony.

The ladies of Turkestan have, moreover, discovered the charm of the small cloche hat long before their European sisters. Even then we saw little fur or brocade caps, amazingly like the fashionable hats worn by our Western ladies. They have also long worn—for fifty or sixty years at least—little boots with a fringed tongue falling gracefully down in front, the only difference being that, in their case, the adornment is put on high boots, not on low shoes as with us. The heels, too, are of a very coquettish height, their under-surface often studded with silver nails, the ends of which are bent up round the sides of the heel and hammered down.

I also visited quite a number of other old settlements where the walls were still existing, but everywhere I found so much damp that I did not think these districts worth archæological excavation. Thus I got up to the fertile spot of Shah-yar, where my arrival attracted large crowds of the peasant population. The Chinese official made his appearance forthwith and entertained me at his house. Here, as everywhere, I met with a most friendly reception from the Chinese no less than from the Turkish natives. They put me up in a clean but somewhat lowly *sarai*—in this part they are called *dan*—whose doors gave no promise of any possible privacy. When

I had got into bed there suddenly appeared a tall young woman in a little Chinese jacket and splendidly embroidered undergarments, accompanied by her attendants, pretty young girls who tinkled pleasing little tunes on long-necked stringed instruments (*tambur*), and all three made themselves quite at home. On closer inquiry I found that the beautiful lady was a well-known demi-mondaine who was anxious to offer her services to the foreign gentleman. I bought a pair of fine earrings from her at a very liberal price, and therewith dismissed the somewhat offended beauty.

Amongst the Eastern Turks this calling is a profession like any other, and many songs in honour of some of these women are sung throughout the land.

Often, too, these demi-mondaines are to be seen on confidential terms with the wives of honest artisans and tillers of the soil.

Unfortunately I did not find in this part one single ruin that would have been worth my while to explore, and so I returned with but negative results to the other members of my caravan.

Meantime the Mirab made all kinds of inquiries, and told me the position of two important settlements in the neighbourhood of the village of Kirish, north-east of Kucha. I started with a bey of the governor of Kucha, and passing the remarkable tower-like *stūpa* to the east of Kucha, close to the ancient city walls of the old town, reached, after a ride of about fourteen miles, the hamlet of Kirish. In a wild valley to the north-east there lies a fairly large group of cave monasteries partly buried with old rubbish; it goes by the name of *Sim-sim* (= *Sesam*), perhaps from some memory of the tale of "Ali Baba" in the *Arabian Nights*.

After that we rode on to another settlement, situated to the south of Kirish, called *Achigh Ilak* (= meeting of the bitter waters), where the temples, few indeed in number but interesting and in an apparently good dry spot, invited excavation.

Later on I took Professor Grünwedel to *Sim-sim*, where we only worked a few days.[1] *Achigh Ilak* was not worked until the arrival of

---

[1] The two Berezowskys who had been sent by the Russians were at Kucha during our stay there.

Grünwedel, for reasons unknown to me, had made an agreement with the Russian scholars, Radloff and Salemann, that the German expeditions should work the more recent settlements of the Turfan district and the Russians the older settlements—which so far had not been touched—in the Kucha district, i.e. the Russians were not to disturb the Germans in Turfan nor the Germans the Russians in Kucha. But when I went to

JOURNEY TO KASHGAR

the fourth expedition, which also excavated with good results at the tower building (a *stūpa*) close to the Kucha old town wall. In *Ilak* there were already large pictures of Buddha, painted on the corridor walls, just as in the later settlements of the Turkish period in the Turfan oasis.

Urumchi, Dr. Kochanowky, the Russian physician and consular agent, told me he was surprised to see me arrive so much earlier than he had expected; he had received letters from the above-mentioned Russian gentlemen requesting him to visit the Turfan settlements with the greatest possible speed in order to secure for Russian science all that was to be found in the way of pictures, manuscripts, etc.

I was annoyed at this behaviour on the part of the St. Petersburg gentlemen, and told the doctor that we had made quite a different agreement with them.

Kochanowsky, however, declared that he knew nothing of such agreements, but a request had come to him to get those things, and, as a Russian official, he was bound to comply with it.

And he did ride over before us to Karakhoja and secured all kinds of antiquities, but was not able to cut the frescoes out of the walls.

Kochanowsky was quite a good fellow, and I could understand his line of reasoning. But it seemed to me that the letter sent by the two St. Petersburg gentlemen had nullified our agreements. I reported the occurrence to Berlin, but begged that the matter might be ignored as no great harm had been done. But some altercation followed, and Kochanowsky wrote me an angry letter in which he repeated that orders given by Radloff and Salemann weighed more with him than private agreements; the Russians had been there first and therefore had the greatest right to these antiquities, etc. I rode over to Urumchi, and, by showing him a copy of my letter, succeeded in convincing him that I had not wished to cause him any annoyance. The letters are now with the papers of the fourth expedition.

When Grünwedel came I asked him whether he would work in Kyzyl. I for my part considered the agreement cancelled. He said he had come to an understanding with Radloff and Salemann, and agreed to my proposal to excavate in Kyzyl and Kumtura. I knew, moreover, that both places lay in the Bai district, and therefore could not be affected by the literal wording of the agreement. Still, if the St. Petersburg gentlemen had not been guilty of this double dealing, I should not have strengthened Grünwedel in his very weak resolve to excavate in these places. To show cunning with the cunning is no part of my creed, but this occurrence had really roused my ire. Kirish lies in the Kucha district, and the older Berezowsky immediately reproached us violently. I had to speak to the old gentleman and smooth him down—he even threatened to expel us by force of arms!

The two Berezowskys were not, by any means, in a position to cut out the mural paintings without injuring them, but since we had already achieved important results there, it was not worth while to carry the matter to extremes, so we gave up excavating in Kirish in order, after peace had been made, to go on farther east.

WORK AND EXPERIENCES IN KYZYL

AFTER finishing our successful excavations in Kumtura, we moved over to the *ming-öi* of Kyzyl; they, too, are situated on the Muzart, about nine and a half miles to the west of Kumtura. Starting from the little Kyzyl rest-house, after a ride of about five miles southward to the old temples of the *ming-öi* the traveller comes to a mountain range that can only be crossed at one spot by a short but steep pass. From one point in this pass it is possible to look down into the wild valley below, and catch a sudden glimpse of the settlement lying stretched out amid its romantic surroundings.

The mountains out of whose precipitous cliffs these temples and monasteries are hewn form a great crescent-shaped range, intersected by the rushing Muzart at both the upper and lower ends (Plates 31–34).

The whole strip of land between the river and the mountain heights consists of rich alluvial soil, and some fruit-trees and fields are cultivated in this district, and there our host had settled about six years before our arrival.

In earlier times the stream followed the direction of the mountain range, and its waters flanked the very foot of the hills.

All these numerous cave-temples were formerly connected with one another by a gallery hewn out of the rock, so that it was possible to visit every temple and monastery without danger of being seen from the river. These galleries, which were only provided with windows at long intervals, are still plainly recognizable.

The cave-temples are of most varying size, some quite small and others, again, about thirty-three to forty-six feet in height, and penetrating the rock to a depth of forty to sixty feet. At the side of many of the temples there are work-rooms, living-rooms for the monks, storerooms with fixed bins for corn and seeds. In such provision stores we still found seeds of madder and carrots, dried grapes, millet, and big dark-blue beans.

The temples are, for the most part, built in one of two styles; the most frequent of these consists of an entrance hall opening at the back into the shrine, the square or rectangular cella. On the farther wall of the cella is fixed the sacred image, a clay statue of

Plate 35

Building with red arched roof. Pictures of benefactors in presumably
European dress on the walls
The "dance of death". Great find of manuscripts here

Plate 36

Frescoes. Tocharist lady, Kum Tura.

A white divinity with a dark-skinned musician, (with Bayblonian harp).

Tocharist painter in the E. Sassanian dress. Second temple building, Kyzyl.

WORK AND EXPERIENCES IN KYZYL

Buddha. To the right and left of this sacred image corridors are hewn out of the rock, and joined to each other by a third corridor at the back. This arrangement is to allow processions to go round the shrine (Plate 38). On the walls there are portrayed scenes from the life of Buddha, and also all kinds of events from the Buddhist legend-cycle. The cella roof is generally a barrel vault, and this roof, in older temples, is painted with pictures of conventional mountain landscapes—in each of which a legend of the rebirth is portrayed (Plate 43). At a later period the rows of mountain landscapes are replaced by rows of seated Buddhas. Right and left of the door, sometimes also on the walls of the side corridors, there are paintings of the benefactors, men and women of royal or noble rank.

Never shall I forget the first time that I opened such a temple, and, after removing the debris, entered the interior by the light of my lantern. For there are no windows anywhere; the whole of these buildings—with the exception of the monks' cells, which often have a little window—must be pictured as perfectly dark.

At first sight the benefactors' pictures remind us most vividly of pictorial representations in Gothic mortuary chapels. There the men stand with legs far apart, balancing themselves on the tips

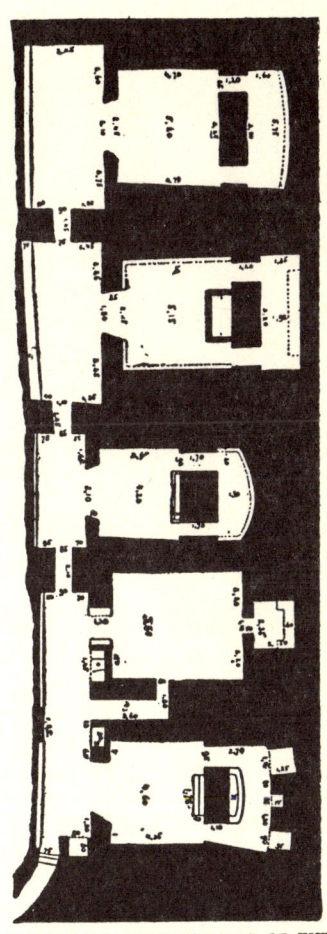

PLAN OF THE MAIN BUILDING OF THE ROCK TEMPLES AT KUMTURA
(*Le Coq's sketch*)

of their toes, in their long coats made of brocade or wonderfully embroidered, with a three-cornered cape. They wear the knights' belt of metal discs and, hanging from this, a long, straight sword with a handle in the form of a cross and a rounded or flat pommel amazingly like the European swords of the Carlovingian and early Gothic period. On the other side they wear a dagger, Scythian in shape, and near it frequently a pocket handkerchief, which was not known in Italy before the sixteenth century. Their hair was parted and cut in a definite style, its colour in some paintings being white, in others, red. The colour of the iris of the eyes is never painted, so that we cannot know if the hair has its natural shade or is powdered or tinted with henna (cf. also pages 116, 117).

Near the knights stand the ladies, all in tight bodices, cut low in the front, with bell sleeves and a little bell trimming on the pointed fronts of the bodice. They wear long trained skirts, and their bearing reminds us strongly of that affected position with shoulders drawn back and body forced forward which we so often see in European paintings from Holbein to Van Dyck (page 125); and even if, on closer inspection, the likeness to our Gothic paintings disappears, the similarity in the women's dress and the men's weapons is both remarkable and striking (see also Plate 36).

If we look up in Chaucer, the Nibelungenlied, or in Wolfram von Eschenbach and Walther von der Vogelweide, the materials that were worn by the European knights and their ladies, we find that they were Persian or Turkish productions. But if the materials are Eastern it is not impossible that the cut was no less so—in fact, that these articles of clothing came to Europe ready cut out.

It is true, so long an interval lies between the date of these temple pictures (about A.D. 700) and the well-attested appearance of similar costumes in Europe, that meantime no definite judgment can be pronounced as to the connection between the styles of East and West. But fashions change more slowly in the East than with us, and the illustration of a man on a valuable Manichæan roll, obtained by Sir Aurel Stein in Tung-hwang, shows exactly the same dress as is worn to-day, more than a thousand years later, by the inhabitants of Chinese Turkestan.

The second type of temple is the Persian building with a dome-shaped roof. The entrance hall of every one of these domed buildings was destroyed, so we do not know whether they had lean-to roofs

WORK AND EXPERIENCES IN KYZYL

or domes like the main temples. The distribution of the pictures was generally the same as in the temples first described, but the sacred image was placed on a finely moulded pedestal in front of the farther wall of the cella, but far enough away to allow plenty of room for the procession to pass behind it.

The results we obtained here far surpassed any earlier achievements. Everywhere we found fresh, untouched temples, full of the

MURAL PAINTINGS, "RED DOME" BUILDING, KYZYL
Above: Gothic benefactors; Dance of Death.   *Below:* Buddhist legend
(*After Grünwedel*)

most interesting and artistically perfect paintings, all of early date, earlier than those in the Kumtura group which we had just visited. There was still not the slightest sign in the painting of any East Asiatic influences. Everything in sculpture and painting alike was

Indo-Iranian, following late antique principles. According to our chronology this settlement flourished between the fifth and eighth centuries A.D. It must have been left at the middle of the eighth century, or perhaps even at that early date it may have been forcibly destroyed (Plate 35).

I succeeded at once, during the early days of our work here, in unearthing an old library in one of the temples that we named the "red dome building," from its vaulted red roof. Here we found early Indian manuscripts in great quantities on palm leaves, birch bark, and paper, as well as writing on wooden tablets. All the pages were cut in the form of the Indian book, the *pothi*.

A complete book of this kind was found here, containing about sixty pages of Sanskrit and Tocharian text in Indian characters.

On one wall of this temple there were paintings of ladies in presumably European dress, as well as a scene reminding the spectator of mediæval pictures of the "Dance of Death" (cf. p. 125).

A few days after our arrival here, as Bartus and I were lying on our cork mattresses at half-past three a.m., smoking our morning pipes, Grünwedel suddenly appeared out of the next room and hurried through ours with many rolls of stencil paper, brushes, and his painting-stool, begging us to send his breakfast into such and such a temple. Herr Bartus exclaimed: "Sir, sir, that will never do for him to be before us; let's get to work now!"

That day was the beginning of the happiest time that we passed together in Turkestan. Success followed success, and, although the food often worried us, the daily recurring surprises gave us such pleasure that we could smile at all life's annoyances. Grünwedel, too, enjoyed the work and the success, and never shall I forget those evenings round the camp-fire.

As our European tobacco had long since come to an end, we had to content ourselves instead with the native product, the best of which comes from the neighbourhood of Bai. It is bright yellow, light, and would not be bad if it did not arrive mixed with fragments of loess, stalks of millet, etc. For about three shillings we bought twenty-five pounds, i.e. twelve pounds net when it was cleaned. Still, we enjoyed it by our camp-fire.

Herr Bartus went with his wonted skill about the business of sawing out the pictures. The painting surface was here a fairly thin layer, and in order to remove the pictures it was essential

WORK AND EXPERIENCES IN KYZYL

to break up the soft rock with hammer and chisel before beginning to saw them out—a task which was very exhausting, even to the Herculean strength of our craftsman.

But the harvest was exceedingly satisfactory; one picture of especial beauty was the painting of a white divinity with a dark-skinned Indian woman-musician from the "temple with the fresco floor" below the "cave of the sixteen knights" (Plate 36).

The process of cutting away the frescoes is somewhat as follows:

The pictures are painted on a special surface-layer, made out of clay mixed up with camel dung, chopped straw, and vegetable fibre, which is smoothed over and covered with a thin layer of stucco.

To begin with, the picture must be cut round with a very sharp knife—care being taken that the incision goes right through the surface-layer—to the proper size for the packing-cases. The cases for transport by carts may be large, somewhat smaller for camels, and smallest of all for horses.

In this part of the work it is sometimes necessary to cut the boundary line in curves or sharp angles to avoid going through faces or other important parts of the picture.

Next, a hole must be made with the pickaxe in the wall at the side of the painting to make space to use the fox-tail saw; in the excavated rock-temples, as we have said, this space often has to be made with hammer and chisel in the solid rock, which fortunately is generally soft.

When the surface-layer is in a very bad condition, men are sometimes employed to keep boards covered with felt pressed firmly against the painting that is to be removed.

Then this painting is sawn out; and when this process is complete, the board is carefully moved away from the wall, the upper edge being first carried out and down, bearing the painting with it, until at last the latter lies quite horizontal on the board, which only touches the wall with its lower edge.

The physical exertion connected with this work is exceptionally great, and at the same time the process requires a light and skilful hand.

The packing, too, is no simple matter.

First, boards must be prepared large enough to take the painting and leave a margin round every side of three to four inches.

Then two layers of dry springy reeds are laid at right-angles to each other on the board, covered with thin felt and then well-picked-out cotton, and on this the first picture is placed, painted side downwards.

This is covered with another layer of cotton, and then comes the second picture, painted side uppermost, and so on.

We have packed up to six pictures like this, but more in one case are not advisable.

On this stack of pictures we put again cotton, felt, and two layers of reeds at right-angles to each other, then a board the same size as the first, and after the empty space between the edge of the picture slabs and the outer edge of the boards has been carefully filled with flax straw, the whole package is firmly roped round.

The chest in which it is to be packed must be large enough to leave an empty space all round the package of three to four inches, and this empty space, beginning, of course, with a covering of the same thickness at the base, must be stuffed with flax straw (all other packing material rubs down too easily) to the required bulk. The package of slabs is carefully placed in the case, the four side spaces and that on the top most thoroughly stuffed with flax straw and the lid nailed on.

We have never had the least breakage in cases packed in this way.

Our division of labour was as follows: I decided the journey, controlled the exchequer, looked out for fresh settlements, and negotiated our intercourse with the Chinese authorities and the Turks.

When a settlement was discovered, Bartus and I cleared out the temples and discovered the manuscripts and antiquities of all kinds. Herr Pohrt sometimes helped in these activities, and at other times devoted himself especially to photography and the taking of temple measurements, etc.

When the temples had been found, cleared out, and swept clean with tamarisk brooms Grünwedel was brought in. He then copied the pictures and made scientific notes, to which we owe his capital book *Altbuddhistische Kultstätten*.

He had little liking for intercourse with Turks and Chinese, for he had an aversion to these people; nor could he communicate with them, since he did not speak nor understand a single word of either Turkish or Chinese.

Unfortunately we had once to regret an accident here. When

WORK AND EXPERIENCES IN KYZYL

we were clearing out one of the cave-temples an avalanche of debris came pouring down from above, burying one of our workers and severely injuring him. But a considerable sum of money for this country (£3) satisfied the man and his family, as well as the Chinese official, who, at the report of this accident, espoused the cause of the unfortunate man. A large family can live here in comfort for a month on twelve shillings.

Here, too, we had a remarkable experience. On March 3rd, when we were each busy working in our own temple, a strange noise like thunder was followed quite suddenly by a great quantity of rocks rattling down from above past the door of my temple.

Herr Bartus, who, as an old sailor, has a perfectly steady head and could climb to the highest temples, had chosen one above mine, and I was afraid he had been hurled down with his excavations. But the next moment—for everything happened with amazing speed—I saw Bartus and his workmen hurrying down the steep slope, and a procession of my Turkis, screaming after! I followed them, too, and in a flash we were down in the plain, pursued by great masses of rock, tearing past us with terrifying violence, without a single one of us being hurt—why or how I cannot understand to this very day!

I turned my eyes in the direction of the river and saw its waters in wild commotion—great waves beating against its banks. In the transverse valley, farthest up the stream, there suddenly rose an enormous cloud of dust, like a mighty pillar, rising to the heavens. At the same instant the earth trembled and a fresh roll, like pealing thunder, resounded through the cliffs. Then we knew it was an earthquake, and saw, too, how the shock moved on and on along the opposite bank. After a few seconds of silence a similar cloud of dust arose in every one of the side valleys, pursuing its way down the stream, but fortunately the earthquake was not of a very violent character. Herr Pohrt, too, appeared with his workers, frightened but not injured in any way.

Then the question arose: Where is Grünwedel? We knew that he had been sketching in the "temple of the sixteen knights," and, as the danger seemed at an end, we all rushed over to this cave. We got up to it without any cause for fear whatever, and were delighted to find that Grünwedel had retreated into a corner and had suffered no injury of any kind. He had certainly chosen the most sensible course, for we were exposed to much greater danger in our flight through the rattling downpour of rocks than he was in the shelter of his temple, although, of course, that might have crashed in, as it did later on, but fortunately when no one was there. This "temple of the sixteen knights or sword-bearers" was one of the most westerly of the group, and was distinguished by having life-sized pictures of the benefactors' family in the corridors to the right and left of the sacred image. They are knights in the great-skirted coats of the eastern Sassanids, adorned with valuable embroidery or made of brocade.

In the back corridor there was a great podium hewn out of the rock, on which there had been a large statue of the dying Buddha; the statue had, however, entirely disappeared. Nor did we find any other treasures whatever in this temple.

On the other hand, there was, in a temple in the immediate neighbourhood, a remarkable head, which, painted after the pattern of a late classical Hercules' head (Plate 40), represents a Buddhist saint, whose identity we were able to determine from a picture in another temple near by. It is Mahakashyapa, one of the Buddhist saints, in the act of kissing Buddha's feet. According to the Buddha legend, the funeral pile prepared for Buddha's corpse will not light until Mahakashyapa has done homage to his Master's feet with a kiss. The latter temple gave us the whole picture, which arrived at Berlin in very good condition, and presents us with the well-known legend, in its surface of thirteen feet by six and a half.

We were not always quite out of danger in these cave-temples. For instance, we used to work in the great cave with one eye continually watching the roof. It had great splits across it, and at every stroke of the pick a quantity of sand or smaller stones fell down on the workmen. Still, we succeeded in emptying the temple without mishap. Its special point of interest was that it was still possible to recognize on the walls remains of very early pictures of a Syrian or Sogdian type. But the most remarkable thing was a splendid frieze, which ran to right and left by the great podiums of the cella, representing, on pearl medallions, Sassanian ducks facing each other in couples, each of the birds bearing in its beak a jewelled necklace. The greater part of this frieze, too, we managed to secure.

I had a narrow escape in the "crash temple." I had cleared away the debris there, finding, as I did so, a great many fragments of

Plate 37

View from a monk's cell. Second buildings, Kyzyl

The "crash" temple. Here the author nearly met with disaster, Kyzyl.

v. Le Coq, Turfan.

Plate 38

Further wall of a *cella* with the pedestal of the sacred image and corridors. Second buildings, Kyzyl

Entrance into one of the corridors *ibid.*

Plate 39

all wooden reliquary, Tuyoq

Painted "lantern" roof, Chikkan Kol

Remains of Hellenistic statues. "Figure" cave, Kyzyl

Plate 40

Head of a Buddhist saint, after the style of a late antique Hercules' head

Indo-Hellenistic fresco, scene from a legend. "Seaman's" cave, Kyzyl

WORK AND EXPERIENCES IN KYZYL

wooden figures, and whilst I was leaning against the wall to the right of the entrance a narrow strip of facing that ran along the lower edge of this wall suddenly fell off. I stepped back a few paces in surprise, and as I did so an enormous block of stone suddenly detached itself without a sound from the wall and crashed violently on to the ground immediately in front of my right foot. I did not stay any longer in this temple! (Plate 37).

We gave the name of the "figure" temple to a very large building close to the "peacock" temple, because rows of exceptionally fine statues, modelled in the Gandhara style, had stood on the podiums, as we could see from the lower portions of these statues that were still extant. On the right and left of the sacred image, at the entrance of the corridors, two pedestals had once stood on which had been placed a god and goddess. Both pedestals had fallen and lay in the dust of the cella, but it was evident from the traces left and the duplicate holes in the floor that they had, in earlier times, stood on each side of the sacred image.

Only a few fragments were left of the female figure; the head was wanting in the male, but the body was perfectly intact, and even the head was found, later on, in the debris. These pedestals had supported half-figures, only the upper part as far as the hips was modelled, and the lower half tapered off into the round stele.

The special interest of this male torso was that it gave a plastic representation of those remarkable coats of mail which are continually reappearing in the paintings. This armour consists of an upper part provided with an enormous protective collar, and this upper part is a scaly coat of mail with the scales all turned upwards. In similar European armour the rounded part of the scales is always the lower edge, the opposite arrangement of the scales only exists still in the armour of Gandhara sculpture and, curiously enough, in the Etruscan. The lower part of the coat of mail was covered with hexagonal scales. This coat is of importance in the history of Chinese armour. The god represented is probably the tutelary deity of children, Panchika, whilst we may presume his companion to be the tutelary goddess, Hariti. The head belonging above the coat of mail is a late antique female head after the style of Juno. It was impossible to induce Grünwedel to take this remarkable torso with us, so I arranged with Herr Bartus to pack it up without his knowledge.

132 BURIED TREASURES OF CHINESE TURKESTAN

Not far from the fine temple with the "figures" I noticed fairly high on a projecting cliff a large heap of dust and stones with a small opening at the top. I climbed up with some of our labourers and saw that here was a buried temple. The pile of sand, etc., was cleared away, in which process several other blocks of stone clattered down from the entrance into the cave-temple.

We then found ourselves in the entrance hall of the temple, containing several tables on which, at an earlier period, numerous little carved wooden figures had doubtless found a place. Now we discovered these figures scattered wildly about under the tables, between wall and tables, and on the ground. On the left side there was another table, and behind it a large wooden nimbus, representing mountain landscapes, also carved in wood. The fairly large Buddha figure that belonged to this nimbus had disappeared.

All these wooden articles still showed traces of a thin surface of stucco and remains of gold leaf and colours, especially of blue, red, and green.

In the centre of the farther wall of this entrance hall a door, still partially provided with beams, opened into the cella of the sanctuary. This was filled to a depth of about one and a half yards with loess debris. On this deposit I found a man's skull and hip-bones. Since the cave had already been half-full, this skull must have belonged to someone who, at a later period, had taken refuge in the temple and died there. The rest of the body may then have been carried off by wolves.

When we had cleared away the masses of sand, etc., the temple paintings were seen to be of quite astonishing beauty. The principal colour was a splendid chocolate-brown with metallic reflections. The dome rose up from a flat roof and was decorated with painted peacock's feathers. These feathers formed a number of bands tapering off to the top, and at the end of each such band an angel was seen floating down to offer the spectator a jewelled chain. The eyes of the peacock's feathers glistened in blue, green, gold, and carmine red.

I wanted to have all these bands cut out so that the whole dome could be reconstructed in Berlin, but Grünwedel opposed this suggestion so energetically that to have insisted on it would have meant the end of all friendly relations, so that unfortunately only two of these decorations came to Berlin.

WORK AND EXPERIENCES IN KYZYL

Damp had affected the colour and given them that metallic brilliance which disappeared, alas! in a few days under the influence of the dry air. Below the flat roof a balcony appears on all four walls, painted in a certain perspective. On the balcony there are celestial musicians, and in the centre of each balcony stands a Buddha with nimbus and mandorla. Below the balconies there are decorative borders with Greek ornaments, and below these again scenes from the life of Buddha, divided off into square pictures by other decorative borders.

The painting here of the temptation of Buddha by the daughters of Mara (Plate 41) is of especial beauty.

Emaciated by his ascetic life, Buddha is sitting on the throne, filled with longing for wisdom. The daughters of Mara, sent to prevent, even at the last moment, the attainment of true knowledge, appear on Buddha's right.

The youngest of them, bold and provocative, steps forward toward the man of abstinence. But they are unable to divert him from his purpose; he looks at them with disapproval, and immediately the three fair maidens are turned into withered white-haired old crones —they are depicted in the picture on Buddha's left.

The ugly old faces had evidently annoyed even early visitors to the temple; we found amongst all the faces that only those of Buddha, the ascetic, and of the three old women had been scratched and disfigured.

The paintings have been secured to a great extent, and to-day this temple, with its dome reconstructed to the ancient measurements, stands built up again in the Berlin Ethnological Museum.

Continuing eastward, rows of other very fine temples are to be seen, amongst which the "treasure cave" deserves special mention. It gets its name from the fact that some Turks are said to have found objects made of gold in its floor. This temple contains paintings which show touches of decided Indian influence, but in which the antique influence, especially in decorative elements, is also very plainly discernible, and which must evidently date as far back as the fifth century. It is situated just at the entrance into the plain of a little brook formed in the north by two streams, one from the west joining that which runs from north to south (Plate 34). The ravine is unspeakably wild and rugged, and the valleys from which the two streams come are narrow, gloomy, gorge-like ravines, enclosed by steep, overhanging cliffs.

In this western ravine we found one of the most remarkable temples (Plate 32). It lies, like most of the temples in the gorge, high on the cliff, and is provided with steps cut in the rock, still in partial preservation, but very dangerous—a fact that made us christen it "the step temple." In the narrow ravines it is essential for all the temples to be situated at quite a considerable height, for in every storm all the water gathers here with amazing speed, fills the narrow inlets of the gorge to the depth of a house, and sends its red-brown waves tearing wildly on to fill the little valley with their deafening roar.

The paintings in this temple, too, showed plain evidence of Indian influence. Unfortunately Grünwedel was not to be induced here, any more than in other temples, to take away all the paintings still extant. He was afraid of an extended stay, and so not until the fourth journey was I in a position to secure the greater number of these especially beautiful paintings, which, alas! had meantime fallen into greater decay. Especially noteworthy was the painting of Mara's temptation of Buddha in the lunette of the dome above the sacred image (Plate 33).

Farther on in this gorge we found some other buildings cut out of the rock. It was very difficult to reach them, for the bottom of the ravine was so covered with masses of rock and rubble in wildest confusion as to make all going very arduous, especially as we were almost stifled by the oven-like heat of the narrow gorge. It is true that here as elsewhere closed galleries hewn out of the rock had run from building to building, but, owing to the great destruction caused by earthquakes, the entrance halls and the connecting corridors had, one and all, been ruined. Many of the temples from which I had cut paintings as late as 1913 were destroyed by earthquakes in 1916.

The buildings, so difficult of access near the source, seemed to be connected with monasteries, and for that reason we were very anxious to examine them more closely. But, to our astonishment, our workers, honest peasants from the village and neighbourhood of Kyzyl, refused to go a single step beyond a certain point in the ravine.

They were so excited and obstinate that I had them summoned

WORK AND EXPERIENCES IN KYZYL

to my presence, and then, in gala costume and my cap of office (an army helmet) on my head, I instituted an inquiry, after the style of a Chinese authority, into their insubordination. It then transpired that just behind the point which they mentioned, there was a shrine, small indeed, but endowed with special powers. These small heaps of stone, with a few sheep or goat-horns lying on them, and close by a couple of willow rods stuck in the earth on which to tie scraps of clothing, yaks' tails, and the like, are called by the Turkis *khojam*—roughly translated, "my pious prince."

Probably this very spot had been the principal shrine of the Buddhist settlement, and was adopted later by the Mohammedans as a holy place.

It appeared that a member of our expedition, quite ignorant of the sanctity of the place, had unintentionally defiled its neighbourhood. I cut a big piece off my shirt and tied it to one stick, two sheeps' heads were laid by the other, the workmen said some prayers near the *khojam*, and all this, with the addition of a fat sheep to the faithful, quite settled the matter.

But the good folk refused, after as before, to work in these places—"*Činn bar!*" ("Evil spirits there!") they said.

One day, after we had already been busy for some considerable time in Kyzyl, the Mirab came to say that he had received information of a fresh settlement quite close to the temple buildings in which we were working, and he was anxious to take me there at once. Behind the group of temples which we called the "devils' caves" a narrow path, climbing over giddy heights, leads to a chain of hills lying behind the main range of mountains. Here I immediately found several cave-temples, some partly filled with sand and others entirely covered, and therefore offering a prospect of good harvests.

Bartus took a large number of labourers and moved away the great heaps of debris that had settled at the foot of the perpendicular cliffs, thus clearing two fresh temples, one of which was perhaps the oldest, and at any rate the finest, of the whole group. This fine temple, when opened, proved to be quite empty, but the walls were all covered with a thick layer (about one inch) of snow-white mould. I fetched Chinese brandy—no European can drink it—and washed down all the walls with a sponge. During the night—

probably as the result of this work—my temperature went up and I had a very bad headache. (No unjust suspicions, please!)

The paintings were the finest that we found anywhere in Turkestan, consisting of scenes from the Buddha legend, almost purely Hellenistic in character (Plate 42). In the corridors there was, amongst others, a fresco depicting the distribution of the relics. The knights appear in Sassanid armour with peculiar primitive helmets formed of crossed metal bands—often, too, bearing a heraldic animal. One of the painters' portraits—for several had put their portraits at the side of the picture—was still in perfect preservation (Plate 36), and shows the dress of the Eastern Sassanids.

The second of these fresh temples was distinguished not only by the beauty and excellent preservation of its paintings, but also by the extravagant use of a brilliant blue—the well-known ultramarine which, in the time of Benvenuto Cellini, was frequently employed by the Italian painters, and was bought at double its weight in gold.

Amongst the pictures one deserving special mention for its beauty is a painting that shows King Ajatashatru taking a ceremonial bath in melted butter. He is seated in the butter-tub and, since no one will venture to give the king by word of mouth the news of Buddha's death, his major-domo is spreading in front of him a cloth on which is depicted an exceptionally well-executed drawing of four notable events in the great monk's life. The first scene in the lower corner to the left shows his birth; immediately above is seen his temptation; in the right hand lower corner the Benares preaching, and, above that, his death. The king looks at the drawing, understands that Buddha is dead, and breaks into lamentation. Below we see the mountain Meru falling down; the sun and moon darkening and leaving their wonted course, with other signs and wonders.

The second picture gives us the burning of Buddha's corpse (Plate 45). He is lying, wrapped round with mummy bandages, in a coffin, with a scroll ornamentation in the late classical style covering one side. The coffin-lid is being let down; in this lid the figure of a dragon appears, the head of the fabulous beast is seen at the front end, and its tail protrudes from the back of the lid. It is a remarkable fact that the representation of the dragon can be proved to exist on early Germanic coffins from about the fifth century to the end of the Carlovingian period, and it is clear that

THE KING'S BATH, KYZYL
Scenes from the life of Buddha, painted on cloth (after Grünwedel)

wherever the pictorial representation appears, one and the same religious view lies behind it. (I have published copies of the Germanic "coffin dragons" in my *Bilder-atlas*.)

The third painting shows the distribution of the relics. The Brahman Drona—unfortunately destroyed—who is making the distribution, is seated on the wall above the city gate; to his right and left appear gods holding Buddha's cinerary urns in their hands. From opposite sides we see Indians riding on elephants or horses— these last exceptionally well painted—each one coming to obtain one of these reliquaries as a palladium for his own city. All these princes are wearing coats of mail with great defensive collars, the remarkable quiver of the Eastern Sassanids, the bridle and horses' head-trappings being also characteristic of the same nation. Little metal tubes are attached to the horses' heads, and in these small bunches of waving feathers are placed. Their manes have three pointed projections, which are either plaits or tufts of longer hair left in the close-clipped manes. This mane decoration, the quiver, and coat of mail were adopted by the Chinese of the T'ang period. Thus China has also to thank Iran for these things appertaining to material civilization.

We then found several other caves that had been used as monks' cells, and were provided with a fixed stone bench and a fireplace, often finely moulded.

One of these cells had a little window in the outside wall from which a wonderful view was obtained of the river and the wild, romantic country through which it flows.

Other cave-temples were of importance in the history of art, as showing how the painting process appeared at its various stages. In some temples the walls were seen smoothed and whitened, in others a network of lines had been drawn as a guide to the painter. This consisted of a series of diminishing rectangles, all standing inside one another, and frequently the rectangles were intersected by a diagonal. The stencils were stretched on a network of this kind, and then came the painting. Sometimes, too, on these guide-lines, inscriptions were found in Sanskrit or Tocharian which seemed to be directions for the painter, such as "Here Buddha comes; here this or that saint," etc.

Another of this second group was a temple close by, which we named the "Sailors' Cave." It consisted of an oblong rectangular

WORK AND EXPERIENCES IN KYZYL

building which displayed on its longer sides scenes from legends in which sailors played an important part. Grünwedel succeeded in determining the subject-matter of both series (Plate 40). Below these pictures there was an acanthus frieze, broken at fixed intervals by representations of the head of a child, of a man, of a late antique Jupiter, or Serapis, of a monk, and lastly, to end each series, a human skull.

Close to this temple we found traces of another, in very bad preservation. A podium was still left, and on this the remains of wonderfully modelled Hellenistic statues. On the farther wall there was a similar podium, and in a recess on the right of this bench we found a curious stele (Plate 47). It consists of an elephant's foot, on which is placed an elephant's head with strangely fringed ears. The trunk winds round the foot, the raised part round each eye-socket gives the idea of a woman's breast, and at the top of the picture there is a woman's head in the late classical style.

It is, indeed, possible that this stele is, as Grünwedel believes, an imitation of those figure supports that have been found in Pompeii: a bird of prey standing on a ball, or the foot of a beast of prey carrying a grotesque winged figure, which, in its turn, supports some objects on both arms. The natives may have seen something similar and copied it in their own way.

On the other side of the brook ravine to the east I discovered, in the principal settlement, a very ruined temple with its roof gone, but its side-walls still about six feet high, standing in a mass of dust. The surprising thing about this temple was the remarkable similarity between its paintings and Pompeian pictures. The profiles especially were quite Greek, but so, too, was the drapery and even the colouring. Grünwedel rather disliked these paintings, which I wanted to take with us as they were. He copied them afterwards, and unhappily had the misfortune, by an awkward movement, to bring down these pictures, which were only hanging loosely on the wall. We have only been able to rescue a few fragments of these very interesting paintings from amongst the debris.

In the rubbish on the floor I found the little gilded wood statuette of a Gandhara Buddha.

From a vehicle drawn by a zebu ox, to be seen on one of the pictures, we called this building the "temple with the zebu wagon."

East of this temple there are several splendid cave-temples of earlier date with roofs—or rather imitation roofs cut in the rock—of a most remarkable shape.

These are the so-called "lantern" roofs still to be found constructed with beams on peasant houses in Armenia, Hindu-Kush, Pamir, Kashmir, and in Little Tibet (Ladakh) (Plate 46, cf. also pp. 92-3). They consist of nothing but wooden squares, made of beams, of which the lowest is the largest and the top one the smallest. They are placed one above another in such a way that the corners of the upper square always lie on the middle point of the side of the square immediately below; the topmost square forms a sort of *impluvium*, and lets air and light into the building, whilst at the same time permitting the escape of the smoke rising from the hearth below.

Temples with such Iranian "lantern" roofs were to be found, not only in Kyzyl but especially in Kirish, on the high range of hills, in the south of the valley, where they all faced north.

The oldest temples of this kind are found in the ancient Buddhist settlements at Bamian in Afghanistan; later specimens executed in very beautiful hewn stone, in those splendid Buddhist temples of Kashmir that display such evident marks of classic influence. Some of these roofs are most richly painted, and display patterns that occur on the temple roofs of Ancient Egypt. Amongst these, many eagles, with two heads and a quite recognizable variant of the classic Ganymede group, also made their appearance.

At a later period, in the more easterly settlements, the builders no longer cut imitations of this wooden construction in the rock, but contented themselves with painting them as patterns in the vaulted roof. Thus converted into mere ornaments these lantern roofs adorn many of the more modern temples in China (Plate 39), but in Korea there exist many Buddhist rock-temples which still show this roof cut in the rock.

Whilst we were thus busy we received news of a third settlement. A very narrow and rough road leads from the second settlement into a small valley lying rather more than a quarter of a mile lower down the mountains, following the course of a little brook. The settlement contains eight rock-temples, of special importance only because the entrance halls, which are generally utterly destroyed, are still standing here—at any rate, in some cases.

In one of the temples there was a picture of a giant leading a

Plate 41

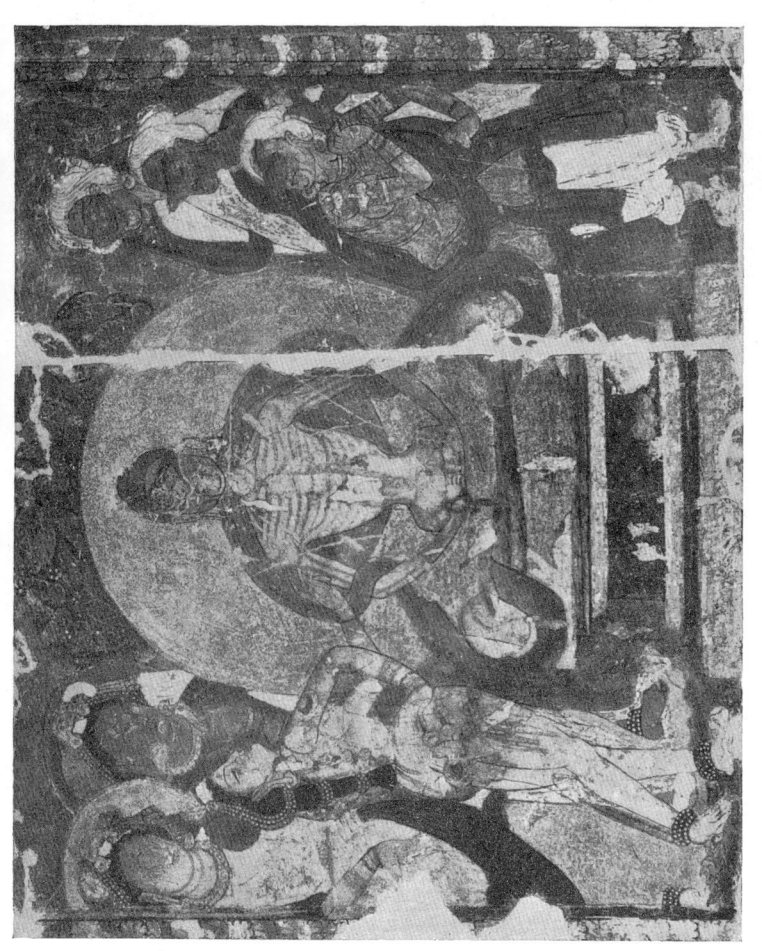

Temptation of Buddha by Mara's daughters. "Peacock" cave, Kyzyl

Le Coq, Turfan.

Plate 42

Buddha preaching — many signs of late antique influence. "Painter's" temple, Kyzy

WORK AND EXPERIENCES IN KYZYL

little boy through water, perhaps analogous with the Christian picture of St. Christopher with the Christ-child.[1]

There were some interesting pictures in a representation of the death of Buddha. For instance, in one of them the mourners appear in the native dress. They are knights and ladies of royal blood, and show their grief by exaggerated movements expressing the most violent pain. The men have drawn their daggers and are wounding their foreheads, and slashing across their chests, a sign of mourning frequently occurring in the East. This remarkable picture is now in the Berlin Ethnological Museum.

After achieving such excellent results we decided to visit the settlements in the Korla-Karashahr oasis. We had visited the *ming-öi* there on our ride to meet Grünwedel in Kashgar, and we looked forward to a rich harvest from the excavations we now intended to carry out in that district.

---

[1] For greater detail I must refer the reader to the *Bilderatlas zur Kunst—und Kulturgeschichte Mittel-Asiens,*" publ. D. Reimer, Berlin, 1925.

WORK IN THE OASIS OF KORLA-KARASHAHR
MY JOURNEY TO KASHGAR

BETWEEN Korla and Kara-shahr there lies, a half-day's easy journey to the west of the latter town, a little hamlet consisting of *sarais*. The mountain range rises in the north-west, and here, too, possesses the same desolate and forbidding character as marks the southern spurs of the Celestial Mountains. About two hours distant from the *sarai* there lies an ancient town with its fortified walls in good preservation on one side only. The town is a long rectangle, intersected on its western side by two parallel mountain chains, running from north to south. On these mountains innumerable temples, both large and small, are to be found, whilst in the south-east there are a great number of Persian domed buildings which serve as burial *stūpas* (Plate 48).

The architecture of the smaller of these domed buildings is often very rough.

If a dome, hemispherical in shape, is put on a square building, the four corners must naturally remain uncovered, but in careful architecture they are each covered by building in a shell-shaped dome.

But in this case the builders saved themselves trouble by cutting strong planks of poplar or mulberry wood to the right size, laying them horizontally over the open corners and covering them with a very thick layer of clay.

A little water-channel rising in swampy ground on the northern extremity of the two mountains chains flows through the centre of the town in a north-westerly direction.

This town, like all others that we visited, is a collection of temples and a necropolis; we did not find any other than religious buildings here.

We worked at this place most arduously, oppressed by terrific heat and swarms of gnats that were very troublesome, especially in the evenings. We were glad we were provided with excellent small-meshed mosquito-nets, or we could not have escaped from the bloodthirsty greed of these insects. The horse-flies that swarmed here were another pest. Whenever Bartus brought out his grey

OASIS OF KORLA-KARASHAHR

pony, the creature was, in a short time, covered with blood, but my brown horse seemed to suffer less. Men, too, are attacked by these unbearable insects and get very serious stings.

We noticed mainly two varieties, a large yellow-brown one with green eyes, and another, long, thinner, and grey in colour, but also with big green eyes.

Strange to say, our food was good here, for numerous herds of sheep and goats feed on the scanty grass of the low land, which, where not covered by salt exudations, produces a little vegetation, thanks to the wet swampy ground.

The excavations that I made in some of the larger temples of the ruined town had unfortunately no special results. This town had been destroyed by fire, and the ruins, which had fallen into the hot ashes, were baked together into great masses as hard as stone. In spite of this, however, it was possible to see that the remains of sculpture were everywhere exceptionally pure in character, following in a masterly way the canons of the Gandhara late classic style. Even the cupolas of the Persian domes were adorned with standing figures of gods, more than life-size, in the late antique style.

No paintings at all had survived in these temples; when, therefore, an inspection of neighbouring cave-temples showed them in many parts blocked with untouched debris we decided to work in these rather than in the ruins of the burnt town.

In these cave-temples we then found a splendid harvest of manuscripts, pictures, and pieces of sculpture; and here for the first and last time Grünwedel expressed a wish to conduct an excavation himself. He took ten labourers and looked for a temple in which to carry out operations, choosing finally a fine temple that promised good results. There he began the work, but as he could not make the men understand and the dust—which in such operations always rises in clouds and is very trying—worried him too much, he soon gave up his attempt in the belief that, after all, there was nothing to be found there. Bartus then fell to work in the same temple, and, when he had cleared the floor, soon brought to light whole layers of splendid big pages written in early Indian script.

Unfortunately this had been the nesting-place of pigeons that used to feed on the red fruit of a kind of briar. Owing to this food, their excreta were always violet-red, and this colour had been communicated to many of the manuscripts.

Here, too, we found wonderful painted statues in great quantities. Their special importance lies in the fact that the paint on them is still in good preservation, which is seldom, or never, the case in the eastern settlements (Plate 47).

One day, when we were working in the most northerly temple, to which we had given the name of the "town-cave" from the representation of a town in one of its frescoes, the sky became overclouded and down came the rain—such rain, too, as we cannot even imagine in Northern or Central Europe.

As I had been told that when rain begins at this time it generally means a storm, I persuaded Grünwedel, who always walked instead of riding, to start at once and go back to the station. He followed my advice and went.

The rain came down faster and faster, so Bartus and I packed together the manuscripts, which I had only just discovered in the "town-cave," wrapped them up in a waterproof cloak, mounted our horses, and rode off. Our workmen preferred to camp in the caves, where they lit a fire and slept on their felt rugs. Scarcely forty minutes had passed since Grünwedel had marched off, but, as we were riding through the lower mountain slopes, I was seized with panic, for strong currents of brown water were rushing out of all the many ravines. It is true they were still but small; in a short time, however, they might have swollen to a dangerous size.

But Grünwedel, being an excellent walker, had fortunately passed all the most dangerous spots before they became too threatening, and we found him in the *sarai*, wet to the skin and shivering with cold. Here, too, the storm was making its presence felt in a most disagreeable manner. The enormous downpour of water penetrated the roof, which only consisted of brushwood and kneaded clay, and ran down through the smoky roof-beams. Soot and mud together had given the water a black-brown tint, and our beds, which had been plentifully besprinkled, were in a truly horrible condition.

Unfortunately this storm caused the death of two men. Three workmen from Korla were on their way to seek work with us, and, with their donkey, had pushed up the mountains over a short but steep path. They had been overtaken by the storm as they reached the first mountain spurs, and only one of the three, exhausted and stiff with cold, reached the caves where our workmen were sheltering.

OASIS OF KORLA-KARASHAHR

His two companions and the donkey had fallen down on the way and perished, and the men, whom we sent to meet them with food and clothing, only found their dead bodies.

It is astonishing how rain like this in the mountains brings down the temperature. The heat, usually prevailing, compels people to go about in quite thin garments; then, when they meet with such a storm and the consequent drop in temperature, their clothing is insufficient and they are soon stiff with cold.

The great "town-cave," whose treasures we secured on this wet day, lay quite to the north, and was so buried with fallen ruins that only the top of the door provided a tiny opening. Moreover, a pyramid of debris stood in the doorway with one slope outside, and the other slanting into the interior of the temple.

I had this pyramid removed by forty labourers, cleared out the temple, and about a yard above the floor came upon an enormous quantity of manuscripts in Indian script, amongst which Tocharian manuscripts were particularly numerous. They lay scattered round the broken remains of a statue of a standing Buddha that had been placed in the centre of the farther wall of the cella.

Judging from these circumstances, I concluded that these manuscripts had once been placed inside the Buddha statue, and later on thieves, who knew that such statues often contained valuables, had broken it open and taken away with them anything of value; but had scattered the manuscripts, which were worthless to them, inside the temple, which even then was already covered with a layer of sand to the depth of a yard or so. The find of manuscripts ended as suddenly as it had begun, for, although I went still farther in, I found the earth firmly welded together by damp. So I gave up the idea of further search. Professor Grünwedel visited Shorchuk once again from Turfan, and studied more minutely the pictures I had already partly cleared from above, but they were unfortunately in a very bad state of preservation.

In the ruined town Bartus made an interesting discovery, for after opening a room which had evidently been a workshop, he found in the debris a large number of stucco moulds.

The whole of this district round Kara-shahr and Korla is, from a geographical and political point of view, both interesting and important; for whilst all other parts of Chinese Turkestan can only be reached either by climbing high and difficult passes—the lowest of which has the same elevation as Mont Blanc—or traversing extensive and dangerous waterless deserts of sand-hills, here we find the one and only convenient approach to the land through the valleys of several rivers in the neighbourhood of Ili, where plentiful water abounds in the mountain streams on all sides, and where a rich vegetation makes life possible for wandering tribes. Such Kalmuck tribes still come from the north-west to Tal. They are Torgut nomads who pitch their *yurts* round about Kara-shahr and live a hard life with their herds.

We once came upon one of these *yurts*, and were invited to tea and a drink by the old Kalmuck owner. Unfortunately the old gentleman was fairly drunk, so that his assurance in Turkish of "*Sizlar bizga yaqin*" ("You are near relations of ours")—no doubt he took us for Russians—was not exactly a compliment.

Just as these Mongols wander about here at the present day, so the nomadic tribes of an earlier period must have used this district as their entrance and exit gate. The Tochari (Yue-chi), on their way from China, undoubtedly at that time passed through this gate to get into the Ili valley. But the western Turks, who were for a long time the rulers in the oasis of Kara-shahr, must also have used this road; for, in our opinion, the founders in Turkish dress often appearing on the walls of these temples do not represent Uighurs but western Turks. According to our chronology the temples in this oasis must belong to an earlier period than that of the Uighurs; for these did not, as far as we have been able to determine, conquer Turfan, the north-east corner of the country, earlier than A.D. 760, whereas we date the Shorchuk temples and their paintings at the middle of the eighth century.

Here the news reached me that Aurel Stein was intending to push forward from Lop to Sha-chou and Turfan, and I then insisted that Grünwedel should at once start for Turfan, where, at his express wish, I had reserved for him the almost untouched temples of Bazaklik, near Murtuk. My own health had suffered so much from dysenteric symptoms that I was now compelled to say good-bye to Grünwedel, Bartus, and Mirab, and start alone on my way to Kashgar.

After taking leave of the expedition I had the cases, which contained all the manuscripts found by us, and some cases of drawing and stencils that Grünwedel had given into my charge, packed on to an *araba* and sent on in advance. I followed on my

Plate 43

Conventional landscapes with re-birth legend. Chief colours, ultramarine and bright red. Painting from the dome of a roof. Kyzyl

v. Le Coq, Turfan.

Plate 44

Distribution of relics. Fresco, Kyzyl

Plate 45

Cremation of Buddha's body. Fresco, Kyzyl
(Mummy bandages. Dragon on coffin lid.)

Plate 46

Splendid apartment with lantern roof in a house in Hindu-Kush (copied from Sir Aurel Stein)

horse, soon overtook the vehicle, and rested alone in the *sarais*, which in this hot summer time—it was the end of June—have very few visitors. I had bread and tea, also a kettle and cup with me, a felt rug to sleep on, and a big frieze cloak for a blanket.

My horse, for protection from thieves, had to share my bedroom. I looked after him myself. I found some lucerne hay in the *sarai*, and, in exchange, handed my *obolus* over to the sleepy host.

It is impossible to miss the way, as the telegraph posts are unfailing guides.

The first halts were the most lonely—from Ashma on I met more people, and just before Yangihisar my attention was called to a remarkable shrine (here usually called *khojam*). It bears the name of *Kara säch mazārī* (the grave-shrine of the black hair), and is a cool spring of sweet water running in a channel filled with a luxuriant growth of a delicate fern with long, slender black stalks. But why the spring was sacred no one could tell me.

In the little places through which I now passed between Bugur and Kucha many people knew me—they were former patients; and when the report of my coming reached their ears—which, indeed, it very soon did—they waited for me at the *sarai* with offerings of milk and, alas! of fruit also. In this district there are particularly delicious plums which have the combined flavour of a fine greengage and an apricot as well. But I had to avoid fruit as the dysenteric symptoms became more and more pronounced. In addition to this, I began to be tormented by toothache. Still, in spite of everything, it was good to ride through the clear air of the plain, which is as invigorating as good champagne. And when the sun was setting, and I was riding on towards the fiery red ball, I rejoiced with every step that brought me nearer home after work crowned with success.

Along this road the traveller passes many smaller streams coming down from the north. They all flow in a deep central bed, bordered on either side by wide, stony slopes. These river-beds must be passed before noon, or, at latest, before 2 p.m. or half-past, for by that time the water from the melting glaciers in the high mountains reaches this part of the plain. The red-brown masses of water come tearing noisily along at a furious rate, and anyone who chances to be caught, even on the stony slopes of the river-bed, has little chance of escaping with his life.

148 BURIED TREASURES OF CHINESE TURKESTAN

When I reached Kucha I was very pleased to find Egambardi, my former servant, who, owing to illness, had had to stay behind at that place. I now needed a servant and especially a cook, for I was much weakened by the bodily ill I have already mentioned.

Egambardi was an excellent cook, and the rice-water (*conjee*), which he managed to make quite savoury, did me good.

Here I waited for my native cart, and, whilst waiting, renewed my acquaintance with a man who, in earlier times, had been the absolute ruler, the lord of life and land of his warlike subjects. This was Mīr Safdar Ali, the *tham* or prince of Hunza, a little bandit state in the Himalayas whose inhabitants, only too well known under the name of the Kanjuti, used to lie in wait for the Yarkand caravans on their way to or from Leh, and carry off both goods and traders, the latter to be sold as slaves throughout the whole of Central Asia.

Mīr Safdar Ali defied the English, so that a small English force, under Colonel Durand, had to be dispatched against him, and after violent resistance on the part of the Hunza people, their incredibly strong positions were carried and the fortified castle of Hunza occupied.[1] The *tham* fled to Turkestan, where the Russians paid him the princely allowance of twenty-five roubles a month in the expectation of being able, at some future time, to make use of this pretender to the crown, against England. They were out of their reckoning here, however, for, as I heard later, this man killed his whole family and that of his vizier as well—fifty-six people, it was said—with his own hand.

He was both feared and hated by his subjects.

In appearance he was European, a tall man of Herculean build, with light eyes and light brown hair and beard! A snow-white lock in the hair on his cheek, below his right ear, increased the strange, almost uncanny expression of his face. He belonged to one of those royal families in the Himalayas who trace their origin back to Alexander the Great.

The Hunza folk, and the people of the adjoining State of Nagyr, call themselves *Burish*; their language, *Burisheski*, stands in a cate-

---

[1] The history of this military exploit, bordering on the fantastic as it does, is related in an extremely readable little book by E. F. Knight, entited *Where Three Empires Meet*, Longmans, London, 1897.

OASIS OF KORLA-KARASHAHR

gory quite by itself, and has no relationship to any other tongue known so far.

Behind Kushtama the river Muzart had to be crossed; it was very full, so the ford was impassable, and I had the valuable cases in their *arabas* placed on a block boat, a prehistoric horror. In a bend, somewhat farther down the stream, there lay a small island with a strong deep current on its left side, but on its right there was a broad expanse of shallow water with scarcely any current.

The men succeeded, by means of a rope from the top of the bend, in getting the boat carried over by the force of the current to the island, and then guided it through the shallow water on the other side, but not without considerable expenditure of time.

Between Chorgha and Djam we were compelled to cross three more swift rivers, over abominably shaky bridges, on the last of which the *araba* with the cases of manuscripts knocked against the side rail, which at once gave way. All the men ran to the rescue, and succeeded in preventing the cart from falling over. All through the endless journey then lying before me I had many and many an anxious time over these precious possessions, entrusted to my care.

In Ak-su I had a little trouble with the Chinese officials. The *tao-tai*, being a new arrival, did not yet know me, and, as I had taken by mistake the passport that belonged to Herr Bartus, whilst my own had been left with him, the official was suspicious. A telegram to Macartney, however, put everything in order.

A Chinese passport is a work of art! It contains in the lapidary Chinese script the name, personal characteristics, etc., of the owner, and thereupon great stamps in the official vermilion. Above the text of the passport there is a triangle drawn in black lines about four inches in height and empty to begin with.

The document, measuring about eight square inches, is drawn up in duplicate, and both copies are folded down the middle lengthways, and are placed one beside the other with these middle folds most accurately meeting. The official who issues it then presses his great vermilion seal in such a way on the contiguous passports that a part of the impression is on the original and the remainder on the duplicate. The traveller keeps the original, whilst the duplicate remains at the office, whence an exact copy of it is sent to the authorities of every place which the traveller visits. The traveller's passport, when presented, is laid against one of these copies, and the seal must fit exactly.

In Ak-su I also visited the *wang* of Ak-su. He is a Turk, but only a titular king, or, as the natives say, a *khizmat-kār-wang*, or subordinate king. Only the *wangs* of Komul and Lukchun are ruling princes with the title of *mamlakat wang*, or kings of the realm. But even their power is considerably restricted by the Chinese officials who keep watch over them.

It now became so unbearably hot that I had to rest during the day and travel by night, the cart following with a soldier from the Ak-su *yamen* (government building).

As I started from Chadir Kol under guidance of a second soldier, it was one o'clock at night and pitch dark. The soldier trotted on, then I heard something go plump, followed by cries for help; in the darkness he and his horse had fallen into a puddle over six feet deep, and I had considerable trouble in helping out first the man and then his horse.

Here the people all at once were unfriendly, and I found out that some English officers had ridden over the same route a little time before. Their servants, Indian Mohammedans, were wearing clothes worn in England for games, and therefore passed as *parang* or Franks. These servants had treated the Turkish landlords and peasants in the high-handed manner peculiar to them, commandeering fowls, eggs, etc., without payment, and putting the money given them by their masters to buy these things—a few pence only—into their own pockets. It is greatly to be desired, in the interests of all Europeans travelling in these districts, that Indian or other Asiatic servants should wear clothing that plainly distinguishes them from the European travellers, so that these awkward misunderstandings may not occur.

The Englishmen themselves, being ignorant of the native dialect, of course, had no idea of their servants' misdeeds.

The rest of the journey to Kashgar passed off without any incidents worthy of mention.

MY RETURN HOME OVER THE HIMALAYAS

When I entered Kashgar, on July 30, 1906, I was again received with the greatest kindness by Sir G. Macartney, the English consul-general (at that time still political agent) (Plate 49). I was very ailing, and Lady Macartney kept me some time as a patient in her house to restore me to health again. Meantime the return journey over Russia was rendered impossible by the outbreak of a native revolution there.

But as soon as I felt better I was most anxious to get my box of manuscripts into safety, and I therefore decided to go homewards over the Karakorum passes—in the West pronounced Karakoram, in accordance with the native dialect—to India. Sir G. Macartney did not like this idea on account of my poor state of health; and as it so happened that an English officer, Captain J. D. Sherer,[1] belonging to the artillery corps of the garrison in Quetta, Baluchistan, and formerly a bear-hunter in Pamir, was visiting in Kashgar, he suggested to this gentleman that he should travel with me and help me over the journey.

Sherer was very pleased to fall in with this plan, and so, as we had to get horses before we really made a start, we travelled over to Khotan together, covering the seventeen days' journey between Kashgar and Khotan in no more than twelve.

The roads here lead through a desert of sand-hills, where not a drop of water can be found for miles together. Since the least divergence from the road means death to the traveller, the track is marked out by small poplar stems in the same way as the *llano estacado* (the staked plain) in Texas—a desert every whit as terrible as that in Turkestan.

In this desert, not far from Karghalik, there lies one of the finest rest-houses in the country, built by Yakub Beg, of good fired bricks. The *sarai* is called *Cholak Langar*, the rest-house of the one-armed man, after one or other forgotten landlord. Here we met the Scottish

[1] Captain Sherer is a son of that Mr. John Sherer, Indian Civil Service, who rode into Cawnpore after the terrible mass murder, at the order of Nana Sahib, of more than two hundred captured English women and children by Mohammedan butchers. Even on his arrival he saw deep wells still filled with the mutilated bodies. A marble monument, Marochetti's mourning angel, now marks the spot where their innocent blood was shed.

newspaper correspondent, David Fraser, with whom we spent a pleasant evening.

Two years later I met him again in London in the Royal Asiatic Society, after my lecture. He had, when accompanying M. von Oppenheim's expedition, I believe, lost an arm by a Bedouin shot, and with a smile alluded to the name of this rest-house as he showed me his empty sleeve.

In Yarkand we visited the Swedish Evangelical Mission, and there I made the acquaintance of the physician, Dr. Gösta Raquette, who by filling up a hole in the stopping of a tooth relieved me of abominable pain. His filling lasted well; on the very evening of my arrival at Berlin, in the following January, as I lay my head on the pillow, that tooth first began to ache again!

Yarkand is a large and fairly prosperous town with good *bazars*. We lodged with the *aksakal* (white beard) of the British-Indian traders, a worthy old Hindu of the name of Rai Sahib Bhuta Ram, who put his country house, situated in a beautiful garden, at our disposal.

Such gardens have but few paths, since in consequence of the artificial irrigation they are often crossed in all directions by water channels. Yet I remember with pleasure a group of splendid old walnut trees, a tree that flourishes in this region. In Kirish, near Kucha, I found a few more, but they are not often to be seen in the north.

As our host heard that old Indian manuscripts were packed in my cases, he begged me to allow him to make a reverential offering to them. I gave the required permission, of course, and he brought flowers and began to scatter them and drops of water on the cases, round which he and some friends walked in solemn procession. When I noticed that my presence disturbed him, I went away after the first glance. But this pious veneration for the intellectual labour of their forefathers expended on these documents had something touching about it.

Here, too, we met a French traveller, Commandant de Bouillane de Lacoste, who afterwards undertook a journey round Afghanistan. We dined with him, and, as he was a big-game hunter too, the conversation between him and Sherer mostly turned on their respective experiences. It was amusing to see that Lacoste considered Sherer's bear hunts—whose authenticity I did not doubt for a second—simply in the light of pure exaggeration.

Plate 47

Statue of a divinity, Shorchuk

Caryatid ? from a pedestal, elephant pillar, Kyzyl

Plate 48

A view of the ruined town at Shorchuk, near Karashahr

RETURN HOME OVER THE HIMALAYAS

All preparations were at last finished, and we began to start on our journey to India. It was not exactly a trifling undertaking, for although the road we had to follow was the usual trade route, in unfavourable weather it offers many obstacles and dangers.

Thus, for example, an Afghan merchant had started from Leh over this route with several hundred ponies, but arrived in Khotan with only thirty-five! The others had died in a snow-storm.

If a caravan is overtaken by such a misfortune, the loads of the fallen animals are all put together in orderly fashion in as sheltered a spot as can be found near the scene of disaster.

Later on they are fetched away, and the caravan code of honour most strictly forbids any interference with these stores belonging to other people. We ourselves often passed such heaps of property.

Our luggage was put on to ponies that had been placed at our disposal by the leader of the Afghan caravans for forty-five roubles each. We rode away from Yarkand on a splendid autumn day; but just outside the city gate there was a stampede of our horses, who were looked after by one man to every four. They had come straight from good food and were full of spirit, and the knocking of the great cases against one another in their march had suddenly produced sudden panic amongst them. In a moment the cases were tossed off, our ponies were scattered all over the plain, and their drivers wildly chasing after the runaways. It meant several hours' delay before the men managed to catch them and load them again. On the following stages the same mishap occurred several times, until at last I was compelled to hire a number of peasant lads from a village near by, so that every pony might have his own leader. This plan answered excellently, and we kept to it until we reached the high mountains, where the extra pony-guides were dismissed, well pleased with their good pay. The ponies' wild spirits were soon subdued by the difficult roads.

As it was already late in the year, we had chosen the winter route (*zamistani*) over Kokyar.

This was the last roof under which we were to sleep for more than eight weeks. The *sarai* swarmed with extraordinarily big fleas that often compelled Sherer to pull his shirt over his head and shake it out. They do not trouble me beyond annoying me with their tumultuous hopping. Compared with lice, fleas may be considered amongst the good things in Allah's creation, and the lice we conquered with the never-failing quicksilver remedy that I have already mentioned.

The journey over the high mountains is accomplished by following the course of a river—in this case the Tisnab. Whenever the cliffs rise in the immediate vicinity of the river, the traveller must either clamber up and continue his journey over their summits, or cross the stream, if the other bank seems to be more promising, and ride on. We often crossed the stream thirty or forty times a day—once, indeed, we did so sixty-four times (Plate 49).

Often there is no ford, and the horses have to be taken through fairly deep water—a proceeding not without danger, for there are deep holes, slippery rocks, and such-like obstacles, any of which can bring a horse down in deep water.

In this way one day the horse that was carrying the tea-service fell in a deep hole. The leathern case, which contained kettles, teapots, sugar basin, etc., had not been properly shut by the careless servants; it burst open, and all my fine Yarkand kettles danced gaily away on the surface of the water, and, as the river banks drew close together immediately below the scene of misfortune, it was impossible to rescue them. A Ladakhi made a quick dash at the tea-provisions and saved them, except the sugar and condensed milk, which disappeared.

Sherer's servants were three very tall, strong young men from Kashmir, exceedingly courageous and clever mountaineers, but in other respects, like most of their fellow-countrymen, incredible cowards, and quite incapable of independent action. The pony-men were partly Turkis, partly Tajiks from Kabul (*Parsiwan*), and there were also amongst them some Baltis, Ladakhis, Afghans, and even one Chitrali. My former servant, Egambardi, from Marghilan, had joined me on this journey, too.

In Yarkand we had met an Afghan of mixed race, the son of one of Yakub Beg's Afghan generals, and the daughter of a Turkish landowner in Kashgar. He was a non-commissioned officer in the Ninth Bengal Lancers, who had come into the country with David Fraser. He was a reliable, faithful man, whom I took with me as far as Rawal Pindi, and my companion in the adventure we experienced owing to Sherer's illness later on.

As soon as travellers come to great heights, from about 13,000 feet, many people find their breathing impeded: many horses, too,

RETURN HOME OVER THE HIMALAYAS

suffer from the rarefied air, yet travellers must always ride, since walking tries the heart too much. The mountain ponies are exceptionally sure-footed, and only have a horrible habit of always going on the extreme edge of the path just above a very deep and often perpendicular abyss. As I am very apt to turn giddy, I found this habit most unpleasant, but my brown horse from Pichang never gave me cause for complaint on this score either.

The rest-camps bore all kinds of names, some of them absurd, from the trivial experiences that one or other caravaner had met with there, as, for example, *Gruč Kaldi* (the rice was left here), *Chiragh Kuldi* (the candlestick was left here); whilst the rest-house, *Daulat Bak Oldi* (the royal prince died here), close to the Karakorum pass, is so called because the Sultan Said Khan of Kashgar, on his return from a successful campaign against West Tibet, died there from mountain sickness (Plate 50).

This is an illness that only attacks strangers, never the Tibetan natives, who, on the contrary, after a continued stay in the Indian plains, always die of emphysema or some other chest complaint. Anyone attacked by mountain sickness [called by the Turks *is* (*yas*) or *tutak*, by the Persians *dam* or *dam-giri*] suffers, with a terrible headache, nausea, etc., begins to rave, and sometimes loses his power of speech. The palms of the hands and soles of the feet begin to swell, and then the patient generally dies between sunrise and breakfast.

Strangely enough, mountain sickness occurs with greater virulence on passes of a lower elevation than the Karakorum; this has an elevation of over 19,680 feet, but mountain sickness is said to occur there less often than on the Saser Pass, which, although somewhat lower, has, nevertheless, a bad reputation for this troublesome complaint.

Although it is usual to take some corn for the horses, they have to be let loose at night so that they can paw all kinds of mountain herbs out of the snow. Whilst doing this they often stray long distances, and I remember how unpleasant it was to wake on many a morning and see not a trace of a horse anywhere. The men had to look for them and bring them up, so that in many rest-camps, and these generally quite the worst, we could not start in the morning until eleven or twelve o'clock instead of at 7 or 8 a.m.

Our journey was favoured by the most splendid weather, and the dangers, as they had been described by our predecessors, often seemed to me quite exaggerated. But I soon saw I was mistaken, for, although my own health was very soon perfectly restored, my travelling companion, in spite of his gigantic stature, began to suffer from the bad effects of the rarefied air. He got mountain sickness in an exceptionally severe form, since he insisted on walking long distances.

I had secured a little flock of sheep at one rupee each. These creatures generally came into the camp in the evening, and the Kashmir servants made us, on most primitive fireplaces, excellent ragouts and other dishes of mutton. But Sherer's illness soon grew so acute that he was scarcely able to sit upon his horse.

We were getting near to the Depsang Plateau, a snow-covered, desolate table-land, circular in form and of tremendous extent. All round the edge of this circle rose the peaks—as sharp as church spires—of innumerable mountains, some quite bare and some covered with ice. To a horseman it seemed as though the world upon which he stood had sunk.

I was so spell-bound by this sight that I paid no attention to the caravan, and when I looked for them they had disappeared behind masses of ice. I fired my gun, however, and an answering shot soon gave me the direction.

We had most beautiful sunshine for our journey across the Karakorum Pass, which, as a rule, is dreaded on account of its storms.

In fine weather this pass offers no difficulties, although it is about 19,680 feet high. But when there is a storm of wind and snow the crossing gives infinite trouble. As we descended from the pass we found edelweiss, and lammergeiers (bearded vultures) as the only living creatures.

The road was everywhere marked by numberless skeletons or dried-up, mummified carcasses of animals. Here and there rose a heap of stones to hide the mortal remains of some trader who had died on the journey.

We passed, too, the great cairn put up to mark the spot where Dalgleish was murdered, although the murderer's Afghan friends had already partly torn down the stones.

On the Indian side of the pass we just succeeded in getting Sherer to the *Burtsi* rest-camp; it gets its Tibetan name from a woody plant,

RETURN HOME OVER THE HIMALAYAS

the root of which is dug out of the earth and forms the natives' only supply of fuel.

Here his strength came to an end, and we had to decide on a day's halt. The valley in which we were camping was a terribly wild gorge, surrounded by gigantic bare heights and penetrated in one spot by a smaller ravine. Enormous masses of rock had been heaped, one on the other, by the raging waters of the melted snows, and the impression of destruction and of the tremendous forces that had spent their violence here made the valley a most fearsome resting-place.

The caravan people were much annoyed at this day's halt. The horses' fodder, that had to be brought with us, as well as wood and our own provisions, were all running very short. On the following morning I went to see how Sherer felt, and was shocked to find that he could not raise his head. His glazed tongue was cleft from tip to root, and twice more from side to side; his teeth were covered with a dingy brown deposit, and his exhausting cough was followed by brown expectoration. He was in a high fever and had been delirious during the night.

In view of this serious development we were obliged to halt for a second day's rest. We took counsel together, however, and it was decided that I should leave Sherer there with the tent (I always camped in the open), all the provisions, his own attendants, and two of the caravan-men who knew the district; go on myself with the caravan over the next three passes, that were the most difficult in the range, as far as Tibet; there get help and come back to fetch him.

But that evening the caravan-men grew very excited, and I heard that they intended to run away. My Turki attendant came to me much upset, to tell me that they meant to start at midnight with the horses and leave us to our fate. Fortunately I had brought with me an extra big sack of wheaten flour—such flour, mixed with glacier water, was the only food of these people. So I handed over this sack to the ringleaders, at the same time, however, threatening them with death if they made any attempt to leave us. All that night I had to sit up with my Mauser rifle in my hand to prevent their treacherous desertion, if they should attempt to carry it out. But all remained quiet.

We started at sunrise. My attendant was only able to bring flour for me, and every day he made, with the help of glacier water, six balls out of it for my food. The flour was white and his hands black to begin with, but after the operation was complete the colours were reversed!

In eight and a half days we had crossed the terrible passes of Murghi and Saser, as well as the easier Karaul Pass, and reached the Nubra valley, in which we rejoiced to catch once again the first glimpses of green fields, trees, and plains.

The homesteads lie about nine to twelve and a half miles from one another. At midday we reached the little Tibet hamlet of Panamik in Ladakh, where I immediately sent word to all the houses and to the nearest homesteads to have bread made, since the Tibetans themselves have none at all and instead eat only malted wheat.[1] Fowls, eggs, milk, everything the poor settlements could offer, was bought at a high price and sent by newly hired coolies[2] to the probable rest-houses; and I also had great loads of

[1] Wheat, sprouted in warm water and dried.

[2] I should most likely have found it impossible to hire coolies at a reasonable wage for the half journey if a high official of the Maharajah, who chanced to be in Panamik, had not visited me. He was a dignified Dogra Brahman who, having been brought up in England, spoke excellent English, and had the bearing and manners of a well-educated Englishman. He induced the coolies to enter my service for a wage of four annas instead of the rupee they had demanded. I shook hands with him, but was astonished at his attempt—as soon as he knew I was a German—to induce me to speak all sorts of ill about the English. Amongst other remarks he said: "*You* shook hands with me, but the English don't. Why should you shake hands and the English not?" This was a somewhat awkward question, but I answered that if the Englishmen did not do so, they no doubt had their own reasons and we parted in all friendship.

But when my men were going to start on their journey back, my Turki attendant, Egambardi, came into my room to say good-bye, wearing a miserable little fur. Now, I had bought him a splendid wolf-skin in Yarkand, so I asked him: "Now that you are crossing the passes in winter, where's the fur that I bought you?" "O sir!" he said, "the *amban* took away that fur and gave me this little bad one."

I was exceedingly annoyed and sent for the man. When he came, I said to him: "You once asked me why English gentlemen would not shake hands with you. If I had known how you behaved I would not have done it myself. Why did you take his good fur from my servant, a poor man, and give him that bad one when you know quite well that he is crossing the passes in the winter?" The Dogra answered in great excitement: "He shall have it back. I will send at once to get it." "Yes," I said, "and you will give him ten rupees' compensation as well." He made further excuses, paid the money, and took his leave, but without any handshake this time.

When I went on the fourth expedition in 1913 to Kashgar, I sent for Egambardi to engage him as attendant again in this fresh journey, and, quite by chance, happened to speak of this incident, saying with a laugh: "But we got the best of it that time." "O sir," Egambardi replied, "that we didn't, for when I got to the next station two of the *amban's* men were waiting for me and took away again money and fur, leaving me only the little old cloak." This experience just shows how little reliance can be placed even on educated officials in this country. It is characteristic, too, that a well-to-do man, to whom I sold my excellent horse, let it die because he was too parsimonious to give it sufficient food.

RETURN HOME OVER THE HIMALAYAS

the deliciously fragrant juniper-wood carried over to the same places. The Tibetans make nothing of running up the steepest paths impassable to horses, with heavy burdens, and were quite able to compass the journey that had taken us nine days with the caravan and laden ponies in considerably less time. I had a drink of nineteen eggs, which was a most refreshing restorative. Then I sent off a messenger to the physician of the Moravian Mission in Leh, Dr. Shawe, with the request that he would come himself or send medicine for Sherer, whose symptoms I described.

I dispatched a second messenger, too, to Sir Francis Younghusband, in Srinagar, Kashmir—seventeen days' journey from Panamik—with a letter, in which I told him that I had reached Panamik, but was obliged to go back to fetch a fellow-countryman of his who had fallen by the way. In the event of our not returning I begged him to have my chests, containing imperial property, fetched from Panamik, where my men were looking after them. I told him in which the money and wage-lists would be found, and begged him to pay off the men and have the chests forwarded to the nearest German consulate—Karachi in Sind. Then I had a stretcher made and, after engaging thirty more Tibetan coolies, went to bed.

At dawn the next morning I rode off with a few provisions, in the company of my Afghan attendant, Rahim Khan, to fetch Sherer. The Tibetans had set out on the preceding day.

We crossed the three difficult passes in the most splendid weather, and at the end of the third day reached the wild ravine, where I had left the invalid.

When we looked down from the bare, precipitous heights enclosing the valley, we could see Sherer's tent, and, standing beside it, his tall Kashmiri attendant, eagerly scanning the heights with Sherer's field-glass. He suddenly caught sight of us and ran into the tent, so that I at once understood that my travelling-companion must still be alive.

We descended the slopes and reached the tent in perfect darkness; and there we actually found my comrade, not only alive, but considerably better than I had expected. Both Sherer and his attendants were delighted beyond measure; they had doubtless scarcely expected that I should, in any case, come back myself, and certainly not so quickly.

The attendants lifted me down from my horse (I was fairly

stiff) and massaged me for two hours as a proof of gratitude. Massage is, moreover, one of the benefits which I learnt to appreciate on these journeys.

But now our difficulties began. Sherer was not able to mount a horse.

The next morning the Tibetans arrived with the stretcher, i.e. two parallel beams joined, ladder-wise, by rungs. My cork mattress was fixed on this, and the invalid firmly fastened on to this primitive bed. As long as the paths were wide enough or in any way passable, Sherer could be carried quite comfortably. Where they were not, he had to be carried on the men's backs over the difficult spots and then return to his stretcher. In this way we approached the Murghi Pass. Here it was quite amazing to see the skill with which the Tibetans carried the stretcher. A narrow path led up to the edge of the ice, and then continued its course just below it. The lower part of the mountain-side is covered with rubble, the upper by ice, and the bearers managed their task by those on the outside dancing and springing from boulder to boulder with the stretcher resting on their shoulders, whilst those on the inner side also danced and jumped, but on the rough glacier ice, with their strong woollen belts slung from their left shoulders and round the stretcher.

In this way they made the journey, whilst I rode in a state of great anxiety behind the strange procession, every minute expecting that those crossing the boulders would follow the crashing avalanches of rocks and take their burden and the other bearers with them, but the agility of these men was so astounding that we pursued our way without mishap.

We went down into the depths again, and passed through the narrow gate-like pass to the second ascent, over which towered masses of rock just ready to fall.

I felt so pleased at the success of our first difficult crossing that I began to whistle softly to myself. Then the caravan leader stopped mo, laid his finger on his lips, and pointed, with an anxious gesture, to the masses of rock suspended above our heads. A single loud note might have been enough to set these rocks in motion, when they would crash down and kill everything beneath them.[1] Thus we crossed the first of the less difficult passes.

[1] Thank heaven, we never got into a stone avalanche. But once, in the first week of our stay in the high mountains, when in a two days' journey we had nearly reached the

RETURN HOME OVER THE HIMALAYAS

We now had to cross the Shayok river, which was not deep but full of ice. The Tibetans threw off their felt rags, held the stretcher up in the air with both hands, and with their continuous cry of "*Kádam aló! Kádam aló!*" marched into the water. Kneeling on my horse I went through the river a little above the bearers, and with an alpenstock belonging to one of the Kashmiris warded off the largest of the ice-blocks shooting down with the current.

We got through without any misfortunes, the men shook themselves like wet poodles, wrapped their rags round them again, took up the stretcher, and the procession went on again to the same cry of "*Kádam aló! Kádam aló!*" The poor invalid was driven nearly desperate by these howls, as he called them, and begged me to stop the cry; but the bearers assured me that without it they would not be able to march on!

Then we came to the foot of the dreaded Saser Pass, and passed the night there in one of the Tibetan rest-houses. These rest-houses consist of low stone walls only, without a roof; travellers lie down in the shelter of the stone walls to get some protection from the wind, which cuts like a knife through any fur.

After a horrible night, we started again at daybreak next morning. Sherer was carried up the first glacier—a precipitous wall of ice—and then we came to the ridge along which we had to reach the second glacier. Here it was impossible to carry the invalid as the path was too narrow, and freshly fallen snow lay in the depths to the right and left of the road. I had foreseen this, and had brought four Yak oxen—first, because these creatures can manage to make their way even in the deepest snow, and, secondly, because I had hoped to be able to get Sherer across on the back of one of them. My mattress was fastened by broad bands on to the back of the strongest of these oxen, and Sherer tied on also with broad belts.

But the beast had scarcely begun to move when the invalid screamed with pain. The motion was so violent that his weakened body could not bear it. We had to take him down again, and at

little rest-house of *Kuda Mazar*, the ground suddenly trembled a little and a muffled rumbling, as of something falling, sounded repeatedly in the distance, each time lasting for four or five minutes. I suggested an earthquake, but the caravan *bashi* said, "*Tash katti*" ("The stones have gone"—i.e. fallen down). Outside *Kuda Mazar* we passed the scene of the phenomenon—for the distance of some miles there were enormous piles of freshly fallen rubble along the foot of the cliffs. We had to pick our way over these heaps of rubble, in constant fear lest the noise of the caravan should loosen more blocks of stone. But we got across unhurt.

L

that moment the sky overclouded and grew dark, a great gust of wind whistled in our ears, and the next minute a most terrible snowstorm had begun.

The caravan-leader came to me whilst we were talking together as to the best thing to be done, and said: "If the foreign gentlemen wish to remain here, they must decide at once; we must go on, as the snow will close the passes." I gave this unpleasant news to Sherer, and, as there was no better alternative, I gave him my well-tested horse and mounted another myself. The Yaks were sent on in front, Sherer came next, and I rode behind him. Then came the rest of the caravan with the baggage-ponies, and in this order we followed this terrible path—in so violent a snowstorm that it was impossible to see what was coming, even at the distance of a few feet only, and the force of the wind was so indescribable as to frighten even the Tibetans.

Sherer bore it all like a hero.

By dint of great effort the second glacier was also crossed, and then came the sudden descent, which proved to be down an unusually rough road. The storm had vented its force in the many hours that we had spent on the pass, and the sun was again appearing through the clouds. On our left we passed a lake quite surrounded by blocks of ice. The blue water, merging into green as its depth increased, combined with the sparkle of the masses of ice glittering in the sun's rays, formed one of the most enchanting sights of the very many offered us in the course of this journey.

The rest-house of *Toti-yailak* awaited us at the foot of the slope, in the midst of a small plateau surrounded by seven glaciers. A tossing stream pursues its tumultuous course on one side of this little valley, where every glacier provides a different wind, each one colder than the other. The night proved the most bitter that we had yet experienced; fortunately my Tibetans had already dragged up great quantities of the fragrant juniper wood, so that for a portion of the night, at any rate, we could sit in something like comfort round the fire, and drink our hot tea.

But then the fire went out, and for the remainder of the night we sat waiting for the daylight in horrible cold. We all had beards, for if washing was an impossibility how much more so any sort of shave! Our breath settled on our beards, and in an instant all was in the tight grip of frost, so I took off my fur coat, buttoned it

Plate 49

The house of the English Political Agent Mr. — now Sir — George Macartney, Kashgar

Crossing the River Tiznab with the caravan

v. Le Coq, Turfan.

Plate 50

Rest-station. *Kulan oldi* (the wild horse died), Karakorum

Tibetan *stupas*, near Panamik

Plate 51

Inscribed stones ("Mani stones") near Panamik

Tibetan monastery, Lamayuru

Plate 52

Group of *stupas* by the roadside, Lamayuru.

The fortress of Dras

RETURN HOME OVER THE HIMALAYAS

over my head, and breathed through one sleeve in which I had fixed the Kashmiri's alpenstock. I had to sit upright all night, as lying down oppressed my heart beyond endurance. All the eight weeks of our journey over the passes I never once had my clothes off, nor washed either hands or face, since the least touch of water at once cracked the skin.

The next morning on we went and reached a narrow little cleft in the rock through which the valley stream had forced its way and formed little banks, on which we found brambles and wild-rose bushes. We heard the note of some partridges, and listened with the pleasant feeling that we were approaching living creatures once again.

In this charming little spot, lit up at the moment by the rays of the setting sun, we spent a restful night, and on the next day successfully managed the last pass of Karaul-Daban. It is steep and sandy but free from ice, and therefore easier to climb; and, when across, we found ourselves once more in the first Tibetan settlement, the village of Panamik, whence I had started in search of Sherer, and where my attendants and the caravan were awaiting us. A messenger had come back from the Leh mission with medicine only—opium for Sherer, since Dr. Shawe could not leave his hospital.

We rested some days in Panamik to recover from the strenuous exertions of the last few days; for getting the invalid over the passes had been particularly exhausting, owing to the anxiety inseparable from his condition.

This fruitful and charming district is inhabited by a cheerful little tribe: the Ladakhis or West Tibetans, a mixed race with a good deal of Aryan blood in their veins, as is shown by their luxuriant hair. The women and girls are specially happy, and with merry smiles are always showing their splendid teeth. Nor is it any wonder that they should be happy in West Tibet, where polyandry is the usual custom, except in the case of some very rich man; a family of several brothers marries a wife whose position is also legally well assured.

The Ladakhis' usual greeting is "*Dju, dju*" and an outstretched tongue, which is somewhat of a surprise at first.

Here we saw fine Tibetan *stūpas* (Plate 50), buildings destined for the ashes of corpses after ceremonial cremation; and we frequently rode past "mani ramparts," very long walls, generally

164 BURIED TREASURES OF CHINESE TURKESTAN

built of layers of slate, but sometimes, too, of granite. The stones of the topmost layer often bear carved inscriptions; the mystic formula *"Om mani padme hum"* ("O thou jewel in the lotus flower"), in particular, is frequently to be seen.

When I took a few of these inscribed stones for the Berlin museum, several Ladakhis noticed my action and complained of it to my attendant. But when he told them that I had worked all over Turkestan in Buddhist temples to get sacred pictures to take for worship into my own country of "Ba-lin," they brought me, of their own accord, more stones than I could carry away.

In many places almost every block of granite or slate lying by the wayside bears such inscriptions (Plate 51).

There are hot springs, too, in Panamik, and Sherer made use of them to get a bath, but I did not venture as the water was very hot; it refreshed him, however.

There was still one more obstacle in our road to Leh, viz. the Khardung Pass, at a height of nearly 19,680 feet. Horses could not cross it, and had to go on a somewhat longer road round the pass.

When we came to the actual crossing we were faced by an almost perpendicular wall of glistening ice, and from the centre of this wall there gushed out a stream of water about one and a half feet in diameter and of tremendous force.

The way leads over narrow zig-zag paths, hewn out of the ice, right up to the summit, and along these a traveller rides on a yak instead of a horse. To avoid having his leg on the inner side crushed against the ice it is essential to ride as on a lady's side-saddle—a method that made me find this ascent anything but pleasant.

After the steep descent that followed, we came by degrees on to better roads.

The rest of the way to Leh was accomplished without any difficulties. Sherer gradually grew a little stronger, and on November 4th I was able to deposit him in the well-run hospital of the good Moravians.

There he had to stay for six months, as his physical condition made it quite impossible for him to bear any more hardships.

Leh is a town that cannot fail to make a great impression on anyone coming from the poor little townships of Chinese Turkestan.

The traveller enters the city by a little door in the fortified wall, and suddenly finds himself in a long, wide *bazar* street, lined with

RETURN HOME OVER THE HIMALAYAS

shops, and, at its upper end, the gigantic castle of the former kings of Ladakh, with its strong white walls, looks down upon the busy street.

And Leh is an exceptionally busy place during the trading season, which lasts until nearly the end of September; then the *bazar*, in spite of its size, is crowded with traders from China, Turkestan, all the Himalaya districts, Afghanistan, and Tibet, but in November there was not a soul about. However, I looked up some of the richest traders in their very beautiful homes, and purchased from them a number of Tibetan wares from Lhasa at bargain prices. I cannot speak too highly of these traders, who with their good looks, dignity, and natural ease of manner were of pure Ladakhi descent but Mohammedans by creed.

The trade with Tibet is partly carried on over paths unsuitable for horses, so a particularly strong variety of sheep is used instead; about thirty-four pounds is said to be the proper load for a sheep.

We were told that the extensive *bazar* ground was sometimes used for polo. On the way between Leh and Srinagar I often saw peasant proprietors displaying both zeal and skill in this knightly game, which has quite taken its place amongst English sports. As far as I know it was adopted from the Manipuris, a people living in the Himalayas on the north-east frontier of India, but it is none other than the ancient *chaugan* game of Persia, whence it has passed on to all the countries where it is now played.

Persia has also given its language to all Mohammedan courts from Teheran to Komul, as well as spreading it through all the Himalayan district and India.

In Leh some dark-skinned servants—Hindustani Mohammedans—tried to incite my Turki attendants on religious grounds, warning them against any food I had touched, etc., for my touch made them unclean. I fetched Egambardi and the other men, and, pointing to the dark complexions, I inquired: "What colour am I?" "White, sir." "And what colour are you?" "White, sir." "And those men?" "Black, sir." "Well, then! We Franks and you belong together. Why, the Hindus won't even recognize each other nor eat together—so when they begin to follow Islam, the old unbelief is still in their minds, and they will not eat with other people! Don't copy them, for Hazrat Muhammad—may peace be with him!—has not written such commands in the blessed Koran."

The Turkis were quite satisfied with this and laughed at the Hindustanis, who, however, were furiously angry.

After one more rest-day I rode on again, and accomplished the seventeen days' journey between Leh and Srinagar in twelve days. The road ran for some distance over the cliffs on either side of the Indus, which tore noisily along in its deep bed at their foot. It was a splendid sight, but so dangerous for a man very subject to fits of giddiness that I was generally compelled in my ride to turn my face to the side of the rock and not to look down upon the river below. In many places the impulse to let myself slide down was so strong that I galloped past the dangerous spots, and these, too, were at last left behind.

We rode down into the Sind valley, where, although it was now November, I had the delight of seeing green pastures, splendid stretches of woodland, and Kashmir's rocky landscape, still bright with the glory of its abundant gentians.

But in this valley, although more blessed than most with beauty of landscape, there grows a poisonous grass, which, when eaten by horses, is said to have a fatal effect. In the Murghi valley, too, a poisonous grass is found, and there I also saw strong plants of aconite as well.

In the last station before Srinagar I camped under an enormous *chenar* tree (*platanus oriental*), one of the most magnificent trees I have ever seen, both for size and beauty of growth.

In Srinagar I put up at Nedou's Hotel, where I found two belated Englishmen. I at once had a bath and a shave, and can certify that, in spite of eight weeks without once taking off my clothes, I was quite clean, for there had been no dust.

At dinner that night I met Mr. Henry Bruce, and afterwards spent a long evening over our wine and cigars with him and Mr. P. Roper, an artist.

I was made to describe my journey and experiences, which I did with all the enthusiasm inspired by strong and recent impressions.

I was not too pleased next morning to hear that my kind new friend, besides being a novelist, whose books, *The Native Wife*, *The Eurasian*, and *The Residency*, deal with delicate social problems in Anglo-Indian life, was also a newspaper correspondent. But when he told me that an article, such as he proposed, dealing with my adventures, would bring him in a large sum of money, I with-

RETURN HOME OVER THE HIMALAYAS

drew my opposition, and a few days later the *Bombay Times* published a long and most flattering account which made me known throughout India—and later in Europe as well.

The next day I visited the Residency to pay my respects to Sir Francis Younghusband, who, as I may mention in passing, was a nephew of the celebrated traveller, R. Barkley Shaw.

Sir Francis, a splendid specimen of the distinguished English soldier, received me in the most friendly way possible, and invited me to take up my quarters in the Residency, a kindness I had to refuse, as I did not want to have to move again with my big baggage and all my packing-cases. But I generally went to the Residency for meals, and had the pleasure, when sitting over the fire with a good cigar in the evening, of hearing the history of the conquest of Tibet from the very lips of the leader of the expedition himself.

Telegrams of invitation reached me from all sides, amongst others one from Sherer's brother in Naushera, and another from Sir Harold Deane, Lieutenant-Governor of the Punjab in Peshawar. The latter invited me to break my journey at Government House, for he was anxious to send me with a squadron of guides into Swat and Bajaur, where valleys, so far unexplored by any European, offer many old Greco-Buddhist ruins, only waiting to be unearthed. The inhabitants of these Hindu-Kush valleys are Mohammedan fanatics. But the squadron of "guides" is recruited from these very valleys, and their members, by the help of their relatives in those districts, can assure the foreigner a safe conduct.

I was just going to accept this offer, but on the way to the telegraph office my eyes developed alarming symptoms similar to detachment of the retina, so that I wired a refusal, thus depriving myself of a valuable opportunity to increase my knowledge.[1]

The Residency doctor, Colonel Edwards, and his wife also welcomed me in the kindest way, and, thanks to some drastic remedies prescribed for me, the disquieting symptoms gradually disappeared. But my strength was flagging, and I was anxious to

---

[1] I suffer from extreme short sight. When, on this tour, we got above the snow-line, my pony-men took some hairs from the yak's tails and pushed them under their caps so that they fell down over their face. I began by wearing black spectacles over my eyeglasses, but found I could not see well enough. So afterwards I rode without any protective spectacles and in a few days got over the horrible snow-blindness; soon, indeed, I could even look at the sun, and my eyes took on that far-sighted look familiar to us in sailors and mountain-dwellers. But when these fresh symptoms appeared I was afraid that I had done myself harm after all.

get home and know that my cases of manuscripts were at last in safety. The transit from Srinagar to Rawal Pindi (via Muttra) is managed by a courteous Parsi, who hires out conveyances called *tonga* and *ekka*. The *tonga* is a light two-wheeled carriage with a seat for two in the front and a similar one in the back. It is drawn by a pair of horses, and, as the coachmen drive quickly, this method of travelling is best, only it is rather expensive.

The *ekka* is an Indian invention—the *tonga* I should consider identical or nearly so with the two-wheeled carriage, once well known in England as a curricle. The *ekka* is drawn by one horse only, and is so clumsy and slow that I preferred to order several *tongas*. But before we left I had still to meet with all kinds of new experiences.

The following morning, at half-past five, a knock came at my door, and I could hear a strange murmur of voices in the hall below. As the knocking grew more insistent, I opened the door, and was amazed to see a number of dignified, white-turbaned men raise their tall forms from the ground. They at once surrounded me, and in broken English each began to praise himself and his own wares, whilst depreciating those of his rivals, whom he reviled in no measured terms. "Sab, not believe him, he liar, he very big t'ief. I good man, honest man! Go 'way, t'ief!" etc., Accustomed as I was to the never-failing respect and good manners of the traders of Chinese Turkestan, whether Turks or Chinese, my first feeling was one of amazement at the shameless importunity of these people. I begged them to allow me to finish my sleep and promised to negotiate with them later on.

They all bowed to the ground, and I went back into my room. But in five minutes the former uproar began again, and when this game had been repeated several times, I grew so angry that I rushed amongst them with a whip.

Then they all fled in wild panic—but in a short time the whole pack were there again!

Then I sent one of the Goanese, by name—*O quae mutatio rerum*—Albuquerque! who, shivering with cold, had just brought up my *chota hazri*, to fetch my sturdy Afghans and Turkis, who soon disposed of these importunate fellows.

Later, I saw them in front of the house, and arranged to meet a couple of silversmiths, father and son, who offered very beautiful and cheap things, at three o'clock that afternoon.

RETURN HOME OVER THE HIMALAYAS

A bevy of boatmen (*handji*) also offered me their boats and services; splendid muscular men they were, with their very pretty wives and daughters to be included in the boat hire. I took a small boat, but without the female addition!

Srinagar reminds one of Venice, with its many canals used as streets, and a boat, hired for a week or a fortnight or even longer, is always at the service of the foreign gentleman.

After a visit to the Residency, I took my boat to the silversmiths, who lived in a fine building on one of the canals. To my amazement, loud lamentations resounded from the house, and when the door was at last opened, I was shocked to hear that both the men whom I had seen in good health in the morning were now dead.

There was cholera in the town, and hundreds of people were dying daily of this terrible complaint, although Europeans are scarcely ever affected by it.

But when one sees how the Kashmiri Mohammedans use the water of the canal, which is, none the less, the common sewer, for bathing, drinking, gargling, etc., the marvel is how anyone at all survives.

The town, with its many bridges and remarkable mosques, invited me to rest, but I was anxious to get home, and, after all too short a stay in this enchanting place, I went on to Rawal Pindi, and thence by train to Bombay. I remember gratefully the kind help shown to me by the *Diwan* (Minister) of the Maharajah.

In Bombay I was met and shown everything by the employee of my cousin, George Volkart, of Winterthur, whose chief, Herr Bickel, was the German consul there.

Bombay is a very fine city which offers in its wealth and splendour a striking proof of its development under British rule.

I took a cabin in an Italian steamship of the *Florio Rubattino* line, and after a wonderful voyage, via Aden, Suez, Port Said, and Naples, arrived at the port of Genoa and, a little later, at the home I was so anxious to reach.

Captain Sherer was not to be deterred from due expression of his gratitude, and a few months after my return I received from the Grand Priory of the Order of the Hospital of St. John of Jerusalem in England, in the tactful way peculiarly characteristic of the well-born Englishman, their solid-gold medal—never awarded either before or since—"For Service in the Cause of Humanity."

ITINERARIES

ROUTE OF FIRST JOURNEY, 1902, BERLIN—TURFAN

(Cf. Detailed Lists)

Aug. 11. Berlin—Wirballen—Rybinsk
by Volga steamboat via Nizhni-Novgorod to Samara
by train to Omsk.
Aug. 28. By Irtysh steamer to Semipalatinsk.
Sept. 2. By mail cart via Sergiopol
to Kopal (Sept. 9)
to Jarkent (Sept. 12)
to Kulja (Sept. 19).
Oct. 3. By *tarantass* to Jin-huo (Oct. 13).
Shi-kho (Oct. 20)
Manas and Urumchi (Oct. 27).
Nov. 17. From Urumchi
Dabanching (Nov. 19)
Turfan (Nov. 25)
Karakhoja (Nov. 26).

LIST OF THE SMALL STATIONS BETWEEN SEMIPALATINSK AND KARAKHOJA
FIRST JOURNEY

(From Semipalatinsk, Sept. 2, via Uluguskaja, Urgalyskaja to Aščikulskaja)

Semipalatinsk (Sept. 2)
Uluguskaja
Argalyskaja
Aščikulskaja
Certatskaja
Qyzilmulla
Arkachaja (here *baba-jaga*, Scythian stone figures)
Algan adyrskaja
Usun Bulakskaja
Egreikaiskaja
Altynkulskaja
Sergiopol (Sept. 5)
Sredne Ayaguskaja
Taldykutuk
Qyzilquskaja
Malo Ayaguskaja (beautiful *baba-jaga* figures)
Guz agug (Sept. 6)
Ukunin Kacskaja
Arganadykskaja
Ašči bulakskaja
Kaidzi bulakskaja
Romanovskaja
Baskanskaja (Sept. 8)
Arsuiskaja
Kopal (Sept. 9)
Akakačku
Sara bulak
Kara bulak
Dzantych agaskaja
Tsakitsynskaja
Kugaly (Sept. 11)
Altyn Emel
Bascinskaja
Aina bulak
Konur Uljon
Koibinskaja
Borochudzir
Jarkent (Sept. 12)
Ak Kent (Sept. 17)
Khorgos

ITINERARIES

Sui-dun
Kuldv (Sept. 19)

From Kuldv (Oct. 4)
Sui-dun
Lao-se-gun
Er-tai (Oct. 7)
San-tai
Si-tai
U-tai (Oct. 10)
Ta-kian-se
Usin-khoho (Oct. 12)
Dzin-ho
Kum bulak
Camp in the open
To-to (Oct. 16)
Kur-tu
Sigu-šo (Oct. 18)
A day's halt (Oct. 19)

Shi-kho (here *kurgans*)
Jan-tse-hai (Oct. 21)
Sen-te-cho-dse
Ulan-ussu
Manas
To-hu-lo
Via Cho-ta-by to Ju-fo-go (Oct. 25)
Via Sanji to Cha-da-yo-pe
to Urumchi (Oct. 27)
Oct. 27 to Nov. 16. Stay in Urumchi
To Turfan
Si-ge-yo-pe (Nov. 17)
Sa-yo-pe
Daban-šen (here, kurgans = cairns)
Bayanho (Nov. 20)
Karaur (Kawurgha)
Kinduk (Nov. 22)
Via Yar-khoto to Turfan (Nov. 25)
Karakhoja (Nov. 26)

Route I. Expedition Turfan—Kashgar, 1903

(March 12 to May 2)

I followed the same route in 1906, leaving Turfan Sept. 12, arriving Kashgar Oct. 14.

Toqsun	Chadir	Yaqa Aruq	Maralbashi
Su-Baschi	Yangi-Hisar	Chorgha	Tushurga
Aighyr-Bulaq	Bugur	Kara Yulghun	Kara Kirchin
Kumush	Awat	Jam	Ordaklik
Qara-Qisil	Yaqa Aryq	Aqsu	Lungku
Ushaq-Tal	Chol Awat	Aikol	Yangi-Abad
Tawilgha	Kucha	Chol Kuduq	Faizabad
Kara Shahr	Toghraq Dan	Chilan	Yamanyar
Shorchuk	Shamal Bagh	Yaqa Kuduq	Kashgar
Dorbon	Kyzyl	Chadir Kol	
Charchi	Bai	Tumshuq	
Ashma	Kushtama	Char bagh	

Route Kashgar—Andijan, First Journey, 1903

Ak-tam (May 17)
Ming-yol
Via Karanguluk to Kanjuga
Ken-su (May 21)
Uksalyr
Kugan (Ulugh Jat)
Igin (May 24)
Irkeshtam

Kirghiz yurt (May 26)
To the foot of the Terak Pass
Snowstorm (May 29)
Cross Terak, halt Jandoi (May 30)
Sufi-Kurgan
Gulcha (June 1)
Langar
Via Madi (Ma-doi) to Osh (June 3)

With the mail-cart to Andijan (June 4)

172 BURIED TREASURES OF CHINESE TURKESTAN

Outward Route Osh—Kashgar, 1913. Fourth Journey

1. Osh-Langar
2. Crossing Taqqa Dawan
3. Gulča (many ladybirds)
4. Kyzyl Kuryan
5. Sufi Karaul or S. Kuryan
6. To the foot of the Terak Pass (Uč ğat)
7. Crossing the Terak Pass. Camp Katta qoniš
8. Crossing Kapqa dawan, Ikizak dawan. Camp Yal pundi
9. Crossing Kičik ikizak dawan—unpleasant descent. Camp outside Irkaš-Tam
10. At 4 a.m. in Irkaš-Tam. Camp Tiyin after crossing Qara dawan
11. At 3 a.m. in Uluy ğat. Crossing Mašrab dawan. Camp in Gumbaz
12. Via Sati dawan to Kyzyl Boi
13. Ming yol
14. Kashyar

Route of the Second Journey Berlin—Turfan, 1904

Berlin—Omsk (Siberian Railway)
Omsk—Semipalatinsk (Irtysh steamer)
Sergiopol
Bakhty
} Oct. 2 to Oct. 8

Chughuchak (Oct. 9—17)
Dolburġin
Saraqusun
Yamatu
Kondalang
Sargaq, in the evening Ulam-bulaq
Sian-sau-fu, in the evening Cha-pai-ze
Shi-kho (left Oct. 25)
Kuitun
Yang-dze-khai
Ala-ussun (Oct. 28)
Manas
Lo-to-ye, in the evening Tu-kho-lo
Cho-to-by, in the evening Zan-ġy (Oct. 31)
Di-hwa-fu (Urumchi, Nov. 1)

Route II. Journey Urumchi—Turfan, 1904

Sai-yo-pa (Nov. 13)
Dabanching, in the evening Ba-yang-kho
Kawurgha (Nov. 15)
Kindik
Yar-Khoto, in the evening Turfan
Kara-Khoğa (Nov.) 18

Route Turfan—Urumchi, Second Journey, 1905

1. Da-dung, Yar-Khoto, Kindik
2. Kawurya (Kowurya)
3. Ba-yang-χo
4. Daban (or Dawan) čing
5. Sai-yo-pa, Ğiği-sos
6. In the morning, Urumchi

Route Turfan—Komul, Second Journey, 1905

1. Lukchun
2. Pi-čang (via Šoga Langari)
3. Čiqtim Kariz
4. Yanči (via Qirq Tu-dung)
5. Otun Go-za
6. Ci-gu-lo-can
7. Lou-dung
8. Taranči (Ch. San-do-lin)
9. Toyuči
10. Astana (via Lapčuq)
11. Čong Komul

ITINERARIES

List of the Stations from Kokyar to Leh, Third Journey, 1906

1. Kokyar
2. Via Otan-su to Pusa
3. Aq Mačit
4. Via the Topa daban (also called Aq qoram) to Čiɣlig
5. Rest-house on the upper course of the Tiznab, called Chalastan
6. Kuda mazari (Onion-shrine)
7. Via Doba to Tušuk Tas
8. Tor Eɣil Aɣzi
9. Via Yangi daban (new pass), cross Yarkand river, to Kulan oldi (the wild horse died)
10. Sasiq Bulaq (evil-smelling stream)
11. Via Kok Art Aɣzi (exit of the green pass) to Egar saldi (he has saddled the horse)
12. Kašmir gilɣa (dangerous quicksands!)
13. Cross Yarkand river endlessly. Rest in Khapalong. In early times robbers from Hunza and Nagyr used to lie in wait here for the caravans
14. Aq Taɣ (white mountain)
15. Wahab ǧilɣa
16. Brangza Karakoram
17. Daulat Bäg oldi (the prince of the realm died). Here Sultan Sa'id Khan of Kashgar died (9. 7. 1533) of mountain sickness
18. Via Depsang Plateau; Karakorum Pass
19. Kyzyl Yar
20. Burtsi
21. A day's halt
22. Murghi Pass
23. Via Čong-Tas (great stone) pass Shayoq river, to Saser Brangza
24. Via Saser Pass to Toti-yailaq (ponies' summer pasture)
25. Via Humalong to Karaul daban; after crossing this, descent into the Nubra valley
26. Via Spango to Panamik
27. Tigar
28. Khalsar
29. Khardung, foot of the pass
30. Over the Khardung Pass
31. Leh.

Route Leh—Srinagar

1. Nimmu
2. Saspul
3. Khaltsi (Khalatse) via Nurla
4. Bot Charbu, via Lamayuru
5. Kargil
6. I camp in the tent of a mining engineer, Mr. Wright
7. Dras
8. Via Matayan to Matsoi (Mat-shoi)
9. I cross the Zodshi Pass, then via Baltal to Sonamarg
10. Via Gund to
11. Kangan
12. Gandharbal
13. In the morning Srinagar

BIBLIOGRAPHY

ARNOLD, SIR THOMAS, C.I.E., Litt. D., Survivals of Sassanian and Manichæan Art in Persian Painting. Oxford, Clarendon Press, 1924.

CARTER, TH. F., The Invention of Printing in China and its Spread Westward. Columbia University Press, New York, 1925.

CHARPENTIER, J., Die ethnographische Stellung der Tocharer. Z.D.M.G., Bd. 71, 1917; Leipzig, 1917

COBBOLD, R. P., Innermost Asia. London, 1900.

DEASY, H. H. P., In Tibet and Chinese Turkestan. London, 1901.

DONNER, Resa i Central-Asien, 1898. Helsingfors, 1901.

DUTREUIL DE RHINS, J. L. (F. Grenard), Mission scientifique dans la Haute Asie, 1890–95. 3 vols. Paris, 1898.

ELIAS, N., and ROSS, E. DENISON, The Tarikh-i-Rashidi. A History of the Moguls of Central Asia. London, 1895.

FORSYTH, SIR T. D., Report of a Mission to Yarkund in 1873. Calcutta, 1875.

FOUCHER, ALFRED, L'Art gréco-bouddhique du Gandhara. Paris, 1905–22. I, II.
Etude sur l'iconographie bouddhique de l'Inde. 1re partie, Paris, 1900; 2e partie, Paris, 1905.
Les Débuts de l'Art bouddhique. Paris, 1911.
Notes d'archéologie bouddhique. Bulletin de l'Ecole française de l'Extrême-Orient, 1909.
Notes sur la Géographie ancienne du Gandhara. Hanoi, 1902.
The Beginnings of Buddhist Art and other essays in Indian and Central-Asian Archæology, revised by the author and translated by L. A. Thomas and F. W. Thomas. London—Paris, 1917.

GRUM-GRŽIMAILO, G. and N., Description of a Journey to Western China, Russian). 3 vols. St. Petersburg, 1896–7.

GRÜNWEDEL, ALBERT, Buddhistische Kunst in Indien. 2. Aufl. Berlin, 1920.
Buddhist Art in India. Translated from the "Handbuch" of Prof. Alb. Grünwedel, by Agnes C. Gibson. Revised and enlarged by Jas. Burgess. London, 1901.
Bericht über archäolog. Arbeiten in Idikutschari, Abhdlg. d. Kgl. Bayer. Ak. d. Wiss., I. Kl., XXIV. Bd., I. Abt. München, G. Franz'scher Verlag, 1906.
Alt-Buddhistische Kultstätten in Chinesisch-Turkistan. Berlin, G. Reimer, 1912.
Alt-Kutscha, Tafelwerk. Berlin, Elsner, 1920.
  (Dieses Buch kann nur mit Vorsicht benutzt werden. Die Tafeln sind vortrefflich; die tibetischen Texte und Karten, die Nachzeichnungen der manichäischen u. a. Miniaturen sind m. E. ganz unzuverlässig. Ebenso die Schilderungen der Kultur der alten Zeit. A. v. L. C.)

HARTMANN, M., Chinesisch-Turkestan. Halle a/S. 1908.

BIBLIOGRAPHY

Hedin, Sven, Geogr. wissensch. Ergebnisse meiner Reisen in Zentralasien 1894–97. Gotha, 1900.
Southern Tibet. Stockholm, 1922.
Abenteuer in Tibet. 16. Aufl. Leipzig, 1923.
Durch Asiens Wüsten. 3 Jahre auf neuen Wegen in Pamir, Lopnor, Tibet, und China. 7. Aufl. 2 Bde. Leipzig, 1922.
Nach Osten. Leipzig, 1916.
Im Herzen von Asien. 5. Aufl. 2 Bde. Leipzig, 1922.
Meine letzte Reise durch Innerasien. Halle, 1903.
Transhimalaja. Entdeckungen und Abenteuer in Tibet. 8. Aufl. Leipzig, 1923.

Huntington, Ellsworth, The Pulse of Asia. London, 1907.

Joyce, T. A., Notes on the Physical Anthropology of Chinese Turkestan and the Pamirs. Journal of the Royal Anthropological Institute, XXIII, pp. 305–20, XIII, pp. 450 *sqq.*

Klementz, D., Turfan und seine Altertümer in "Nachrichten über die von der K. Ak. d. Wiss. zu St. Petersburg im Jahre 1898 ausgerüsteten Exped. n. Turfan." St. Petersburg, 1899.

Kuropatkine, A. N., Kashgaria (Eastern or Chinese Turkestan), transl. W. E. Gowan, Calcutta, 1882.

Le Coq, Albert von, Chotscho. Königlich Preussische Turfan-Expedition. Berlin, 1913.
Die Buddhistische Spätantike in Mittelasien. Teil I—VI. Berlin, 1922–24.
Bilderatlas zur Kunst und Kulturgeschichte Mittel-Asiens. Berlin, 1925.
Die Abdāl. Baessler-Archiv, Bd. II, 1912.
Sprichwörter und Lieder aus Turfan. Baessler-Archiv, Leipzig, 1911.
Köktürkisches aus Turfan, ibid. 1909.
Chuastuanift, ein Sündenbekenntnis der manichäischen Auditores. Anh. z. d. Abhdlg. der Kgl. preuss. Ak. d. Wiss. Berlin, 1911.
Dr. Stein's Turkish Khuastuanift from Tun-huang, R.A.S. London, April 1911.
Türkische Manichaica aus Chotscho I. Anh. z. d. Abh. d. Kgl. Preuss. Ak. d. Wiss., 1912.
Bemerkungen über türkische Falknerei. Baessler-Archiv, Leipzig, 1913, und Nachtrag, ebenda, 1916.
Türk. Manichaica aus Chotscho. II. Anh. z. d. Abh., 1916.
Türk. Manichaica aus Chotscho. III. Anh. z. d. Abh., 1922.
Volkskundliches aus Ostturkistan. Berlin, 1916.

Lüders, H., Das Sāriputraprakaraṇa, ein Drama des Asvaghosa. Berlin, 1911.
Die Praṇidhibilder im neunten Tempel von Bäzäklik. Berlin, 1913.
Die Śakas und die "nordarische Sprache." Berlin, 1913.
Ueber die literarischen Funde von Ostturkistan. Berlin, 1914.
Die śākischen Mura. Berlin, 1919.
Zur Geschichte und Geographie Ostturkistans. Berlin, 1922.
Kleinere Sanskrittexte 1. Bruchstücke buddhistischer Dramen. Berlin, 1911. 2. Bruchstücke der Kalpanāmaṇḍitikā des Kumāralāta. Leipzig, 1926.

Müller, F. W. K., Handschriftenreste in Estrangelo-Schrift, aus Turfan, I. Sitzber. d. Kgl. preuss. Ak. d. Wiss. Berlin, 1904.

MÜLLER, F. W. K., Handschriftenreste II. Anh. z. d. Abhdlg. d. Kgl. preuss. Ak. d. Wiss Berlin, 1904.
Eine Hermas-Stelle in manichäischer Version. Sitzber. d. Kgl. preuss. Ak. d. Wiss., 1905.
Der Hofstaat eines Uighurenkönigs. Festschrift Vilhelm Thomsen. Harrassowitz, Leipzig, 1912.
Ein Doppelblatt aus einem manichäischen Hymnenbuch (Mahrnâmag). Abh. d. Kgl. preuss. Ak. d. Wiss. Berlin, 1913.
Manichäische Texte aus Turfan (in Vorbereitung).

MONNERET DE VILLARD, U., Arte manichea. R. Istituto Lombardo di Scienze e Lettere Rendiconti. Vol. LVI, fasc. XVI—XX. 1923.
Sull' Origine della Doppia Cupola Persiana. Architettura e Arti Decorative, fasc. IV, Anno I. Milan, 1921.
La Scultura ad Ahnâs, note sull' Origine dell' Arte Copta. Milan, 1923.

OLDENBURG, S. VON, Russkaja Turkestanskaja Ekspedicija (Russian). St. Petersburg, 1914.

PELLIOT, P., Les Âbdâl de Païnâp. Journ. as., Janv.—Fév. 1907.
Trois ans en Asie Centrale, conférence faite à la Sorbonne le 10 Décembre, 1909, dans Bulletin du Comité de l'Asie Française, Janvier 1910.
Rapport de M. Paul Pelliot sur sa mission en Asie Centrale (1906–1909), dans Comptesrendus de l'Acad. Inscr. et Belles-Lettres, 1910, 58–68.
Les Grottes de Touen-houang. Paris, 1922–24.

RADLOFF, W., Proben der Volkslitteratur der nördl. türkischen Stämme. VI. Teil. Dialekt der Tarantschi. Deutsche Übersetzung (amüsante und lehrreiche Märchen), etc., St. Petersburg, 1886.

REGEL, A., Über s. Reise nach Turfan. Petermann's Mitteilungen 1879, Heft X—XI; 1880, Heft VI; 1881, Heft X. Gotha.

SHAW, ROBERT, Visit to High Tartary, Yârkand and Kâshghar. London, 1871.
Deutsch: Reise nach der hohen Tatarei. Jena, 1876.
ed. N. Elias, History of the Khojas of Eastern Turkestan. Supp. J. As. Soc. Beng., vol. LXVI, part I, 1897.

SMITH, R. A., The Stone Age in Chinese Turkestan. "Man," 1911, XI, pp. 81 *sqq*.

STEIN, SIR AUREL, Sand-buried ruins of Khotan. Personal Narrative of a journey of archæological and geographical exploration in Chinese Turkestan carried out and described under the orders of H.M. Indian Government, by M. Aurel Stein. Vols. I, II. Oxford, Clarendon Press, 1907.
Explorations in Central-Asia, 1906–8. "Geographical Journal" for July and September, 1909.
Ruins of Desert Cathay. Personal Narrative of Explorations in Central-Asia and Westernmost China. Vols. I, II. London, Macmillan & Co., 1912.
Ancient Chinese Figured Silks Excavated by Sir Aurel Stein at Ruined Sites of Central-Asia. Drawn and described by F. H. Andrews. London, Bernard Quaritch, Ltd., 1920.
Serindia. Detailed Report of explorations in Central-Asia and Westernmost China, carried out and described under the orders of H.M. Indian Government by Sir Aurel Stein. Vols. II—III text; Vol. IV plates; Vol. V maps. Clarendon Press, Oxford, 1921.
Ancient Buddhist paintings from the Caves of the Thousand Buddhas on

BIBLIOGRAPHY

the Westernmost border of China. Recovered and described by Sir Aurel Stein with an Introductory Essay by Laurence Binyon. Published under the orders of H.M. Secretary of State for India and with the co-operation of the Trustees of the British Museum. London, B. Quaritch, Ltd., 1921.

SYKES, ELLA, Through Deserts and Oases of Central-Asia. London, 1920.

THOMSEN, VILHELM, Ein Blatt in türkischer "Runenschrift" aus Turfan. Sitzber. d. Kgl. preuss. Ak. d. Wiss. XX, 1910.

    Dr. M. A. Stein's MSS. in Turkish "Runic" Script from Miran and Tung-hwang, R.A.S. London, 1912.

WALDSCHMIDT, E., Gandhara, Kutscha, Turfan. Leipzig, 1925.

WEBER, WILHELM, Die ägyptisch-griechischen Terrakotten. 2 vols. Berlin, 1914.

YOUNGHUSBAND, F. E., Heart of a Continent. London, 1896.

ZATURPANSKIJ, DR. CHOROS, Reisewege und Ergebnisse der deutschen Turfan-Expeditionen. Orient. Archiv. Bd. III. Hiersemann, Leipzig, 1913.

INDEX

Abdal race, 39
Araba, 114
Art—
  Early Christian, 18
  E. Asiatic connection with Hellenistic, 28, 43
  Greco-Buddhist, Greco-Christian, 18
Aurel Stein, Sir, 26, 112
Avalanches—
  stone, 160

Bactria, 18
Bakhty, 48
Bazaklik—
  monastery settlement of, 85
Benefactors—
  portraits of, 89, 123 *seq.*
Bœhmeria, 81, 96
Buddha—
  early type of, 17
  legends, 130, 136, 141
Buddhist—
  art in Turkestan, 18
  mural paintings, 62
  settlements, 18
Burial mounds, 20 *seq.*, 88

Cella, 57, 88
Civilization—
  movements of, 19

Domed tombs, 55

Earthquakes, 134
Ekka, 168
Electæ, 33, 58
Electi, 33, 58
Explorers—
  of E. Turkestan, 25 *sqq.*

Fata Morgana, 38
Frescoes—
  of Indian Monks, 71
  method of removal, 127 *seq.*

Gand-hara, 17
  art, 79
  sculpture, 131
Ganymede group, 89
Garuda, 89
Gold Medal—
  of Order of St. John of Jerusalem, 169
Gumbaz, 81 *seq.*

Hunza folk, 148

Jenghiz Khan, 23, 39

Kalmucks, 39
Karakhoja, ancient, 56
  buildings of, 76 *seq.*
  frescoes, 77
  religious documents of, 77
Kariz, 53
Kashgar, 20, 149
Khojam, the, 135, 147
Khojas, the, 24
Komul oasis, 103
  melons of, 103, 105
  mosque and royal tombs of, 103
Korla-Karashahr oasis, 107, 109
Kucha oasis, 107
Kumtura—
  ming-öi of, 115
Kyzyl, 122 *sqq.*
  monks' cells of, 123, 138
  paintings at, 117, 132 *seq.*

Ladakhis, 163, 165
Llano estacado, 151
Loess dust, 37, 51, 60, 63

Manes, 30 *sqq.*
Manichæan—
  art, 22
  frescoes, 61
  manuscripts, 58 *seq.*
  religion, 32 *seq.*, 45
  sects arising from, 33 *seq.*
  stronghold of, 35
Mani ramparts, 163

INDEX

Ming-öi, 18
Mirab, the, 53
Mīr Safdar Ali, 148
Mongols, 19 *seq.*
Mountain sickness, 155
Muzart, River, 122
  fossils of, 115
  the crossing of, 149

Paintings, mural—
  classification of styles, 28 *sqq.*
Palao, 66
Passports, Chinese, 149

Roofs—
  construction of domed, 142
  lantern, 92 *seq.*, 140

St. Christopher, 141
Sangim, 83 *sqq.*
Sassanian painting, 22, 58, 136 *seq.*
Sculpture—
  casts of, 80 *seq.*
Shrine of the Seven Sleepers, 56, 93
Silk-routes, 19, 23
Sir George Macartney, 111 *seq.*, 151
Sogdians, 20, 22, 27
  mural frieze of, 130
  script of, 22, 27, 59
Stencils, 81, 87
Stupas, 57 83
Sven Hedin, 25, 44

Tarantass, 46 *sqq.*
Telega, 46
Temple buildings—
  architecture of, 77
  method of renovation, 77 *seq.*
Tochari, the, 20 *seq.*, 45
Tonga, 168

Tungans, 49, 74
Tung-hwang, 26, 106, 112
"Turfan" expeditions, 25
  city of, 54 *seq.*
  grapes of, 93
  minaret of, 55, 57
  oasis of, 51 *sqq.*
  ruler of, 65
Turkestan, E., 35
  animals of, 39, 49, 71, 91
  architecture, 41
  character of people, 42
  Chinese rule, 39 *seq.*, 50, 52, 65
  climate, 51, 62 *seq.*
  education, 42
  fairy tales, 113
  fish, 109
  food, 63 *seq.*
  industries, 41
  insects, 36 *seq.*, 51 *seq.*, 142 *seq.*
  irrigation, 53 *seq.*
  language, 40 *seq.*
  population, 39 *seq.*
  position, 35
  religion, 41, 45
  subordinate kings in, 150
  surface, 35
  vegetation, 37, 52, 93
  wastes, 37 *seq.*
  women's dress, 118 *seq.*, 124
Turkish "Runic" script, 59
Tuyoq, 93, 96

Uighurs, 21 *seq.*, 35, 56
Uighur script, 62
Urumchi, 49 *seq.*

Yakub Beg, 24, 94, 151
Yue-chi, 21
Yurts, 49, 146

Some other Oxford Paperbacks for readers interested in Central Asia, China, and South-east Asia, past and present

CAMBODIA
GEORGE COEDÈS
Angkor

MALCOLM MacDONALD
Angkor and the Khmers*

CENTRAL ASIA
PETER FLEMING
Bayonets to Lhasa

ANDRÉ GUIBAUT
Tibetan Venture

LADY MACARTNEY
An English Lady in Chinese Turkestan

DIANA SHIPTON
The Antique Land

C. P. SKRINE AND PAMELA NIGHTINGALE
Macartney at Kashgar*

ERIC TEICHMAN
Journey to Turkistan

ALBERT VON LE COQ
Buried Treasures of Chinese Turkestan

AITCHEN K. WU
Turkistan Tumult

CHINA
All About Shanghai: A Standard Guide

HAROLD ACTON
Peonies and Ponies

VICKI BAUM
Shanghai '37

ERNEST BRAMAH
Kai Lung's Golden Hours*

ERNEST BRAMAH
The Wallet of Kai Lung*

ANN BRIDGE
The Ginger Griffin

CHANG HSIN-HAI
The Fabulous Concubine*

CARL CROW
Handbook for China

PETER FLEMING
The Siege at Peking

MARY HOOKER
Behind the Scenes in Peking

NEALE HUNTER
Shanghai Journal*

GEORGE N. KATES
The Years that Were Fat

CORRINNE LAMB
The Chinese Festive Board

W. SOMERSET MAUGHAM
On a Chinese Screen*

G. E. MORRISON
An Australian in China

DESMOND NEILL
Elegant Flower

PETER QUENNELL
A Superficial Journey through Tokyo and Peking

OSBERT SITWELL
Escape with Me! An Oriental Sketch-book

J. A. TURNER
Kwang Tung or Five Years in South China

HONG KONG AND MACAU
AUSTIN COATES
City of Broken Promises

AUSTIN COATES
A Macao Narrative

AUSTIN COATES
Macao and the British

AUSTIN COATES
Myself a Mandarin

AUSTIN COATES
The Road

The Hong Kong Guide 1893

INDONESIA
S. TAKDIR ALISJAHBANA
Indonesia: Social and Cultural Revolution

DAVID ATTENBOROUGH
Zoo Quest for a Dragon*

VICKI BAUM
A Tale from Bali*

'BENGAL CIVILIAN'
Rambles in Java and the Straits in 1852

MIGUEL COVARRUBIAS
Island of Bali*

BERYL DE ZOETE AND WALTER SPIES
Dance and Drama in Bali

AUGUSTA DE WIT
Java: Facts and Fancies

JACQUES DUMARCAY
Borobudur

JACQUES DUMARCAY
The Temples of Java

ANNA FORBES
Unbeaten Tracks in Islands of the Far East

GEOFFREY GORER
Bali and Angkor

JENNIFER LINDSAY
Javanese Gamelan

EDWIN M. LOEB
Sumatra: Its History and People

MOCHTAR LUBIS
The Outlaw and Other Stories

MOCHTAR LUBIS
Twilight in Djakarta

MADELON H. LULOFS
Coolie*

MADELON H. LULOFS
Rubber

COLIN McPHEE
A House in Bali*

ERIC MJÖBERG
Forest Life and Adventures in the Malay Archipelago

HICKMAN POWELL
The Last Paradise

E. R. SCIDMORE
Java, Garden of the East

MICHAEL SMITHIES
Yogyakarta: Cultural Heart of Indonesia

LADISLAO SZÉKELY
Tropic Fever: The Adventures of a Planter in Sumatra

EDWARD C. VAN NESS AND SHITA PRAWIROHARDJO
Javanese Wayang Kulit

MALAYSIA
ISABELLA L. BIRD
The Golden Chersonese: Travels in Malaya in 1879

MARGARET BROOKE
THE RANEE OF SARAWAK
My Life in Sarawak

HENRI FAUCONNIER
The Soul of Malaya

W. R. GEDDES
Nine Dayak Nights

A. G. GLENISTER
The Birds of the Malay Peninsula, Singapore and Penang

C. W. HARRISON
Illustrated Guide to the Federated Malay States (1923)

BARBARA HARRISSON
Orang-Utan

TOM HARRISSON
World Within: A Borneo Story

CHARLES HOSE
The Field-Book of a Jungle-Wallah

EMILY INNES
The Chersonese with the Gilding Off

W. SOMERSET MAUGHAM
Ah King and Other Stories*

W. SOMERSET MAUGHAM
The Casuarina Tree*

MARY McMINNIES
The Flying Fox*

ROBERT PAYNE
The White Rajahs of Sarawak

OWEN RUTTER
The Pirate Wind

ROBERT W. SHELFORD
A Naturalist in Borneo

CARVETH WELLS
Six Years in the Malay Jungle

SINGAPORE

RUSSELL GRENFELL
Main Fleet to Singapore

R. W. E. HARPER AND HARRY MILLER
Singapore Mutiny

JANET LIM
Sold for Silver

G. M. REITH
Handbook to Singapore (1907)

C. E. WURTZBURG
Raffles of the Eastern Isles

THAILAND

CARL BOCK
Temples and Elephants

REGINALD CAMPBELL
Teak-Wallah

MALCOLM SMITH
A Physician at the Court of Siam

ERNEST YOUNG
The Kingdom of the Yellow Robe

*Titles marked with an asterisk have restricted rights.